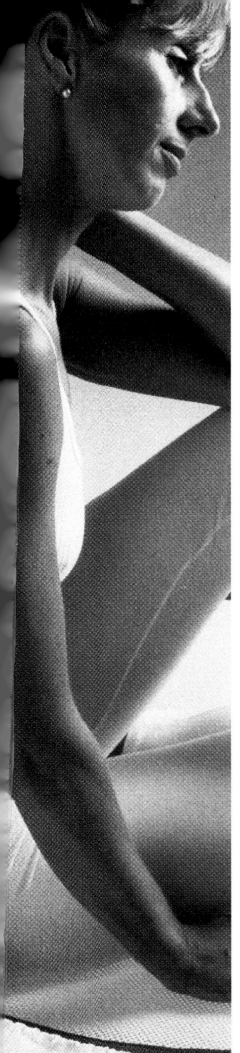

BOUNCING BLITZ

Bounce *just for the sake of bouncing!* Bounce *for fun!*

Bounce *to recharge your batteries.* Bounce *to grow.*

Bounce *for emotional stability.* Bounce *to be positive.*

Bounce *to strengthen your immune system.* Bounce *for recovery.*

Bounce *away fatigue.* Bounce *to boost your brain power.*

Bounce *for mechanical rhythm.* Bounce *to be busy.*

Bounce *to release tension.* Bounce *to calm your nerves.*

Bounce *to shift your perspective.* Bounce *for eyes that see.*

Bounce *for a bonny baby.* Bounce *to oppose gravity.*

Bounce *to stimulate your senses.* Bounce *for the stars.*

Bounce *for rejuvenation.* Bounce *to banish wrinkles.*

Bounce *for free-flowing lymph.* Bounce *for better blood.*

Bounce *to activate your lifestyle.* Bounce *to be happy.*

Bounce *for sweet dreams.* Bounce *to jog your memory.*

Bounce *to stimulate your metabolism.* Bounce *to relax.*

Bounce *for a better body.* Bounce *to clear your skin.*

Bounce *for self-control.* Bounce *to beat the blues.*

Bounce *back with me!*

STARBOUND

Michele Wilburn

ORION

*I dedicate my work to two
extraordinary women with vision:
Anthea Sieveking, distinguished
photographer of children, who
inspired me to write this book; and
Rosie Cheetham, my publisher, who
dared to follow her instinct and bring
you* STARBOUND.

Text copyright © Michele Wilburn 1993
Photographs © Orion Publishing Group 1993

First published in Great Britain in 1993 by
Orion
An imprint of the Orion Publishing Group
5 Upper St Martin's Lane, London WC2H 9EA

A CIP catalogue record for this book is available from the
British Library.

ISBN 1 85797 134 5 (csd)
ISBN 1 85797 083 7 (tpb)

Editor: *Alice Millington-Drake*
Creative Director: *Peter Bridgewater*
Design: *Annie Moss*
Photography: *Larry Bray*
Illustrations: *Michael Courtney*
Cover design: *Carroll Associates*

Printed in Great Britain by
Butler & Tanner Ltd., Frome and London

WARNING

AS WITH ANY EXERCISE PROGRAMME, YOU SHOULD CONSULT YOUR
DOCTOR BEFORE COMMENCING. EVERY CARE HAS BEEN TAKEN TO
PRESENT THE TECHNIQUES AND PROGRAMMES WITH REGARD TO
THE SAFETY OF THE READER. HOWEVER, THE AUTHOR AND
PUBLISHERS CAN ACCEPT NO LIABILITY FOR INJURIES THAT MAY BE
SUSTAINED AS A RESULT OF FOLLOWING THE EXERCISES IN THIS
BOOK OR USING THE BOUNCE UNIT EQUIPMENT.

CONTENTS

FOREWORD

My parents were wonderful teachers and always worked in small schools in the New Zealand countryside. Because my father was always the headmaster, home was the schoolhouse and the garden was a playground, designed for action. Swimming pools, tennis courts, athletic training facilities and gymnastic equipment were all part of the package. With my brother and two sisters, life was simply a rollercoaster from one exciting activity to the next. I recall spending much of my time hanging upside down from the monkey bars, learning new tricks and enjoying a jumbled view of the world. To this day, wherever I am living, I search for the best set of bars and head for a swing at least twice a week!

I followed in my parents' footsteps and trained to become a teacher. Three years in the classroom proved enough, so I decided to explore the world and expand my horizons. In my early twenties, after a particularly turbulent emotional experience, my metabolism was thrown out of kilter. I lost a stone in weight, then ballooned with a change in lifestyle and diet, to gain three stone in the next three months. I had left my teaching post and was spending time in a ski resort, eating too much pasta, and developing a passion for chocolate and cream cakes. I tore a ligament in my knee in a skiing accident which gave me the final excuse to sit in the snow and overindulge. The ski season came to an abrupt end, the snow melted, but my fat cells seemed doomed to stay.

Although looking back, I realize my career as an exercise coach began with daily programmes I developed for the children during my three years as a teacher, those three months in the snow were the most influential in shaping my life and work, if not my body! Overweight, I set off to travel the world with a friend on a working-holiday. She had also gained weight, so together we formulated wonderful plans to shed the pounds. I vividly recall my first workout – ballet-barre style – standing behind a tomato-sorting conveyor belt in North Queensland, Australia. Between us we developed a system of leg lifts and pliés to trim our thighs and tighten our buttocks. One of us would sort and toss the tomatoes while the other practised the kicks and tucks. Of course the farmer got his kicks as well simply by watching us. My initiation into the field of serious exercise was definitely stamped with fun.

It was in the sun on Hayman Island, on the Barrier Reef in Australia, that I experienced my first taste of exercise to music, with the original dancercise programmes. As I travelled around the world a few times over the next few years, I gathered techniques and tips from some marvellous teachers. Although I enjoyed a variety of occupations, which included dancing the can can, singing for my supper, and acting as an extra on film sets, I always returned to coaching exercise classes. After all, it was easier than returning to the classroom. Teaching women was less strenuous than teaching children, and I always found them easier to control!

In the early eighties, I settled in London to develop programmes tempting ladies into serious slimming action with before and after shots – exercise became a fun-filled experience. Training with Janet Balaskas, Director of the International Centre for Active Birth in London, was a wonderful preparation for the birth of my child and slowed me down sufficiently for my entrance into motherhood.

Romani, my daughter, proved to be as energetic as myself. My exercise regimes collapsed as the responsibilities of motherhood stepped in. Especially in those first few months it was hard to find time to call my own. Arranging babysitters and then dealing with a distraught baby on return often put me off going out at all. I took up walking in the park when it wasn't raining and fitted in my pelvic pulls somewhere between feeds. I desperately missed the daily workouts which had been so much an integrated part of my lifestyle. Somehow exercise in the home never seemed to give me the lift I sought.

When Romani was nearly a year old, I returned to New Zealand. I was invited to stay with friends for a weekend party, and in my hostess's living room I was intrigued to spot a mini-trampoline. Following careful instructions, I tried my first bounce. I had often used a trampoline as a child, but this was a completely different experience. Certainly not a piece of equipment to start performing tricks from. Nevertheless I was captured, not only by the wonderful feeling of freedom I experienced as I took myself through dance exercise routines, but by stories my hostess related about the magnificent healing that was stimulated when people bounced regularly. She herself was a wonderful example of energy and vitality, and her

entire lifestyle was truly an inspiration to me. Within a week I had purchased my first 'bouncer'.

When packing to return to London, I was heart-broken at having to leave the bouncer behind. However, it was lucky that I did. My father suffers with multiple sclerosis and was quickly losing the ability to walk. My mother tempted him into using the bouncer daily, a habit which he has bravely kept up ever since, for nearly five years now. Although his condition is still severe, we are sure he has benefited greatly by bouncing gently using a balance bar. In fact, I believe he would be confined to a chair by now without the additional boost that bouncing has offered his system.

In England, I attended a course for bounce coaching and was delighted to find a large number of exercise teachers who had discovered the joys of bouncing. I was amazed to hear the equipment had been around since the late seventies, yet I'd never seen bouncers anywhere. It became clear that the bounce movement had gained momentum as the fitness boom peaked in the mid-eighties. Although bouncing received a small amount of popular press at the time, it was simply never developed to hold the platform that it so rightly deserves.

Over the past three years I have developed my Starbound programmes by working with top pioneers in many fields. When I first set out to interview doctors and complementary health practitioners, I found the medical profession had reacted positively to bouncing as a form of exercise for many years.

Physiotherapists use the equipment for rehabilitation, operation recovery and general recuperation from injury. Pioneers in visual improvement use bouncers in therapeutic programmes. Mental toughness coaches are placing the equipment in their consultation rooms. Kinesiologists recommend the exercise as a means of enhancing lymphatic response. 'Switched-on' companies place bouncers in quiet rooms to allow staff the chance to release stress and tensions. Schools are setting up bounce classes for children because of the wonderful opportunity bouncing provides for the development of motor skills. Old people's residences are helping the elderly by encouraging them to walk with a balance bar for support. Gymnasiums are placing them between circuit stations because they offer a great means for speedy heart-rate elevation, which in turn enhances the conditioning process. Therapists are using them to speed the breakdown of tension locked in the muscles. Children are using them for fun. I've been busy developing Starbound programmes for you to use at home and in class situations for extension of new skills.

All of my classes now centre around the use of the bouncer, with the format varying according to the age, need and capability of my clients. I began teaching Starbound classes at the Gym at the Sanctuary, Covent Garden, in the heart of London. New clients consistently express amazement at the versatility of the equipment and the wide variety of techniques we perform to develop new and challenging skills. They are delighted to have found a form of exercise which leaves them feeling energized and revitalized at the end of each session rather than drained and drenched in perspiration.

The fitness boom has matured but is far from over. In my experience people are looking for exercise which is kind to their joints, challenging yet relaxing for their minds, and calming yet uplifting for their spirits. I firmly believe there is no quick fix. To achieve any goal you need to plan for steady and consistent action within realistic time zones.

Most people find they are able to achieve their aims not only because bouncing suits them as a form of exercise, but because they are likely to continue as they reap positive benefits while having fun.

The versatility of the equipment is really astounding. The entire family can use it, whether old, young, fit, able or infirm. Stress impact to joints and ligaments is dramatically reduced, while stimulation of the immune system is boosted due to healthy lymphatic response. Muscular, skeletal, endocrine, fluid and organ systems are enhanced simultaneously. Cellular metabolism is fired providing an excellent catalyst for healing, weight and inch loss, and general well-being. Numerous written testimonies, that I have gathered from people around the world, refer to improved blood pressure, and balanced cholesterol and stress levels. Others speak of sleeping more soundly at night and living more energetically by day. Many are using their bouncers in lifestyle programmes to eradicate painful symptoms arising from ailments such as arthritis, allergies, back problems and asthma.

There can be no doubt that your bouncer is more than just a tool for developing fitness. Every time you bounce you invite an ever-improving lifestyle. I've been using my bouncer around the house and garden every day for over five years, tapping my Starbound programmes to empower and activate my life.

Starbounding is fun! Starbounding is certainly for everyone! A bouncer in the house provides the perfect focus for an 'all in one' concept of optimum health and fitness. If bouncing your way back sounds too simple, the positive influences you experience as you follow your Starbound programmes regularly will probably surprise you. Benefits you are about to reap, coupled with an additional zest for living and abundance of energy, will offer you more bounce per ounce than ever before.

BOUNCING RESOLUTIONS

BOUNCING RESURRECTION

Millions of people around the world have been allowing their bouncers to gather dust because they haven't known how to use them. I'm inviting you to share numerous programmes I have designed to enable you to tap the potential your bouncer has to offer.

With insight, Harvey and Marilyn Diamond, authors of the international best-seller *Fit for Life*, and also *Living Health*, announced recently: '. . . The fact is that resistive rebounding will probably revolutionize the fitness movement in the next decade, not only for world class athletes, but for everyone interested in fitness, from the weakest to the strongest, from the clumsiest to the most fleet of foot.'

Since the concept of bouncing from a mini-trampoline was introduced nearly twenty years ago, as the most efficient and effective form of exercise ever devised, the reality has slowly dawned. Your bouncer is not a gimmick to be passed off as yet another fad. It stands on its own as the most powerful piece of equipment in the field of health and fitness, offering the perfect tool to rebalance your energy levels, bringing health and vitality back into your life. Your bouncer won't accomplish positive changes by being talked about, stored, avoided or even admired. However, it will work wonders for you if you work on it.

BOUNCY ALTERNATIVES

If you're lucky enough to make it to the gym, you're probably restricted to an hour, three times a week. Yet your body is designed to move actively and vigorously. Most health problems that have surfaced over the last fifty years are due to our tightly bound and hectic lives. The development of transport systems offers efficient delivery to our destinations, but at what cost? Buying food from shops, sitting at desks and earning livings with active minds but restricted bodies doesn't allow for the exercise we need to stay healthy. If your daily work involves both mental stimulation and safe physical activity you are one of the lucky ones. Most of us don't have this fortune and need to seek healthy options.

EXCUSES, EXCUSES

Experts have placed the general population into four categories to define attitudes to exercise. A small minority fit regular activity into their daily routines. Others would rather be chained to their chairs and not move a limb. Illness and disability restrict the capacity for an unfortunate few. Yet the majority clearly state that they would welcome more exercise if only it was easier to weave into their already overburdened daily timetable.

GO WITH THE FLOW

But how many of us simply lack the self-discipline to make time for exercise? You cannot afford to neglect the responsibility that you alone must carry for the state of your health. I have created your Starbound programmes by blending movement and relaxation techniques from gymnastics, dance, body conditioning, yoga and trampolining to provide a perfect combination for opening your energy flow and stoking your motivation to keep active. If there was a bouncer in every home, workplace, classroom and old people's residence, everyone would have the chance to move their body freely, fully and regularly.

BOUNCING SOLUTIONS

Recent surveys reveal the average person watches television for more than twenty hours a week. Yet the main reason put forward for not being able to fit exercise in is a simple lack of time. If you're one of those couch potatoes, you can always watch your favourite programmes while you bounce.

Exercise routines in a glossy magazine may temporarily inspire you, but how many times have you got down to the nitty-gritty and been disappointed to find them inadequate and dull? As you bounce you naturally overcome the inertia that threatens to dampen your enthusiasm. Each time you leave the mat, your body effortlessly opposes the force of gravity, creating feelings of buoyancy and exhilaration, heightening your senses and spurring your body into action.

You're spoilt for choice when you bounce in the privacy of your home. Whatever the weather, you can enjoy bouncing to your favourite music, by yourself or in the company of friends. In winter, you'll soon be shedding your woollies, turning the heating down as you turn your internal radiators up high. On a warm summer's day head off to the garden for a breezy bounce and burst of fresh air.

Once you've purchased your bouncer, you'll save money on expensive gym fees, travel expenses, shoes and special clothing. No need to arrange babysitters, sit in the traffic, find a place to park or jostle with crowds on public transport. Without a doubt, a bouncer in the house takes the hassle out of exercise.

Your Starbound programmes are geared to offer you a natural kick out of life. They provide you with the chance to succeed, where other forms of exercise may have failed for you. Bouncing puts the fun back into fitness, inviting spontaneity and variety, offering ingredients you need to spice up your life.

BOUNCING THROUGH THE AGES

People have always bounced. Leaping and jumping is a natural act tapped by the young in their play, forming an important part of recreation and physical education. Bouncing epitomizes fitness as you spring into step, energizing your being with zest and vigour. With your bouncer you are able to reclaim your natural instinct to jump.

As far back as the middle ages, travelling acrobats specialized in plank leaping, jumping over a variety of objects, including each other. Eskimos stretched walrus skins between stakes in the ice, bouncing zealously off and upon them. Inspired by the trapeze artist who ends his act dropping into a net, George Nissen set about designing the first trampoline around 1936. Throughout World War Two, the American Armed Forces adopted the equipment as part of their training programme to aid the development of aerial orientation, coordination and motor skills.

SKELETAL HEAVEN

Starbound programmes are designed to remove the struggle when achieving fitness, so with ease and pleasure you realize your aims. The aerobic pound is definitely out. When you jump up and down on the spot with a high impact landing, your spine is absorbing up to five times more force than when you walk. As you land, vertical shock waves spread up from your ankles through your bones and spine, and minor nerve damage may well occur at the root of your pelvis.

Although new exercise programmes have been surfacing to prevent injuries sustained from high impact aerobics, many problems have merely changed form. Many teachers are setting up bounce classes, determined to eliminate long-term possibilities of harsh impact injuries to your muscles, ligaments and joints.

JOGGING YOUR MEMORY

Jogging is considered damaging. Although your body is designed to run, it isn't designed to run on a concrete surface, which is what pounding the pavement involves. Because many joggers are not aware of the facts, they end up with micro-trauma injuries to their heels and ankles. Shock is transmitted up through your hips to your spine, through each vertebra and disc to your skull. Even though your discs have a shock-absorbing capacity, the shock is only reduced at each level. It can go right to the top of your spine and deflect off your skull setting up additional standing waves.

BUOYANCY FROM YOUR BOUNCER

You can bounce buoyantly without worrying about potential shock impact to your joints, skeleton or muscles. The impact your body absorbs on a quality bouncing unit is equivalent to walking on a carpeted surface. Vulnerable knees, ankles and backs are relatively stress-free. The impact is spread not only over a greater range, but a longer period.

As you bounce, the first portion of your weight deforms the surface of the mat as it gives. By the time you have been going down for several milliseconds, which spreads the impact, tension will be spread along with the abruptness to which it is applied to your ligaments and joints. Further damage, due to possible ripping in your muscle fibres, is prevented by the excellent balance of eccentric and concentric muscle contractions. Additional protection is offered to your spinal nerves, at the base of your spine, because the peak force isn't nearly as high.

Simply to maintain your balance when you bounce, your posture must be naturally aligned, which in itself offers protection from injury. Those of you who are overweight or suffering signs of wear and tear are able to relieve tensions and become fitter, as you gently loosen stiff muscles without straining your joints.

A TOTAL PERSPECTIVE

As you embark on your bouncing adventures aim to use your sessions to balance your mental alertness and for relaxation, as well as to beautify, tone and cleanse your body. Tired of watching people in exercise classes with tight unhappy faces, straining to the beat with sweat pouring from their brow, I have designed your programmes so you can bounce with awareness, to sharpen your senses. Your emotional and mental attitudes are even more important than your vital statistics.

Many societies in the past have woven a thread between sport, religion and philosophy. As ancient teachings from the East blend with scientific discoveries from the West, there has been a surge back to a total perspective which salutes harmony between mind, body and spirit. Your Starbound programmes reflect this trend, providing you with a variety of techniques you can blend with meditation and relaxation to develop personal strength and agility.

DON'T BECOME A STATISTIC

Billions of pounds are spent each year curing ills that a simple daily bounce could prevent and cure. Between 1901 and 1980, the proportion of deaths in the United States attributed to major chronic illness rose from 46% to 81%. In the Western world, cardiovascular disease and cancer account for more than two-thirds of all deaths. We are conditioned from early in life to expect a downward slide in the state of our health. It is implied that life is one slippery slope of ailments. High blood pressure, low blood sugar, bronchial conditions, obesity and constipation are among the minor complaints that settle in, gradually creating conditions for the onslaught of more chronic disease. Although hereditary factors may predispose you to the development of certain diseases, inactivity is one of the main triggers to set them off.

SELF-INVESTMENT, SELF-HELP

Although popping pills has been accepted this century, the prevention and cure of the many ailments crushing the hopes of millions around the world cannot be found in the medicine cabinet. Many things creep up on you to disturb the balance of your health. Poor sleeping patterns, thoughtless food habits, sudden changes, emotional traumas, mental tensions and a variety of stress triggers are among the culprits that serve to throw you out of kilter.

Although chemists' shelves are stocked to offer instant remedies for everything from chilblains to headaches, in many cases we need a change in perspective. Too many people treat their body like a car, filling it up with fuel, rarely taking time to check the oil and water, then waiting for it to break down before devoting any more time or money to it. If this sounds familiar, don't drown yourself in an ocean of guilt; take stock and shape up. Bouncing back to a prime state of health needn't be a difficult affair. With your bouncer as the perfect focus of support to cushion the changes, you'll find new patterns slip into place.

TAKING POSITIVE CONTROL

There are many ways you can use the different Starbound programmes to activate your lifestyle. Throughout the book you'll find Resolution Plans filled with guidelines to help ensure you gain optimum benefit from your bouncer. If you really want to change a habit, you have to be prepared to follow a daily plan of action, or your wishes will remain unfulfilled. To attain your targets you need to assess areas for change, then set appropriate goals and strategies to pave your way to success. Throw away thoughts of self-denial. Place positive disciplines upon yourself, tap your inner forces of resolve and feel your confidence and self-image grow.

TRANSMISSIONS

CELLULAR POTENTIAL

By adulthood, your body is an amazing network of billions of microscopic particles, or cells, which attempt to maintain themselves, even against all odds. While some have multiplied to stimulate your growth, and to repair wear and tear, others have simply increased in size. Every cell depends on bountiful supplies of rich oxygen and an abundance of essential nutrients from your food. In the heart of every cell, tiny chemical furnaces, known as mitochondria, are busy in the processes essential to your metabolism. Oxygen and nutrients combine to create energy for the life processes of each cell.

COMMUNAL NEEDS

Because they are bathed in intercellular fluid, no two cells ever come into contact with each other. Plasma, the fluid in which blood cells are suspended, seeps out of tiny capillaries all over your body, carrying supplies of nutrients from your digested food and oxygen from the air you breathe. It merges with the intercellular fluid, from where each cell should be able to obtain its share of goodies for healthy growth, maintenance and repair.

A continuous exchange takes place between oxygen and nutrients, and carbon dioxide, wastes and debris from your cells. If your circulation is flowing freely, once the exchange has taken place, fluid is reabsorbed into your capillaries to re-enter your bloodstream or is carried away by your lymphatics to be cleansed and filtered.

Snags and rocks restrict the flow of a river gathering debris while water flows on regardless. In the same way, wastes and toxins build up in stagnating tissues creating breeding grounds for disease, even though circulation continues.

For tip-top functioning your cells need to be housed in a pure and wholesome environment. Just as problems posed by pollution unsettle our earth, so they stand to unsettle your body. Waste products are toxic to the system, resulting in poor circulation to and from the cells and in a stagnation of cellular fluid. Eventually these cesspools of pollution strangle and shade your potential for radiant health.

BOUNCY CELLS

About two-thirds of your body is comprised of fluid which regulates numerous functions, acting as a reservoir for nutrients while controlling many electrical and chemical processes. A variety of poor conditions and thoughtless habits are chiefly responsible for polluting your internal waterways and tissues, opening the doors for disease. Unbalanced food intake, negative attitudes, reactions to stress, environmental pollutants, drugs, alcohol and overindulgence in many forms combine with a lack of regular exercise to trigger poor and sluggish circulation.

The strength and vitality of your health depends on the proper functioning of the billions of cells throughout your body. As you bounce, combined forces positively influence the nourishment and strength of each and every one.

COMBINED FORCES

Since Isaac Newton was compelled by a falling apple to investigate gravity, a few more solid deductions have been made about this powerful force. Physical development depends on the fact that you have to oppose gravity to muster strength. From birth you challenge this force, at first lifting your head, then crawling, walking, running, jumping and moving against it in a variety of ways. One of the four fundamental forces of the universe, gravity continually influences your posture and development.

Poor relationships with gravity are responsible for many cases of spinal compression, impaired circulation, disc degeneration and a diminished functioning of glands, tissues and cells. When your body becomes restricted intercellular fluid stagnates, result-

● The unique way your body is subjected to the force of gravity, combined with the vertical upward and downward movement on the bouncer, and changing forces of acceleration and deceleration, puts all cells from the tiniest to the largest bone under consistent rhythmical pressure.

● Bouncing is gentle yet strengthening for all systems in your body.

ing in a further build up of wastes and debris around your cell walls. If you want to experience the benefits of additional cellular stimulation, take the reins of the G-Force (the term given to the force of gravity) in the most natural way and bounce to harness its power.

The measure of the force of gravity affecting your body at rest is 1 g. Speedy motion in a horizontal plane or a change of position in a vertical direction will increase the G-Force acting on your body. Compared to jumping from a hard surface, bouncing from a yielding mat enables you to make the most of the G-Force values, without the shock impact.

When bouncing, the pull of the G-Force is measured at the lowest point on the mat as you are about to turn your jump. On a large trampoline it is likely you would go up to 8 gs (about eight times your body weight). However, on a small bouncing unit it is unlikely you would exceed 3 gs, and the usual G-Force values range between 2 to $2\frac{1}{2}$ gs. This provides the perfect level for stimulating the most efficient training, according to NASA studies on the effects of trampolining.

SPACED OUT

Since man has been exploring outer space, astronauts have been faced with the effect of zero gravity which threatens to weaken their bones and tissues through lack of stress upon their body cells. For this reason, four NASA scientists carried out the first-ever research into the use of the trampoline, with evidence surfacing to suggest that bouncing is superior exercise.

Dr Wade, exercise physiologist at The London Hospital Medical College, informed me that much exercise in space is performed bouncing off the walls of the craft so that astronauts can keep themselves fit by applying some stress to their bones. As he explained, the bone cells of these astronauts benefit from the bouncing motion. The amount of work performed by your cells when jumping will exaggerate the normal effects of gravity. As you land on your bouncer you are decelerating with the additional force coming up. Your falling weight is placing extra stress on your cells which will help to strengthen them.

BENEFITS AS YOU BOUNCE

● *Every cell is influenced from all directions by the atmospheric pressure pushing on it, coupled with the influence of a direct gravitational pull.*

● *Forces of gravity are stimulated more powerfully because of the direct vertical plane. The G-Force is tapped to optimum advantage.*

● *At the top of each bounce every cell is relatively stress-free, offering a feeling of weightlessness, while at the bottom of the bounce the G-Force at work on all body cells is increased by up to three times the normal amount depending on the intensity of your jump.*

● *The forces of acceleration and deceleration combine with the force of gravity to impose a further challenge on your cells, encouraging them to adjust and strengthen their walls and processes.*

● *The G-Force measured at your ankles, back and forehead is almost equally distributed when you bounce, compared to floor exercise where your ankle joints take more than twice the impact of your lower back or forehead.*

INNER OCEANS

Merging Rivers

An extraordinary network of blood and lymph vessels interconnect to transport fluids throughout your body. Blood is constantly referred to as your 'river of life', bringing health, strength and vitality as it flows. Your heart pumps blood which carries ingredients such as hormones, gases, oxygen and nutrients through a variety of vessels. To remain healthy, every cell has to receive a full quotient of nutrients, at the same time disposing of waste products and carbon dioxide.

The most important exchanges in your circulation take place through billions of capillaries. Their walls consist of only one layer of cells, enabling products to pass easily into your intercellular fluid and waste products and carbon dioxide to return into your bloodstream. Over 40,000 miles of these tiny vessels weave their way through your tissues and organs in the closest possible contact with your cells. New capillary routes are continually springing up due to demand. For every two pounds you gain in weight, for example, you have to grow over a mile of capillaries.

SILENT SUPPORTS

As you bounce, the supply of blood to your muscles is dramatically improved which in turn stimulates your lymphatic flow. Little is said about the magical properties of lymph, or of the important role your lymphatic system plays in supporting the quality of your health. Lymph is a colourless, watery tissue fluid that circulates in the lymphatic vessels of the body. It becomes milky when draining fats and wastes from your intestines. About 10% of fluid and all blood plasma proteins enter your lymphatics which are often described as the rubbish bin of your body. Dead cells, bacteria, viruses and plasma proteins are among debris from intercellular fluid, rendered harmless in your lymphatics, before re-entering the bloodstream.

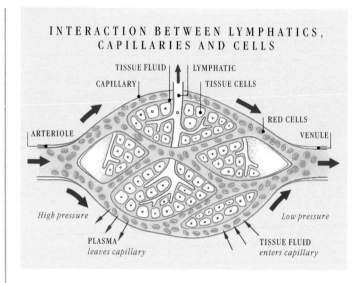

INTERACTION BETWEEN LYMPHATICS, CAPILLARIES AND CELLS

TISSUE FLUID — LYMPHATIC
CAPILLARY — TISSUE CELLS
RED CELLS
ARTERIOLE — VENULE
High pressure — *Low pressure*
PLASMA
leaves capillary
TISSUE FLUID
enters capillary

LYMPHATIC MAZES

Believe it or not, you have more lymph vessels than blood in your body, although they flow in one direction only, from the smallest capillaries to the largest ducts. Blood and lymph are interlaced throughout your body, merging to help each other, often running parallel routes, until they blend again when lymph is tipped back into your bloodstream, via the large subclavian veins behind your collarbone.

Along your lymph pathways bead-like nodes are found which vary in size from a pinpoint to a cherry. They act as deprogramming stations for your cancerous cells, prevent viruses from invading further and filter debris from your circulation. Without a doubt, your lymph nodes are one of the most important stations of defence in your body. Antibodies and lymphocytes (white blood cells famous for fighting off germs and bacteria) are produced and activated within them. Many other warriors, such as phagocytes and white blood cells that engulf and eat debris and bacteria, line a network of tiny passages operating in your nodes.

FAT CHANCE!

● Your lymphatics have many other roles to play. Fat, for the most part, isn't initially transported in your bloodstream but absorbed through the intestinal wall into lymphatic vessels known as lacteals. It is picked up in the form of droplets, or as free fatty acids and glycerols, to be transported through your lymphatics before entering your blood.

THE LYMPHATIC DRAINAGE SYSTEM

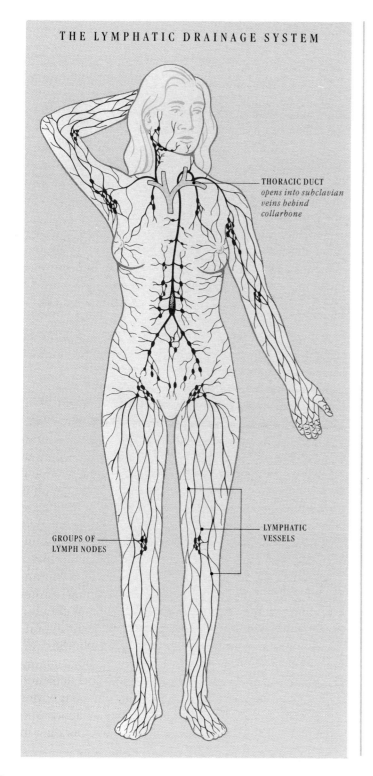

THORACIC DUCT
opens into subclavian veins behind collarbone

GROUPS OF LYMPH NODES

LYMPHATIC VESSELS

INVISIBLE PUMPS

Your blood is taken on its journey by the pumping of your heart. But even though lymph flows for thousands of miles throughout your body it has no such pump. The flow is regulated by a series of valves, which depend on definite stimulants for activation. On an x-ray you see a string of pearls with valves that open as the muscle belly is filled and compressed. You depend on an increase in pressure below the valve to open the leaf and shunt the lymph forward. Bouncing offers one of the most powerful forces to activate conditions which pump your lymph. To create an increase in pressure you depend on:

- Deep and full breathing.
- Changes in gravitational pull.
- Muscular contractions and stimulation.
- Changes in atmospheric pressure.
- Activation of calf, thigh and abdominal muscles.

All of these conditions are fulfilled effortlessly as you bounce.

There has been much research connecting lymphatic response to the changing G-Force as you bounce. It is considered that:

❶ Bouncing up against the downward pull of gravity closes one-way valves, regulating the flow of fluid.

❷ Moving down again releases pressure in the valves. Increased G-Force when you depress the mat produces a healthy surge of fluid through your body. As the pressure in your tissues changes, the flow of lymph is shunted on. Your body thrives on the change in speed and direction that occurs twice with each jump.

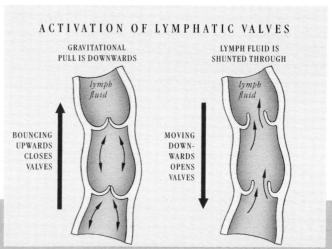

ACTIVATION OF LYMPHATIC VALVES

GRAVITATIONAL PULL IS DOWNWARDS

LYMPH FLUID IS SHUNTED THROUGH

lymph fluid

lymph fluid

BOUNCING UPWARDS CLOSES VALVES

MOVING DOWN-WARDS OPENS VALVES

INCREASE YOUR FLOW

Lack of activity, shallow breathing, poor food habits, convalescence and clustered blood plasma proteins can all create a sluggish lymph flow. As you bounce the normal rate of flow may increase by three to fourteen times. Lymph naturally flows very slowly with about 4 fluid ounces moving every hour. When you are inactive between $\frac{1}{5}$ and $\frac{2}{5}$ of a teaspoon of fluid is drained each minute as opposed to up to 4 teaspoons when you bounce.

At the bottom of each bounce your cells are compressed which helps to lure wastes, plasma proteins and toxins from the surrounding tissue fluids. The mutual exchange between your capillaries and cells is excited into action. Lymph and body fluids flow freely under these conditions.

Trapped Plasma Proteins

If your circulation becomes stagnant, blood plasma proteins, such as globulin, fibrinogen and albumin, accumulate and cluster causing a fragmented stockpile of rubbish in your tissue spaces, and severe problems for your cells. They cause a sad loss of energy, blocked electrical circuits, pain and disease. Up to 50% of these proteins can leak out of your bloodstream over a twenty-four hour period if blood capillaries have dilated due to poor nutrition, reactions to stress, improper exercise or injury.

Once released into your intercellular fluid, plasma proteins depend entirely on your lymphatics to return them to your blood. They are simply too large to enter the tiny walls of your blood capillaries. Because they carry a negative charge, trapped plasma proteins attract sodium which in turn causes fluid retention. If surrounded cells become swamped with fluid, they in turn are deprived of oxygen and nutrients, and are simply unable to operate. For healthy functioning, a cell must remain in a dry state with just enough fluid to fill the crevices around it.

BEWARE! BEWARE!

If any number of offenders cause your capillaries to dilate too quickly reactions snowball, with a burst of plasma proteins spilling over into your intercellular fluid.

❶ Refined sugars, salts and overprocessed foods (like biscuits, crisps and ice cream) all serve as a poison to your capillaries causing them to dilate. Plasma proteins escape.

❷ Your hormonal response to stress triggers a release of hormones which dilate your capillaries. Plasma proteins surface.

❸ When injured, your cells release poisons, like histamine, which dilate your capillaries pulling plasma proteins and fluid from your bloodstream, creating inflammation and pain. Plasma proteins cluster.

❹ As they become trapped they cause pressure in your intercellular fluid, influencing the onset of high blood pressure. Plasma proteins rob your cells of oxygen.

❺ When they cluster around your cells they create an imbalance in potassium and sodium, upsetting the pump that generates electrical activity. Trapped plasma proteins switch your generators off, dulling your energy supply, causing pain and damage.

❻ Overdosing on fats in your diet robs your body of oxygen, making it impossible for your cells to complete their energy cycles. Red blood cells carry oxygen through your bloodstream. If they are not charged with a rich supply they cluster, causing cellular jams. Trapped proteins appear at the scene of the crime.

Immune Overhauls

Because 90% of modern-day illnesses and afflictions are immune related, treatments are often best stimulated by the activation of lymph. Many headaches, for example, are lymph related. There are over 300 lymph nodes in your neck, head and throat area – more than anywhere else in your body. The function of these nodes is mainly to drain toxins from your brain. If

STRESS-FREE DRAINAGE

● If fatty deposits build up in nodes and lymph vessels blockages occur within your lymphatics.

● A back-log in the flow of lymph encourages plasma proteins to cluster. If lymph piles up damage

may occur to your valves with serious implications for your immune system.

● Bounce daily to move fatty deposits and toxic residue to prevent degeneration in your tissues.

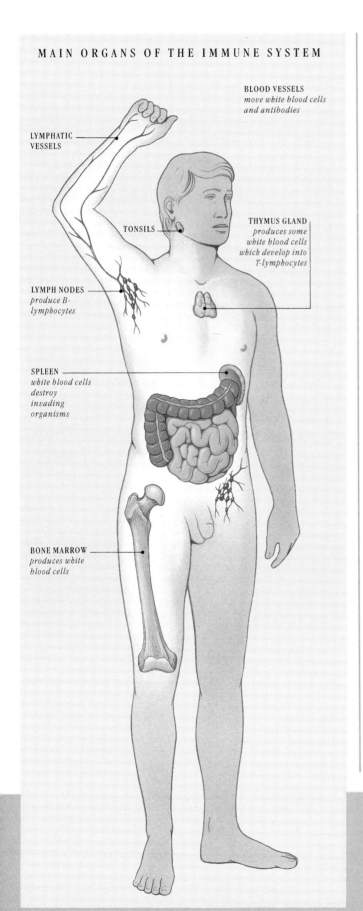

MAIN ORGANS OF THE IMMUNE SYSTEM

BLOOD VESSELS
move white blood cells and antibodies

LYMPHATIC VESSELS

TONSILS

THYMUS GLAND
produces some white blood cells which develop into T-lymphocytes

LYMPH NODES
produce B-lymphocytes

SPLEEN
white blood cells destroy invading organisms

BONE MARROW
produces white blood cells

blockages in your lymph become stagnant toxins are not able to drain efficiently. Because of the forces at play when you bounce, all fluid systems are activated simultaneously, offering a perfect boost for your lymphatic and, therefore, your immune response.

Your immune system, of which your lymphatic vessels are an important part, is the mother of all systems. If it is geared for immediate action when any form of invasion occurs, it will function well and you shouldn't fall ill. Your lymphatic vessels link your immune organs, which include your bone marrow, tonsils, thymus, lymph nodes and your spleen. This busy network produces and circulates blood cells and antibodies to fight infection, filter bacteria, and eliminate parasites and debris from your body.

MUSTERING IMMUNE ARMIES

When any type of invader enters your body, in the guise of bacteria, viruses, fungi, pollen grains, chemical substances, or with any potential to create a burden for your body defences, it is known as an antigen. Like an army in defence, your immune system constantly monitors your body for anything out of place, immediately sending in appropriate soldiers, or defender cells, when battle is announced. Your white blood cells have intricate abilities to attack antigens. B-lymphocytes produce antibodies, while T-lymphocytes recognize and directly attack invading viruses. They also protect you from cancer, identifying and destroying cells that have gone haywire. Among the lymphocytes lying in wait, you have thousands of varieties of cells, each responsible for making only one type of antibody. They multiply to produce an army of like cells as soon as they come in touch with the antigen they match. Following the destruction of antigens, scavenger cells, known as phagocytes, come in to devour the debris from the battlefield.

As viruses enter your body they worm their way into your cells which replicate. The best and only way to prevent these invaders taking over is to stimulate your immune system to stay on top. As you bounce, your capacity to develop and maintain immunity is given the boost it needs to conquer any alien forces.

BOUNDLESS ENERGY

SODIUM POTASSIUM PUMPERS

Although it sounds like the latest craze in fizzy drink, your sodium potassium pumps involve the rotation of sodium and potassium ions, in and around every cell in your body, generating an electrical field which surrounds each cell wall. An intricate balance of potassium and sodium in and around your cells keeps the generation of electrical energy constant. If a cell becomes swamped due to clustered plasma proteins and wastes, the surrounding electrical activity is dimmed, creating short circuits in your energy flow.

SHEER MUSCLE POWER

For sheer survival you rely upon the quality of your muscles to give your body strength, mobility and energy. All motion depends upon muscle tissue sweeping into action with a succession of chemical and electrical interactions occurring throughout your body. To illustrate the subtle communication that takes place, look at what happens when you move the biceps in your upper arm.

❶ Inelastic tendons attach your biceps to both your shoulder blade and your forearm, with a mass of

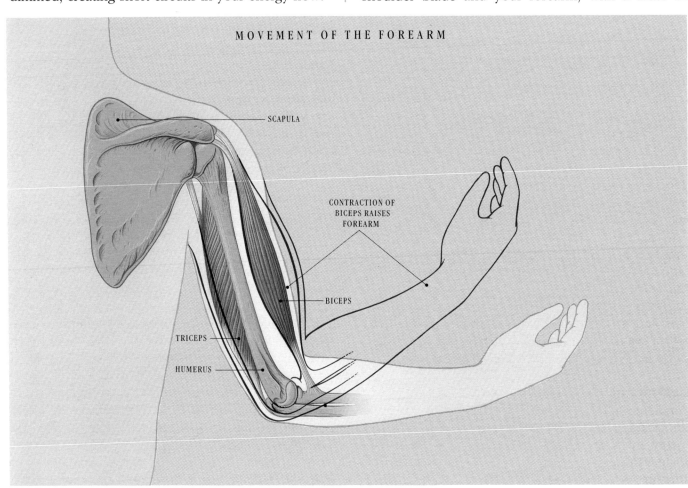

MOVEMENT OF THE FOREARM

SCAPULA

CONTRACTION OF
BICEPS RAISES
FOREARM

BICEPS

TRICEPS

HUMERUS

muscle cells forming your biceps tissue sitting between the tendons.

❷ As the instruction to move your biceps is sent from your brain, the message is transmitted to special endings on your muscle, not actually in contact with the muscle itself. The message is then taxied over a small bridge between your nerve and muscle by the chemical acetylcholine.

❸ When the taxi arrives at the muscle it fits like a glove, initiating an electrical impulse which causes your muscle to contract, bringing your forearm up.

SHORT CIRCUITS

As complicated as the process may seem it occurs every time you move any part of your body. Millions of muscle fibres and chemical molecules work with nerve fibres through transmissions of electrical impulses.

As they work your muscles give off waste products, among them carbon dioxide and lactic acid. Problems arise if your muscles become tense or blocked, bunching up and pressing on surrounding blood and lymph vessels. If they become trapped in their own wastes – making the delivery of nutrients and oxygen an impossible task – the delicate transmission of electrical impulses and muscle fibre response is severely impeded. Imbalance in the tone of your muscles shifts the balance of your health.

When the electricity at home blows a fuse you hunt for the wire and reconnect the circuit. So, what happens when you blow a fuse in your body circuit? The electrical field around every cell needs to be 'switched on'. When trapped plasma proteins, excess fluid and a build up of wastes from cellular metabolism swamp your cells, the switches for your electrical circuits throughout your body are impaired.

MANIPULATING MERIDIANS

Meridians, which can be tapped by modern technological methods, are the pathways along which the energy in your body flows. Along their channels, points can be identified which are electromagnetic in structure, surrounding the capillaries in your skin.

Energy is believed to flow through your body in a complete circuit following these clearly defined meridians. If the flow of energy is restricted, or your circuits are operating on overload, balance has to be restored before your energy will flow fully again.

Life is loaded with energy, although it remains a mystery. Light is invisible unless it hits a solid mass and is reflected back to your eyes. Constant energy pours out of each of us, as well, channelled through our senses, speech, movement and especially our thought.

Wise teachers of ancient times have always referred to energy but in different terms. Indians called the higher energy 'Nam' and the lower energy 'Prana'. Chinese tagged it 'Tao' or 'Chi'. Greeks saw it as 'Logos of the Music of the Spheres', Hippocrates referred to 'Nature's Life Force', Wilhelm Reich called it 'Orgone Energy' and Dr Stone considered it 'Electromagnetic Energy'. Whatever it is labelled, most people agree that energy is the force that gives us life, providing personal connection between mind, body, spirit and emotions. Many orthodox practitioners are now combining the knowledge of oriental practitioners, surrounding the energy pathways in your body, with the more scientific western approach.

PALM YOUR ENERGY

Observe the vibrations of your subtle energy 'first hand'. In the Rhythm Bounce (p. 29), rub the palms of your hands together with your fingertips facing away from your body. Continue this motion for at least one minute. Stop bouncing and hold your palms facing and a few inches apart. Move your hands closer together, and then wider apart. Keep them between one and six inches from each other. You should feel the subtle movement of magnetic energy.

THE KIRLEON CONNECTION

Every living being, whether plant, animal or human has a measurable living energy field around them. When this energy can move through the whole body, including bones, skin, muscles, fluids and organs, in the right relationship, it will create charisma and

INNER ENERGIES
● Many changes take place while you bounce related to the subtle movement of your energy.

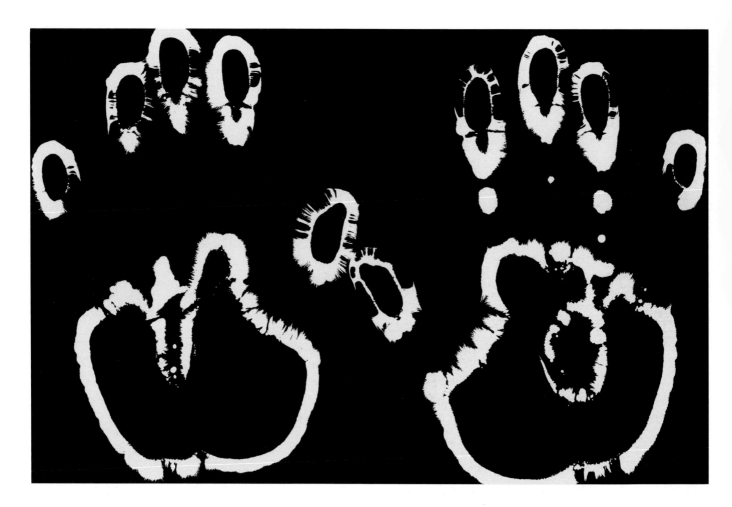

A Kirleon photograph recording the electrical interference patterns in my hands was used as a tool for counselling to monitor what was happening in my energy fields.

radiate light. If your supply becomes run down, your body will soon let you know. When depleted of energy all of your body systems run below par.

BOUNCING ENERGY IN

As you bounce you are creating subtle waves of energy rhythmically throughout your whole being. Muscles are stimulated into action, joints are oiled by circulating fluids, bones are strengthened by their resistance to gravity, while fluid and energy are eased forward in the course of their flow. Stiffness you have been holding gently melts away. As you invite elasticity and suppleness in to play, your breath deepens and your spirit is recharged. The elasticity and friendliness of the mat to your body reinforce a fluid mental attitude of vitality, vigour and positive encouragement. Energy is truly tapped as your mind is calmed, refreshed and rebalanced. The vital forces in motion favour your soul as much as your body.

ZONING IN

The use of your bouncer exerts a powerful influence upon your neurolymphatic reflex zones. This simple test will show you how positive this influence can be. Try it with a friend and see for yourself.

ENERGY IN MOTION

● Many therapists describe emotion as 'energy in motion'. They consider we use our body as an armour to shield our reactions to stress.

● Energy becomes trapped if it reaches muscles that are tensed or locked.

● Wilhelm Reich was among the first pioneers to view the process of therapy as facilitating the free flow of energy throughout your body.

❷ Now, rub your hands up and down the complete lower edge of your ribs on both sides. This is the neurolymphatic reflex zone for your quadricep muscles. Repeat the test again. Now that your neurolymphatic zone has been activated do you find it simpler to resist the pressure? Do you feel more power?

❸ Bounce freely for about thirty seconds without rubbing your zones. Repeat the test again with your friend. Do you have more power than in either of the previous tests?

MAGNETIC ATTRACTIONS

The bouncer is hailed by many therapists as 'the rocking chair of the nineties'. In their opinion, constant rhythmical bouncing creates a consistent and forceful flow of lymphatic fluid which, coupled with mechanical energy arising from the mat, energizes every cell. Every living thing pulsates with a natural rhythm. This is reflected in nature in the waves that lap upon the shore, in the unfolding of the seasons as summer follows spring, and in the cycles of the moon with the natural ebb and flow of the tide. Life moves forward in a pulsating rhythm which also binds your body, influencing the intricate timing of your hormonal and chemical output, as well as many other patterns within your 24-hour circadian cycles.

POSITIVE VIBRATIONS

The positive rhythmical vibration that is stimulated when you bounce reaches the core of your being, building on the supply of kinetic energy in your cells, organs and tissues. Following intense research, it is not difficult to see why so many people in poor health claim miraculous results and boosts in their general energy levels with a simple vibrational bounce a few times a day.

Scientists have discovered that animals and humans exposed to increased frequency vibration, develop increased heart rate and metabolic activity. Responses measured during whole body vibration resemble those during mild exercise, leading to the suggestion that it could be used in place of exercise.

❶ Stand straight, bending your knee at a right angle. Lift your thigh parallel to the floor. Take a deep breath in. As you exhale have your friend press down with a firm hand on the front of your thigh. Try to push against the pressure by moving your thigh upward. Register the amount of force you need to muster to push your thigh.

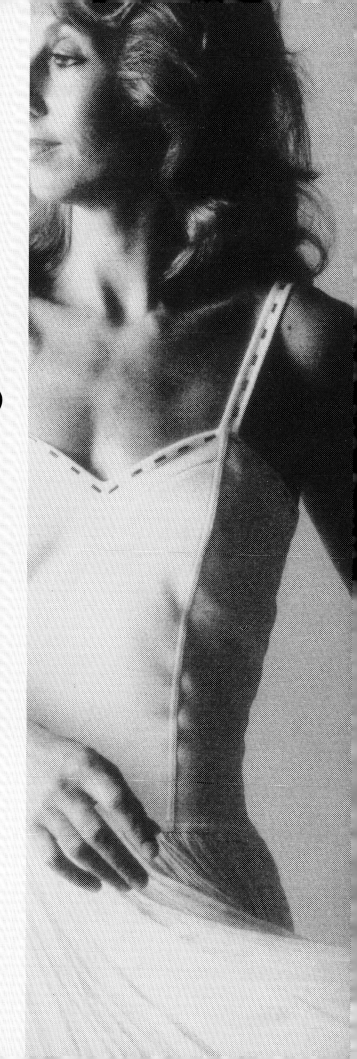

THE STARBOUND WORKOUT

PREPARING FOR ACTION

THE PERFECT TOOL

Before you purchase a bouncing unit, bear in mind the following pointers:

● Does the bouncer carry a guarantee?

● The outer cover should be of thick vinyl or fabric and completely cushion the springs.

● The mat must be of high quality material, to prevent jarring, with strong stitching. The surface should be at least 40 inches in diameter.

● The quality of the spring steel determines the quality of the bounce and longevity of the spring itself, which should be rust-resistant.

● Check you can replace the mat and springs, if necessary, due to wear and tear.

● The legs should be long enough to keep you off the floor at all stages of the bounce. Check that the legs have quality caps that will not mark the carpet.

PERFECTLY PLACED

You can bounce almost anywhere, providing you leave enough clearance from surrounding furniture. If possible, use a mirror to check your posture, and as an aid when choreographing routines. Do keep your bouncer in a main living area, making it accessible for constant use. You can always sew your own covers by joining a strip of fabric, elasticating each side, then slipping it over the existing cover. Or place a sheepskin rug over the mat to create a cosy base from which to stretch, condition and relax in the evening. Don't feel the need to hide your bouncer from the visitors. The chances are it will become the perfect conversation piece.

A bounce in the garden offers the perfect chance to pick up an extra burst of sunlight. Pure sunlight is undoubtedly a great source for the stimulation of Vitamin D, which is essential for transporting calcium to your bones. Bouncing in the morning or the afternoon means you can avoid the sun at its peak. Never leave your bouncer sitting outside.

DRESSED FOR LEISURE

There's no need to dress for the gym, as long as you are comfortable, in loose-fitting garments which enable you to move freely. Many women find they are more comfortable in a sports bra or support top. If you bounce in bare feet, you provide a subtle massaging effect and ensure better foot control. If you suffer from tight calves or achilles tendons, training shoes will help to ease tension in the beginning. Beware bouncing in slippery shoes, socks or tights.

BALANCE BARS

If you have any doubt about your balance or stability, always use a balance bar. They attach very easily to the legs of your bouncer, and provide a grip for your hands at about waist height. Vertigo and exhaustion often run together, so check you are not overdoing it. If you are continually losing your balance, try widening the stance of your feet to provide a firmer base for your body. Any turns about the mat will be slowed down if you keep your arms out wide from your sides. If you lose balance, always stop and establish the correct position before continuing.

STRIKING THE BALANCE

You'll have great fun designing programmes, striking the balance between using your bouncer spontaneously or for planned sessions. Adapt techniques from each of the different programmes to incorporate different elements into each session.

Prepare for your session before you begin, with your skipping rope, resistance bands, cushions for stretch, and other aids you may want to use, close at hand. Choose music that is suited to your mood or prepare your Starbound video. If you have children, check they are fully occupied or plan to include them into your session. If you want complete time-out for relaxation and meditation, take the telephone off the hook.

SAFETY ZONES

Certain boundaries need to be observed to ensure total safety on the bouncer. NEVER BOUNCE:

● When you are under the influence of alcohol.

● When you are overly tired.

● From the bouncer to the floor.

● When your body is in the crucial stages of a virus or infection.

● On a mat that is torn or frayed.

● On a full stomach.

● On the spring cover of your mat.

WHEN WILL YOU BOUNCE?

As you explore the variety of techniques available, you'll soon realize your bouncer serves a number of purposes. The following hints may serve as a reminder:

● A bounce in the morning will set you off on a positive footing. Even a couple of minutes will make a positive difference to your day.

● Whenever you feel sluggish take a bouncing break.

● Bounce if you are feeling low, stressed, worried or upset.

● Bounce to tank up on oxygen supplies, and boost your brain power, if you are sitting at a desk, working or studying.

● Bounce for a couple of minutes every hour if you are typing, or working a computer, to help avoid repetitive strain injuries.

● Plan your full Starbound Workout sessions in advance, preferably booking them into your weekly timetable.

MEDICAL CHECKLIST

If you score over five points in the following test, take it along to your health practitioner and have a check. Usually there is no need for concern, but it is best to err on the safe side as you plan for long-term health and fitness.

AGE		OBESITY LEVEL	
Under 35	0	Normal weight	0
35–44	1	More than 20% overweight	2
45–54	2		
55 and over	4		

BLOOD PRESSURE		MEDICAL HISTORY	
Under 140/90	0	Previous cardiac trouble	6
Under 160/95	2	Diabetes mellitus	5
Over 160/94	4	Heart disease in family	2
Unknown	2	Lower back pain	5
		Heavy smoking	2
		Previously inactive	1

IF IN DOUBT

Always check with your practitioner before you embark on any of the bouncing programmes if you suffer chest pain, dizzy spells, osteoporosis, arthritic or joint pain, or have any worries about your health. If you are taking any medication, suffer from prolapsed womb, detached retinas, thrombosis phlebitus, or suffer any chronic disorder which requires permission to exercise, you must consult your practitioner.

T O P I C A L   T I P S

BEGINNING TO BOUNCE

● It isn't unusual to experience a slight feeling of panic when you first step on a bouncer. Take it very slowly, keeping your feet low to the mat, giving yourself a chance to reorientate.

● Pace yourself according to your level of fitness and ability. Finish all sessions, for at least two weeks, feeling as though you could have done more.

● Any temporary feelings of nausea may relate to the reorientation of the organs of balance in your inner ear. Sudden changes and repositioning of the head can create these sensations. Don't forget to breathe fully.

● As your programme commences, you may notice some immediate changes occurring with your body. Minor headaches, sniffly noses, discharges, changes in bowel habits and skin irritations may temporarily occur. They're often signs that your body is throwing off toxins and wastes while entering a cleansing state. Keep bouncing gently through this period while your body readjusts to the changes taking place.

● Muscles deteriorate without use, so remember residual benefits will eventually be lost when you stop bouncing for prolonged periods.

● Master skills and techniques with care and attention, gradually building up your repertoire.

● You'll be delighted as your senses of sight, sound and smell are switched back on. Energy, joy and vitality will replace the fatigue and dulled responses you may have been harbouring.

2 STARBOUNDING

Your Starbound Workout is designed to offer you a variety of techniques divided into five sections:

1 LYMPHATIC REFLEX ZONES

2 THE WARM-UP

3 BOUNCE TARGET ZONES

4 CONDITIONING

5 STRETCH AND RELAXATION

Take time to become familiar with the techniques from the Starbound Workout. One-star techniques offer the simplest foundation from which to work on your bouncer. As you progress you simply learn to adapt new routines adding two-star and three-star techniques to your sessions. You will possibly be ready to practise most techniques immediately, but whatever your fitness level, don't push yourself too far too soon. Learn one new technique at a time and add it to your sessions. Remember to ease rather than stress your body into new patterns.

Techniques in the Starbound Workout are laid out to offer you clear guidelines for instruction. Once you become familiar with each technique, the fun begins as you create new routines yourself, by combining the techniques in different formats. Some people prefer to memorize small routines created to specific music, while others create new patterns spontaneously each time they bounce.

You obviously can't perform all techniques set out in all sections of the Starbound Workout every time you bounce. Simply choose sequences you feel most appropriate to your needs. Although most routines are marked for repeats '× 8' to each side, this is only an approximate guide. Vary the counts according to your choreography.

If you are using the bouncer for a few minutes as a pick-me-up, or for a bit of fun, make the most of your time and practise any variety of techniques from different programmes throughout the book. Remember to stretch your calf and thigh muscles (pp. 44–6). Adapt sequences from those such as Bright Eyes, The Kiss of Life, Alarm Bells! Stress! or Better Backs.

Alternatively, if you are planning your Starbound Workout to fulfil your aerobic fitness requirements and to condition and tone, you'll need to plan your sessions by selecting techniques from each of the five sections – always warming up before working in your Bounce Target Zones. When you are selecting your conditioning techniques remember to balance sessions to ensure all muscles receive your attention. Don't be tempted to overindulge your trouble spots!

Before starting to work through these programmes, it is important to understand the basic posture, rhythm walk and rhythm bounce from which your routines will develop.

POSTURAL PRESCRIPTIONS

Throughout your routines, become aware of lengthening your spine to encourage structural balance. When you are posturally aligned, you should centre your breathing in your belly, with a relaxed abdomen. Bouncing calls upon a body-centred approach so you'll naturally sharpen your postural commitments throughout your programmes.

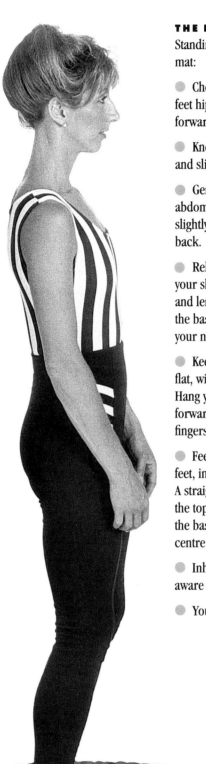

THE POSTURE STANCE
Standing in the centre of your mat:

● Check your toes are in line, feet hip-width apart and facing forward.

● Knees should be released and slightly bent.

● Gently contract your abdomen, tilting your pelvis slightly forward, to flatten your back.

● Relax your shoulders, keep your shoulder blades released and lengthen your spine from the base through the back of your neck.

● Keep the top of your head flat, with your chin slightly in. Hang your arms loosely, forward from your sides, with fingers relaxed.

● Feel your weight over your feet, in line with your hips. A straight line should run from the top of your head through the base of your neck to the centre of your spine.

● Inhale deeply to become aware of your breathing.

● You are ready to bounce!

THE RHYTHM BOUNCE ✪
From the Posture Stance, push into the mat from your hips, with your knees loose and relaxed and your feet remaining completely low to the mat at all times. Establish a rhythm as the movement flows easily and smoothly.

THE RHYTHM WALK ✪
Raise your left heel, keeping the ball of your foot flat to the mat as your opposite heel depresses the mat. Establish a rhythm as you alternate feet, walking on the mat. The different heights of the raised heel will determine your rhythm. Arms should correspond with the movement of the opposite leg. For example, your left arm moves forward as your right heel lifts off the mat.

◄ **1 ENERGIZER**

Place your left hand over your navel. Stroke down the centre of your sternum with your right hand. Move your eyes from side to side. Reverse hand positions and repeat.

Lymphatic Reflex Zones

I was taught the following techniques by registered lymphologists who use them to direct electrical energy in the body for pain relief and healing processes. I often use them at the beginning and end of my workout. Any of the techniques can be practised at any time, either on their own or interspersed with other exercises.

● Pace your rhythm evenly, moving in either the Rhythm Walk or the Rhythm Bounce.

● Practise any of the breathing techniques (pp. 135–7) to activate your breath. Try this pattern: Inhale, exhale, inhale, exhale, inhale, exhale, exhale, exhale. Empty your lungs completely.

● Stroke each zone, either with all fingers coned together or with a flat palm. Use long quick motions as if you were striking a match over the zone. Stroke the area for between thirty and sixty seconds.

▲ **2 POLARIZER**

Place your left hand over your navel. Rub above and below lips with index and middle fingers of your right hand. Reverse hand positions and repeat.

▲ **3 EQUALIZER**

Place your left hand over your navel. Stroke your coccyx (tail-bone) with your right hand. Move your eyes up and down. Reverse hand positions and repeat.

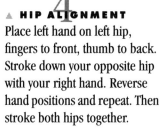

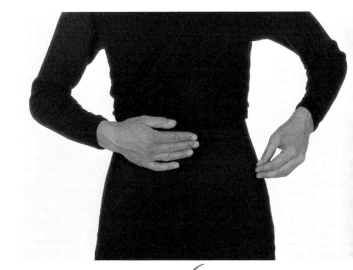

▲ SPINE AL**5**IGNMENT

Hold the large bone at the base of your neck with thumb and fingers of your left hand. Hold your tailbone with the thumb and fingers of your right hand.

▲ ILEOCE**6**AL VALVES

Place your right hand over your navel. Stroke your left hip with your left hand. Reverse hand positions and repeat.

▲ HIP ALI**4**GNMENT

Place left hand on left hip, fingers to front, thumb to back. Stroke down your opposite hip with your right hand. Reverse hand positions and repeat. Then stroke both hips together.

◄ UPPER**7**TENSION

Place your right-hand fingers under your rib cage on the right side. Stroke the right side of your neck with your left hand, down the side of the neck behind the ear and out across your shoulder. Reverse hand positions and repeat.

▲ SINUS/PITUITARY 8

Stroke the coned fingers of both hands on your chest below the collarbone.

▲ THYROID 9

Touch the coned fingers of both hands to your throat on each side of your neck just above the collarbone.

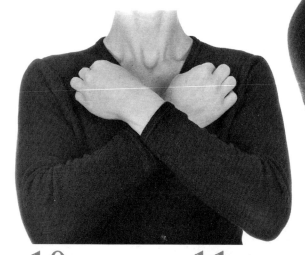

▲ LUNGS 10

With your wrists crossed, stroke below your collarbone.

EYES 11 ▶

Place your left hand over your navel. Cone your right-hand fingers over your left eye. Reverse hand positions and repeat.

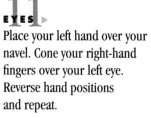

12 ▲ HEART

Place your right-hand fingers below your left collarbone. Place your left-hand fingers on top of your right hand.

13 ▲ KIDNEYS/ADRENALS

Hold your hands on your waist, thumbs facing forward, fingers pressing into your back. Squeeze and massage.

14 ▲ GALL BLADDER/LIVER

Place your left hand on your right shoulder. Stroke out under your ribs, from the base of your sternum, with your right hand.

15 ▲ SPLEEN/PANCREAS

Place your right hand on your left shoulder. Stroke out under your ribs, from the base of your sternum, with your left hand.

16 ◄ TRANSVERSE COLON

Place your right hand on your left shoulder. Stroke across your midriff from right to left with your left hand.

DESCENDING COLON

Place your right hand on your left shoulder. Stroke down your left side from waist to hip with your left hand.

ASCENDING COLON

Place your left hand on your right shoulder. Stroke up your right side from hip to waist with your right hand.

The Warm-Up

Following your Lymphatic Reflex programme take the time to warm your body from top to toe. Warming up takes place in three phases:

❶ Mobility
❷ Pulse Raising
❸ Stretching

The colder the weather the more important it is to warm up properly. The intensity of the warm-up should relate to the intensity of the session to follow. Never stretch until your deep body temperature has been raised. Always loosen and relax your shoulders before working on your neck and back.

MOBILITY

Borg Scale 8–11. Duration: Approximately 5 minutes Loosen and limber to:

● Take your joints through a full range of motion.
● Increase your supply of synovial fluid to lubricate and protect your joints.
● Relax and prepare your muscles from top to toe.

◀ CROCODILE WALK 2
Place outstretched fingers on shoulders. Start the shoulder roll with your elbows, leading them forward, up, over and around. Repeat × 4 and reverse direction. Roll alternate arms back × 4, and then forward × 4.

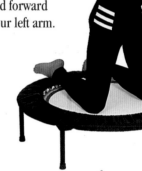

SWINGBALL ▶ 3
Holding your right arm straight, rotate it forward, over and behind, moving through a full circle. Back × 4 and forward × 4. Repeat with your left arm.

◀ DOUBLE SHOULDER ROLLS 1
Kneel on the bouncer mat. Roll both shoulders up towards your ears, back, down and around. Back × 8 and then forward × 8.

◀ PAPER PRESSES 4
❶ Bring your arms up from your sides, rolling them inward in front of your body until the backs of your hands and little fingers touch. Exhale.

❷ Open your chest as you swing your arms behind your body, squeezing your shoulder blades together. Roll your thumbs up and back as you open your palms. Inhale. Repeat × 8.

● If you feel discomfort while kneeling adapt techniques and perform them while sitting at the edge of the mat with both feet on the ground or standing on the bouncer.
● In any position keep buttocks tucked under, back straight and stomach gently contracted.

FOCUS WHEEL 5 ▸

Sit on the bouncer, relax your shoulders and concentrate on your breath. Focus on a point directly in front. Slowly rotate your head to fix your eyes at a point behind. Hold for 3 seconds. Exhale. Return your head to centre. Inhale. Slowly turn in the opposite direction. Exhale. Repeat × 4. Focus on a point further behind each time.

SIDELINER 6 ▸

Kneel on your left knee, placing your right foot on the floor to your side. Check knees are aligned and lower back is flat. Raise your right hand to touch your right ear, keeping elbow in line with your side. Reach out over your head, extending fingertips, feeling the stretch through your right side. As you raise your right hand, ease left arm in front of abdomen toward opposite thigh, or place hand on hip. Return to starting position. Repeat × 8 to each side.

▲ WINDMILL 7

Kneel or sit on the bouncer with your legs wide, spine aligned, buttocks tucked under. Contract your abdomen. Gently rotate your trunk from your waist, keeping your hips still. Aim your left hand toward right buttock and move your right hand across in front of your body at shoulder level focussing on your index finger. Pause and change sides. Repeat × 8.

STEAMROLLER 8 ▾

Kneel on all fours. Place your hands on the bouncer rim at shoulder-width. Keep your back flat. Contract your abdomen as you hump your back, exhaling, tucking your chin toward your chest. Relax, inhale and repeat × 4.

▾ EGGBEATER 9

Move your body forward and place your hands on the floor at shoulder-width with fingertips aligned. Circle your hips to the right × 8, then left × 8.

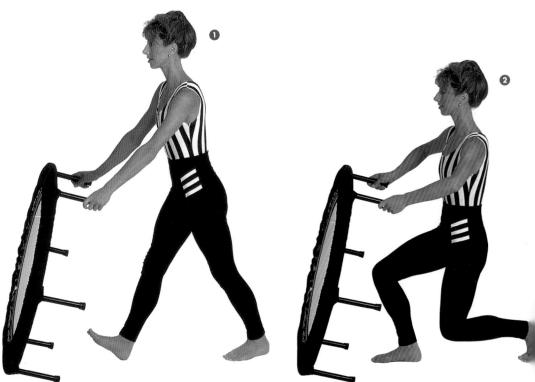

10 LUCKY DIPS ▶

❶ Tilt the bouncer on the rim, to rest on two legs. (It will balance firmly on its own.) Stand facing the mat. Take your left foot back, flat to the floor with toes pointing forward. Flex your right foot and raise toes.

❷ Bend your knees to dip your left knee towards the floor (flattening your front foot while raising your back heel). Keep your back straight, with your buttocks tucked under. Return to starting position. Repeat × 8 with each leg.

11 FLIP FLOPS ▶

With the bouncer on the rim, lean forward slightly to hold two legs with outstretched arms, feet hip-width apart, toes in line. Lift heels alternately rolling through to the ball of the foot. Repeat × 8.

12 STAPLE GUNS ▾

With the bouncer on the rim, stand facing the mat with your legs wide, feet facing forward (at 45°), toes in line. Lean forward to place your hands on the rim for support. Gently lunge from side to side, warming your groin and inner thighs, keeping your knees angled over your toes.

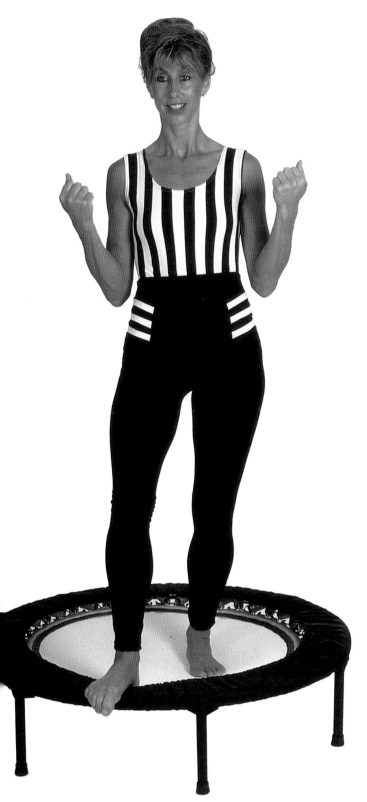

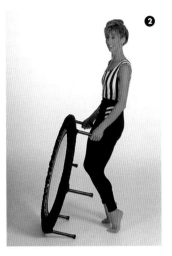

13
ROCKING CHAIR ▲

❶ With the bouncer on the rim, stand with feet parallel and hip-width apart. Slowly rock back on the heels of both feet, with legs straight, trying to lift your toes.

❷ Roll forward onto your toes, keeping your knees loose and buttocks tucked under. Repeat × 8.

14
◄ **GRIPPER**

Stand on the bouncer. Take your weight on the left foot as you extend your right foot to the edge. Grip the rim with your toes, hold for 2 counts. As you release the grip, lift only your toes simultaneously off the frame. At the same time work your hands. Flex your fingers and clench your fists. Repeat × 4 to each side.

● In forward lunges, such as Lucky Dips, keep your front knee in line with your ankle.

PULSE RAISING

Borg Scale 10–12 approximately. Duration: 5–7 minutes.

As you raise your pulse:

● Gradually increase the intensity of your movements, keeping your feet low to the mat as you commence your routines.

● Become familiar with the shape, size and surface of your mat.

● Gradually work arm movements into your routines.

● Practise simple routines for the session to come.

● As you become familiar with your two-star and three-star techniques in the Bounce Target Zone section, you can include them in your pulse raising activities.

The sequences in this section are classified as one-star techniques, and can be included in your Bounce Target Zone routines. Because the following techniques are performed from the foundation of the Rhythm Bounce, they require double-foot strike landings: both feet depress the mat at the same time.

◄ LET'S TWIST ✪ ►

Keep your feet low to the mat as you jump to twist your hips and arms in opposite directions. Relax your upper body and keep your knees soft and toes aligned.

◄ TOE TAPPER ✪

From the Rhythm Bounce, extend your right leg forward, point your toes and tap the mat in front. Return to starting position. Repeat × 8 and change legs.

◄ SHUFFLE ✪

Stand with your feet parallel, hip-width apart and flat to the mat. Jump and slide alternate feet forward and back. As you shuffle, swing your opposite arm to leg, with your elbows bent at a right angle, swinging back behind your waist and punching forward.

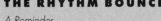

THE RHYTHM BOUNCE

A Reminder

● From the Posture Stance, push into the mat from your hips with knees loose and relaxed and your feet low to the mat at all times. Establish a rhythm as the movement flows easily and smoothly.

HEEL FLAK ✪ ▷

Marking time in the Rhythm Bounce, extend your right leg forward, foot flexed and toes pointing upward. Tap your heel to the mat and return to starting position. Alternate legs × 8.

SLINKY SKIER ✪ ▷

Stand with your feet parallel and hip-width apart. Bounce to both sides of the mat, swinging your arms in front of your body. Repeat × 8.

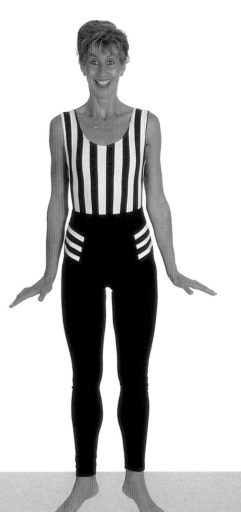

JUMP JACKS ✪ ▲

With your feet hip-width apart and hands by your sides, make a small jump to spread your legs just wider than your hips, raising your arms just higher than shoulder level. Jump back to starting position on the next bounce. Repeat × 8.

THE MUMMY ✪ ▷

Stand with your heels and knees together, feet flat to the mat, toes pointing apart in a v-shape. From the Rhythm Bounce, mummify your entire body, tightening all your muscles, but with knees soft. Bounce rhythmically, clockwise around the mat. As you bounce, lock your facial muscles in different expressions for counts of 4 and then release.

THE SHAKER

● From the Mummy, relax your body completely. With feet flat to the mat, shake and release both arms at the same time. Shake out your right and then left leg. Clock the mat in both directions × 8, releasing tensions.

The following techniques are performed from the foundation of the Rhythm Walk. They require single-foot strike landings: one foot at a time depresses the mat.

▼ JOGGER ✪

From the Rhythm Walk, speed your movement, leaning your trunk forward slightly as you lift your heels behind your body. Aim to form a right angle at your knees.

HIGH FLIER ✪ ▶

Alternately lift each knee in front, aiming to bring your thigh parallel to the mat, with a right angle at knee and hip. Point your toes as you lift your foot, rolling through the ball of your foot as you depress the mat. Keep your back straight, with buttocks tucked under and abdomen contracted.

◀ FIREWALK ✪

Imagine you are a firewalker, trying to avoid the burning embers. Dart about the mat performing steps at top speed. Keep your lower back flat and abdomen contracted.

THE RHYTHM WALK

A Reminder

● Raise your left heel, as your right heel depresses the mat. Establish a rhythm as you alternate feet, walking on the mat. Arms should correspond with the movement of the opposite leg.

STEP AND TOUCH ✪ ▷
Step to the right side of the mat, following through with your left foot to meet the other on the mat. Reverse directions.

STEPPING UP
Stepping from the ground to your bouncer mat offers fun elements to your bounce sessions, providing an excellent means for raising your pulse. Use these techniques in routines interspersed with other movements. Aim to step to the inside of the cover, lifting your feet high over the rim. When stepping up strike the mat with a heel-ball-toe action. Step down close to the bouncer with a toe-ball-heel strike. Check your floor surface is suitable, avoiding concrete, or wear shoes. Happy stepping!

❶

CENTRE STAGE ✪ ▷
❶ Stand on the ground facing your bouncer. Step up with your right foot, and follow through with your left. As your left foot lands, clap.

❷

STREETWALK ✪ ▲
❶ From the Rhythm Walk, step your right foot forward and mark time with your left.

❷ Then step your right foot behind, marking time with your left again. Continue to repeat the routine very quickly × 8. Change feet.

❷ Step your right foot back to the floor, following through with your left. Repeat × 8. Then repeat with your left foot leading × 8. Vary the number of steps with each foot leading × 4, × 2, and × 1.

● Always take your heels down to the mat to avoid bouncing on the balls of your feet. You will land with a toe-ball-heel strike.
● Keep your knees soft at all times.
● Keep your back straight, abdomen gently contracted, and buttocks tucked slightly.

ARMS

As you are raising your pulse with your one-star techniques, you can include different arm movements to vary your routines.

❶

❷

◀ BACKBITING

With your arms extended behind away from your sides and fingers outstretched, clench your fist into your shoulders. Immediately extend your lower arms back, through the sides of your body, stretching your fingers open. Repeat × 8.

▼ DRAGONFLIES

Squeeze both hands to form tight fists. Then stretch your fingers apart. Repeat.

CONDUCTOR ▲
❶ Clench your fists into your chest, with your elbows extended at shoulder level.

❷ Press down, straightening your arms. Return to starting position and repeat.

FIREWORKS ▼
❶ Reach up with fingers outstretched. (Always keep them within visual range without tilting your head.)

❷ Clench your fists as you pull your arms into your shoulders.

❸ Extend them out to the side, opening your palms. Bend your arm, clenching your fists back into your shoulders. Repeat × 8. Instruct yourself: reach – tuck – open – tuck.

❶ **❷** **❸**

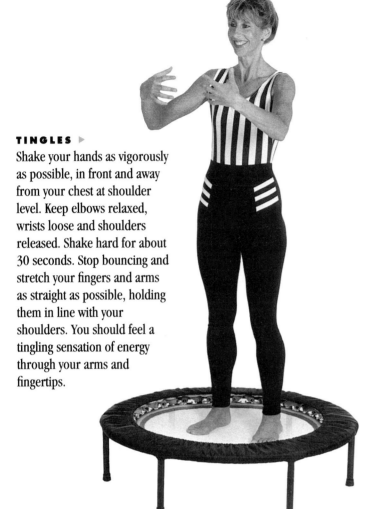

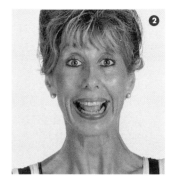

TINGLES ▷

Shake your hands as vigorously as possible, in front and away from your chest at shoulder level. Keep elbows relaxed, wrists loose and shoulders released. Shake hard for about 30 seconds. Stop bouncing and stretch your fingers and arms as straight as possible, holding them in line with your shoulders. You should feel a tingling sensation of energy through your arms and fingertips.

SMILEYS ▲

❶ Press the heels of your palms over the outside of your jaw and massage, by rotating your palms clockwise × 4, then anticlockwise × 4.

❷ Open your mouth, lips about one inch apart. Elevate your cheek muscles and lips simultaneously, imitating an upward smile and squeezing tightly. Repeat × 8.

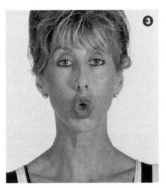

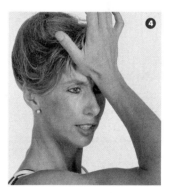

FACIAL TONERS

These simple facial toners will help loosen tension in your face and scalp. The muscles in your face need warming up as well.

FREESTYLE

For about a minute, bounce freely and screw your face into weird and wonderful

contortions. Hold each position for about 3 bounces before changing.

❸ Tense the muscles of your neck, sounding oo, then ee. Repeat × 8.

❹ Frown really hard. Hold the frown tightly pressing the heel of your palm on your forehead for 3 bounces. Release and relax.

❺ Complete the routine by exaggerating the sounds of the vowels A E I O U.

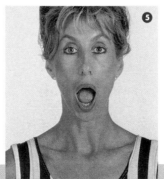

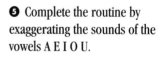

● Keep elbows soft, wrists and shoulders relaxed.
● When raising arms to the side keep them aligned and slightly forward from your shoulders.

STRETCH

● Remember tight, inflexible muscles often invite injury. Always include a period of static stretching after you have raised your pulse.

● The height of the bouncer offers the ideal surface from which to stretch in a variety of positions and from a variety of levels.

● Stretching protects your muscles and joints, making them less susceptible to wear and tear.

● You should stretch before and after every session.

● Ease into your stretches, avoiding jerky movements. Extend each stretch in the pre-bounce warm-up for between 10–15 seconds.

● Ease into your stretch to a point of tension, but never through it. Imagine your breath is moving in to open the tension in your muscles and joints.

● Stretch a little every day to encourage flexibility.

● Spice up your stretch routines adding sound and breath techniques (pp. 130–1, 135–7).

Rubber Legs and Elastic Bands are important stretches, so always include them in your warm-up and cool-down routines.

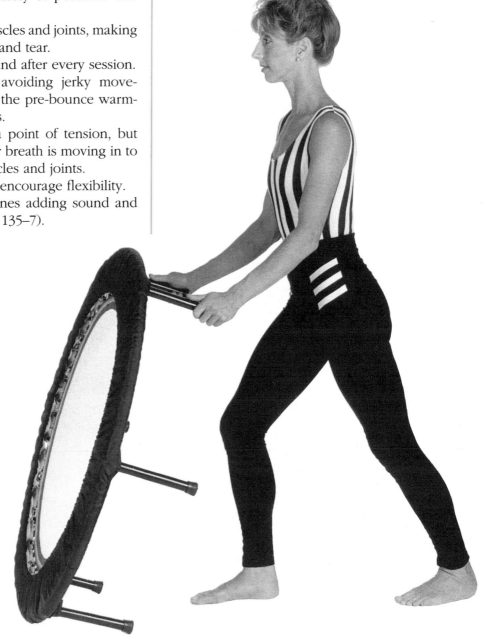

RUBBER LEGS ▶

(Gastrocnemius, calf muscle)
Turn the bouncer onto the rim and grip the legs with outstretched arms, elbows bent. Lean your trunk forward slightly, bending your front leg with knee aligned over ankle at a right angle. Straighten your back leg, with the heel flat to the floor. Keep both feet facing forward. Feel the stretch through the calf of your back leg, moving it further back to intensify the stretch. Breathe deeply. Hold the position for at least 8 seconds. Reverse sides.

YOUR BOUNCER BAR

● Use your bouncer as a bar for support only and avoid leaning your weight onto the frame.

● When gripping the legs or frame, keep your hands and shoulders loose.

● Be sure to keep your back straight by tilting your pelvis through gently and contracting your abdomen, with buttocks tucked.

● Your neck must remain in line with your spine.

2 ELASTIC BANDS ▼

(Soleus, underlying calf muscle and achilles tendon)

From Rubber Legs, walk your back leg in so the toe of your back foot is in line with the heel of your front foot. Bend your back knee, gently easing your leg lower, on your back foot. Your front foot should be completely released from bearing any weight. To help balance you may prefer to keep your front foot flat to the floor. Keep your back flat and buttocks tucked under. Breathe deeply as you hold the stretch, then reverse legs.

3 PEG LEGS ▼

(Quadriceps at front of thigh)

Turn the bouncer onto the rim and grip with your left arm outstretched. Bend your right leg behind to grip the upper portion of your foot in your right hand. Keep your buttocks tucked under, knees hip-width apart and relaxed, gently easing your heel towards your buttocks, feeling the stretch in the front of your thigh. Hold, breathing deeply. Change legs and repeat.

CIRCUS TRICKS 4 ▼
(Hamstrings, back of thighs)

❶ Stand facing the bouncer. Place your left foot on the mat. Lean your trunk forward, from your hips, bending your right knee over your toes, contracting your abdomen, and keeping your spine aligned. Place your hands on your hips. Keep your chest higher than hip level. Feel the stretch in your hamstrings at the back of your left thigh.

❷ As you advance, place your hands on the rim to support your upper body, intensifying the stretch by lowering your trunk towards your thigh.

● To extend the stretch to include your calves, try raising your toes from the mat, holding for a further 8 counts. Change legs and repeat.

BANANA SPLITS 5 ▶
(Hip flexors)

Kneel on the bouncer on your left knee with your right leg bent and extended forward onto the floor. Keep your body aligned, knees over toes, hips facing forward. Gently press your hips forward, buttocks tucked under. Feel the stretch through your hip flexors. Keep your neck long in line with your spine, chin tucked in. Change legs and repeat.

6 KNITTING NEEDLES ▲
(Groin, inner thigh)

Kneel on your right knee, tucking your heel under your buttocks. Extend your left leg directly out to the side (foot at 45°), gripping the rim in front of your body with your right hand. Your left arm is supporting your body from the floor. As you ease into the stretch, through your inner thigh and groin, gently lower your elbows.

7 LAZY LIZZIES ▼
(Abdomen)

Lie flat on your stomach on the bouncer, placing your hands shoulder-width apart on the floor to support your body. Slowly raise the upper portion of your chest, stretching through your abdomen. Keep your hips relaxed into the mat. Breathe fully.

8 ◄ JINGLES
(Hips, buttocks, lower back)

Sit cross-legged on the bouncer, with your right heel in front of the left. Turn to the left and place both hands on the rim, either side of your left knee. Gently open your chest as you ease forward with your upper body straight over the left knee. Keep your buttocks flat to the mat, feeling the stretch in your right hip, buttocks and lower back. Repeat to the other side.

● When leaning forward into a stretch, remember to keep your back straight and abdomen firmly contracted.

47

Bounce Target Zones

One of the main aims of the Starbound Workout is to provide you with an opportunity to bounce within your 'target zones' to improve the level of your aerobic fitness. This enhances the ability of your lungs to absorb more oxygen, and your heart to pump blood, which carries the oxygen and nutrients to your muscles to produce energy. Your lungs provide the perfect rendezvous for your respiratory and circulatory systems. Little air sacs lie side by side with tiny blood capillaries in your lungs, where the exchange of fresh supplies of oxygen takes place for carbon dioxide and waste products from your blood. When you bounce within your target zones a progression of positive changes occurs throughout your entire body. Your heart and lungs are powerfully stimulated in many ways.

BOUNCING PARAMETERS

Bouncing within your aerobic target zone relates directly to the ability of your body to use oxygen to fuel your activity. For a steady development of aerobic fitness, to strengthen the functioning of your heart and lungs, you need to bounce in your target zone:

❶ Between 60% and 80% of your maximum heart rate
❷ For between 15 and 60 minutes
❸ At least every second day

If you want to improve your aerobic capacity four sessions a week should be perfect, with a day off to rest between sessions. If you simply want to maintain your present level of fitness, three sessions a week will stabilize your fitness level.

THE BORG SCALE OF PERCEIVED EXERTION

Researchers have been finding that stopping to read your pulse while you are exercising is not as accurate as desired. For your Starbound Workout, learn to assess how hard you are working according to the Borg Scale of Perceived Exertion. As a tool for measurement you'll find the scale easy to learn and

BENEFITS AS YOU BOUNCE

● *Your circulation speeds up with more oxygen absorbed.*
● *An increased supply of carbon dioxide and wastes are removed.*
● *Your chest wall becomes more flexible, deepening your breath, encouraging a faster exchange of gases from your lungs.*
● *Your heart performs more work for less effort with a longer rest between beats.*
● *Blood capillaries multiply, carrying more oxygen and nutrients to your cells.*
● *Red blood cells multiply to carry additional supplies of oxygen around your body.*
● *Raised blood cholesterol and triglyceride levels lower.*
● *High density lipoproteins, which help prevent heart attacks, multiply.*
● *Blood thins with less chance of clotting.*
● *Venous return (the supply of blood and lymph returning to your heart) will improve.*
● *In turn, bloodstasis (the pooling of blood in your legs and abdomen) is relieved.*
● *Clustered blood plasma proteins are carried away in your lymph.*
● *Growth, maintenance and repair of your cells, along with the production of energy throughout your body, is improved.*
● *Immune system is strengthened, helping you to resist viral infections and other invaders foreign to your body.*
● *You'll notice an increased resilience to stress with a better balance in your blood pressure. If you suffer with palpitations they are likely to diminish.*

COOL-DOWN
● Just as you warm-up to prepare your body, plan for a gradual decrease in the intensity of your activity toward the end of your Bounce Target Zone and again at the end of your Conditioning routines.

SAFE AND SOUND
● If you are overweight, unsteady or unfit avoid all techniques that require you to land or balance on one leg.
● Adapt by tapping your toes to the mat instead of lifting, as in Kangaroo Jazz.

● Develop techniques slowly as you improve your strength and balance.

use. It is extremely accurate and will allow you to rate the effort you are putting into your bounce session, enabling you to stay within the required target zone for your age.

You can assess the intensity of your bouncing simply by becoming aware of how you feel. By multiplying your scale score by ten you'll get an accurate guide to your associated heart rate value.

RATE YOUR EFFORTS

BORG SCALE	LEVEL OF EXERTION	HEART RATE
6	very very light	60
7		70
8	very light	80
9		90
10	fairly light	100
11		110
12	somewhat hard	120
13		130
14	hard	140
15		150
16	very hard	160
17		170
18	very very hard	180

BOUNCE TARGET ZONE GUIDELINES

The following chart shows the maximum heart rate for your age followed by the required level of Perceived Exertion (BSPE) you should experience at the different stages of your target zones.

TARGET ZONES

AGE	MAXIMUM HEART RATE	× 60% BSPE	× 70% BSPE	× 80% BSPE
20–29	200–191	12–11	14–13	16–15
30–39	190–181	11	13	15–14
40–49	180–171	11–10	13–12	14
50–59	170–161	10	12–11	14–13
60–69	160–151	10–9	11	13–12

The amount of bouncing you perform within your target zone will depend on how fit you are and how long you have been bouncing.

● Always build up gradually. Remember to assess the effort you are putting into your session by becoming thoroughly familiar with the Chart for Perceived Exertion.

● When you are a beginner you will find it quite challenging enough to perform short sequences using the one-star techniques, as outlined in the pulse-raising section of your warm-up.

● Before you know it you'll be bouncing to greater heights with more competence, confidence and ease. Continue to challenge yourself and develop new skills by utilizing the two-star and three-star techniques outlined in the following programme.

● The timechart (*below*) gives progressive guidelines to suggest how long you might bounce within your target zones as your programmes are developing.

T O P I C A L   T I P S

TARGET ZONE BOUNCING

❶ While you are still a beginner stay low in your target zone, between 60% to 65% of your maximum heart rate.

❷ Assess your heart rate a few times throughout the session. Are you bouncing in your required zone?

❸ The fitter you become the lower your heart rate should read, which indicates you are able to perform more work with less effort.

❹ You can use the 'overload principle' as a guide for improvement. This implies you have to bounce at a level slightly higher than your comfort zone to progressively increase the time and intensity at which you bounce.

❺ You should always bounce at a level that allows you to talk or sing comfortably with a little extra effort required to sustain your voice and breath. If you are having difficulty speaking while you bounce, the chances are you have moved out of your target zone.

TARGET ZONE TIMECHART

● *Guidelines only*

Weeks 1–8: 15 minutes per session (one-star Rhythm Bounce techniques, introducing two-star techniques when ready)

Weeks 9–12: 16–20 minutes per session (combine one-, two- and three-star techniques when ready)

Weeks 13–16: 21–25 minutes per session (combine one-, two- and three-star techniques)

Weeks 16 plus: 26 minutes plus per session (combine one-, two- and three-star techniques)

The following techniques are arranged in groups with progressions from two-star to three-star techniques. The sequences are performed from the foundation of the Basic Bounce and the Lift Off.

THE BASIC BOUNCE ✪✪ ▼

From the Rhythm Bounce, raise both heels off the mat together, only just allowing the balls of your feet to leave the mat. Keep your head aligned with your back straight and chin in.

THE LIFT OFF ✪✪✪ ▶

From the Rhythm Bounce, both feet leave the mat simultaneously; your toes pointing downward at full lift-off. Keep your feet parallel, knees slightly bent, abdomen contracted and lower back flat.

50

REMEMBER: POSTURE!

● Check your feet are hip-width apart and facing forward. Knees should be released and slightly bent as you bounce. Heels down as you land.
● Gently contract your abdomen, tilting your pelvis slightly forward to flatten your back.

PETITE POINTER ✪✪ ▼

From the Basic Bounce, kick your right leg forward and back to starting position. You can either repeat kicks alternating with right and left legs or perform a specified number to the left and then to the right. Begin with alternate legs to encourage better balance. Your feet can be flexed or toes pointed for variation in your routines.

SPEEDY POINTER ✪✪✪ ▼

Kick alternate feet forward quickly, tensing your upper thigh. Keep knees slightly bent and back long. The swap over actually takes place in mid-air so you need to have good balance before you include this technique in your routines. As you land the ball of your foot strikes the mat first, rolling quickly through to your heel.

SHUFFLE TURN ✪✪✪ ▽
❶ Perform the Shuffle but hold your right leg forward for a count of 4 small bounces before changing direction.

❷ Swivel through 180° (half-turn about the mat) to face the opposite direction. Use your back foot as a guide, turning to the outer edge of the foot.

❸ Bring some height into the turn as you become more advanced. Remember to roll into your feet as you land.

◁ **DOUBLE SHUFFLE** ✪✪✪ ▷
❶ Turn on a diagonal to face the right. Shuffle right leg forward × 2 (with left arm punching).
❷ Jump to face a left diagonal position with your left foot forward × 2 (right arm punching). Repeat, alternating directions.

JACK IN THE BOX ✪✪✪ ▼

❶ Bounce the Shuffle keeping your right foot forward for a count of 4 bounces. Then lift your left heel back to form a right angle between your knee and thigh as you hop on your right foot.

❶

❷

❸

❷ Land in the Shuffle, on both feet.

❸ Then immediately lift your right knee to form a right angle between your thigh and calf, as you hop on your left foot. Repeat × 4. Reverse the entire sequence with your left foot forward. As your reactions speed up try leaving out the centre shuffle bounce, speedily moving from your right to left foot.

● Control your leg movements to protect your back.
● Keep all knee lifts low while you perfect the different techniques.

❶

◀ **TOE TWISTER** ✪✪

❶ With feet wider than your hips lift your right heel, as you bounce, twist and swivel the ball of your right foot. Turn your knees and toes out towards the right as you swing arms in front of your body to the left.

❷ Bounce and turn the knees and toes inward, swinging your arms in the opposite direction. Repeat × 8. Change feet and repeat.

❷

54

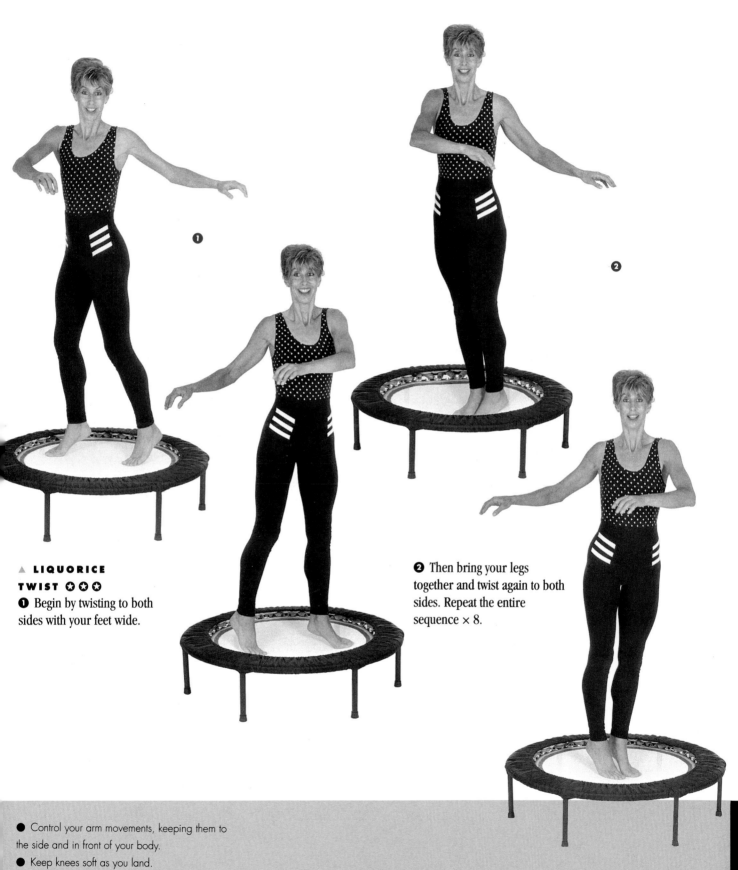

▲ LIQUORICE TWIST ✪ ✪ ✪

❶ Begin by twisting to both sides with your feet wide.

❷ Then bring your legs together and twist again to both sides. Repeat the entire sequence × 8.

● Control your arm movements, keeping them to the side and in front of your body.
● Keep knees soft as you land.
● Be sure the whole of your foot is striking the mat with a toe-ball-heel action.

SEAFARER ✪✪✪ ▶

Once you have mastered the Side Sling try leaving out the centre bounce. Keep your upper body in a stationary position as you swing opposite arm to leg.

▲ SIDE SLING ✪✪

Open your arms out to each side. Marking time with the Rhythm Bounce, extend your left leg to the side, returning it to a centre bounce before extending the alternate leg. You can point your toes or flex your feet. Use your arms to begin with to stabilize your balance then vary routines to accompany your legs.

BACK TO CENTRE

● If you are practising techniques which require you to balance on a single foot always keep a centre bounce between each change of side.

◄ HEART STRING ✪✪✪

Raise your right arm toward the ceiling in line with your side. With your left hand touching your heart, swing your left leg out to the side to create an imaginary diagonal heart string. Bounce back to a central position then immediately reverse arm and leg positions. Vary the counts of your leg swings, eventually leaving out the centre bounce as you master the technique.

◄ KNOCK-KNEED SKIER ✪✪

Keep your knees, ankles and feet pressed together as you bounce to either side of the mat. Imagine you are holding ski poles at either side or in front of your body at waist height, moving them from side to side corresponding with your feet.

SKI CORNER ✪✪✪ ►

From the Knock-Kneed Skier, on every fourth count jump a quarter turn to your right. Clock around the mat, then change direction. As you perfect this technique you can make larger turns until you do half turns to face in the opposite direction.

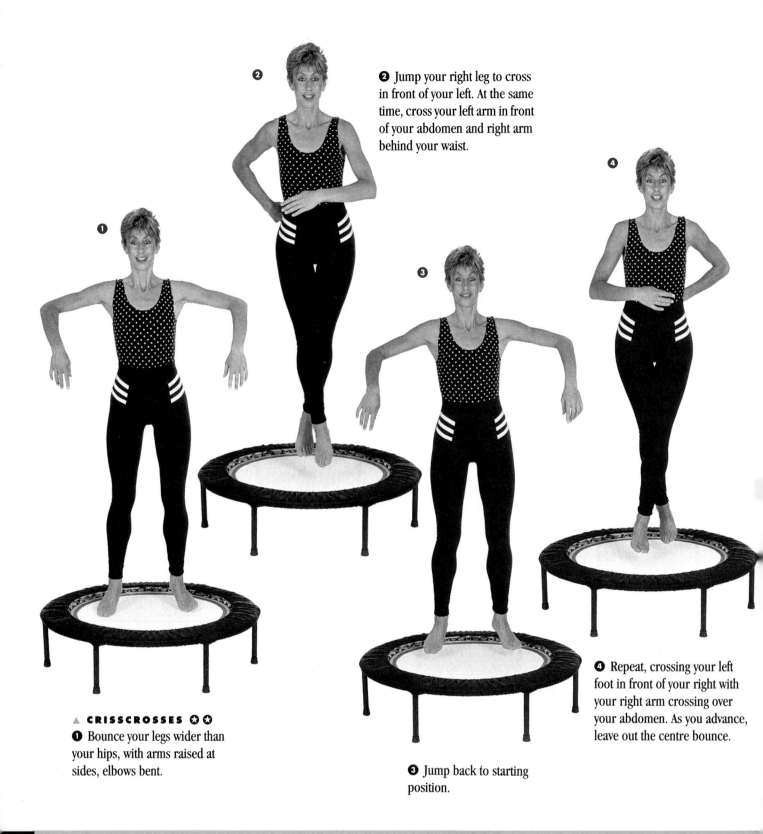

2 Jump your right leg to cross in front of your left. At the same time, cross your left arm in front of your abdomen and right arm behind your waist.

▲ **CRISSCROSSES** ✪✪
1 Bounce your legs wider than your hips, with arms raised at sides, elbows bent.

3 Jump back to starting position.

4 Repeat, crossing your left foot in front of your right with your right arm crossing over your abdomen. As you advance, leave out the centre bounce.

58

HAPPY LANDING
● Keep your knees soft as you land.
● Never slide your feet, but instead always jump your movements.
● When you become more confident, leave out the centre bounce.

▼ JACK KNIVES ✪ ✪ ✪

❶ With both knees slightly bent, turn your toes out as you jump, with your arms to the side, palms facing upward.

❷ On the next bounce rotate your legs from the hips to turn your toes slightly inward, rolling your arms down in front of your abdomen.

HOPSCOTCH ✪ ✪ ▶

❶ Bounce from the Basic Bounce to bend your right knee, raising your heel behind toward your buttock.

❷ Bounce back to centre, then repeat to other side. (Don't kick your leg back from the hip, but bend from your knee.) Begin this technique with your hands on your hips. As you advance, extend your left hand behind toward right heel, then your right hand toward left heel. For variety, leave out the centre bounce and speed up.

◄ HIGH JUMP ✪ ✪ ✪

Perform the Lift Off but pull both knees up together. Always start low and gather momentum for more height. Do 4 ordinary Lift-Off bounces in between the High Jump until you become fitter. As you advance, bring your arms and knees in toward your chest.

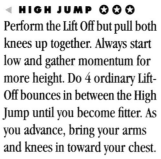

FROG LEAPS ✪ ✪ ✪ ▲

Build up from the Lift Off into as high a bounce as comfortable. As you gain momentum, open your knees out as you tuck your heels in toward your thighs. Aim to touch your hands in front of your body. This technique requires strong pelvic floor muscles, and is only suitable for advanced programmes.

BOX CURLS ✪ ✪ ✪ ▶

Gaining momentum in the Lift Off, lift your heels behind, opening them out slightly. Aim to touch outstretched hands to each side. As you become really fit, this combines energetically with Frog Leaps to intensify routines.

HIGH JUMPS

● These techniques are only for those with extreme confidence and skill. Don't attempt them too soon.

● Always jump in the centre of the mat.

● Keep your back straight, knees soft and abdomen gently contracted.

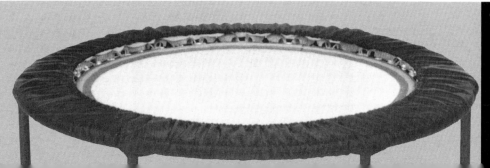

◀ PELVIS PINCHES ✪ ✪ ✪ ▶

❶ Bounce and raise your right knee, foot flexed, heel turned in and toes facing out. At the same time, pull down with your left arm, bending your elbow to shoulder level, at the side of your body.

❷ Bounce back to centre, before repeating on alternate sides.

ZIG ZAGS ✪ ✪ ✪ ▶

❶ Extend your arms at shoulder level out from your sides. Flex both lower arms toward the ceiling with your fingers free. Marking time in the Basic Bounce, lift right knee up toward your right elbow.

❷ Bounce back to centre, then bring it across toward your left elbow.

❸ Bounce back to centre, then bring your knee back to a centre lift as you press your elbows together in front of your chest. Open your arms and repeat with the other leg.

◄ THREADING NEEDLES ✪ ✪ ✪

● Hold your arms out at shoulder level. Bounce, then lift your right heel in toward your left inner thigh, reaching the fingertips of your left hand towards your heel.

● Immediately release, bounce back to centre and change legs. As you advance, leave out the marking bounce in between, to speed up the action. Keep your upper body fixed with your chin in and abdomen contracted.

TIN SOLDIERS ✪ ✪ ✪ ▲

Cross your right ankle in front of your left, knees soft, arms stiffly held to your sides. With your back straight, push down through your hips and bounce clockwise around the mat. Reverse directions.

DON'T FORGET TO BOUNCE

● Remember to jump the entire movement.
● If you lock one foot to the mat while moving your other leg you may strain your supporting knee.

▲ CROCHET NEEDLES ✪ ✪ ✪
❶ Stand facing your bouncer. Step up with your right foot.

❷ Bounce and lift your left knee bringing your hands to touch it. Step your left foot straight back to the floor. Alternate legs. Keep your back straight.

◄ CHORUS KICKS ✪ ✪
❶ From the floor, step up with your right foot.

❷ Bounce and kick out with your left, bringing it back to the mat. Keep your back straight and your kick low to begin with.

❸ Step down, leading with your right foot. Step up with your right × 8 and then left. Experiment with different sequences.

TIP-TOP STEPPING
● Aim to step to the inside of the cover, lifting your feet high over the rim.

● When stepping up, strike the mat with a heel-ball-toe action. Step down close to the bouncer with a toe-ball-heel strike.

● Check your floor surface is suitable, avoiding concrete, or wear shoes.

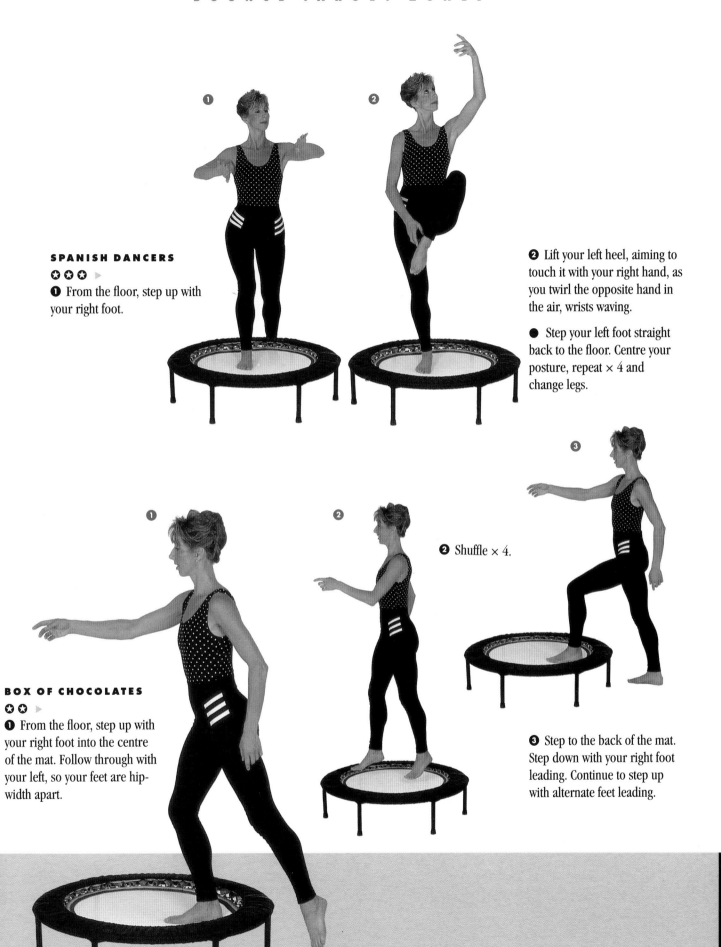

SPANISH DANCERS
❂ ❂ ❂ ▷

❶ From the floor, step up with your right foot.

❷ Lift your left heel, aiming to touch it with your right hand, as you twirl the opposite hand in the air, wrists waving.

● Step your left foot straight back to the floor. Centre your posture, repeat × 4 and change legs.

BOX OF CHOCOLATES
❂ ❂ ▷

❶ From the floor, step up with your right foot into the centre of the mat. Follow through with your left, so your feet are hip-width apart.

❷ Shuffle × 4.

❸ Step to the back of the mat. Step down with your right foot leading. Continue to step up with alternate feet leading.

The following techniques require single-foot strike land-ings – one foot at a time depresses the mat – often with a Basic Bounce in the centre of the mat to mark time.

◀ **BALLET STEP** ✪ ✪
From the Rhythm Walk, roll through the foot until it is vertical. Keep your bottom tucked under and back flat.

OLYMPIC TORCH ✪ ✪ ▶
Keeping your back straight, lift alternate knees to form a right angle with your body, keeping heels tucked under. Sprint off the mat, pressing your soles down firmly. No centre bounce. Keep your abdomen contracted and buttocks tucked under.

KNEES UP MOTHER BROWN ✪ ✪ ▶

From the Rhythm Bounce, raise your right knee at right angles. Keep a bounce in between knee lifts. Instruct yourself: bounce – right knee lift – bounce – left knee lift; vary the counts of knee lifts.

▼ KANGAROO JAZZ ✪ ✪

Mark time in the Rhythm Bounce. Hopping on your left foot, tap your right foot forward × 2. Tap to the side × 2. Then behind × 2 (in line with your left heel). Repeat, then change legs. Repeat with each foot tapping once in each direction.

CAN CAN ✪ ✪ ✪ ▶

Extend your arms to the side at first to help your balance. Hop on the spot with your right leg, bending your left forward, either slightly extended or at a right angle. Clock the mat a full circle to the right with 8 hops, then change legs and clock to the left.

INJURED
WALLABY ✪ ✪ ✪ ▶

Extend your arms to the side at first to help your balance. Hop on your right leg, bending your left up behind at a right angle. Clock the mat a full circle to the right. Keep your bouncing foot steady, mapping your way around the outside edge of the mat. Lean your trunk slightly forward from the hip. Reverse directions, and then change legs.

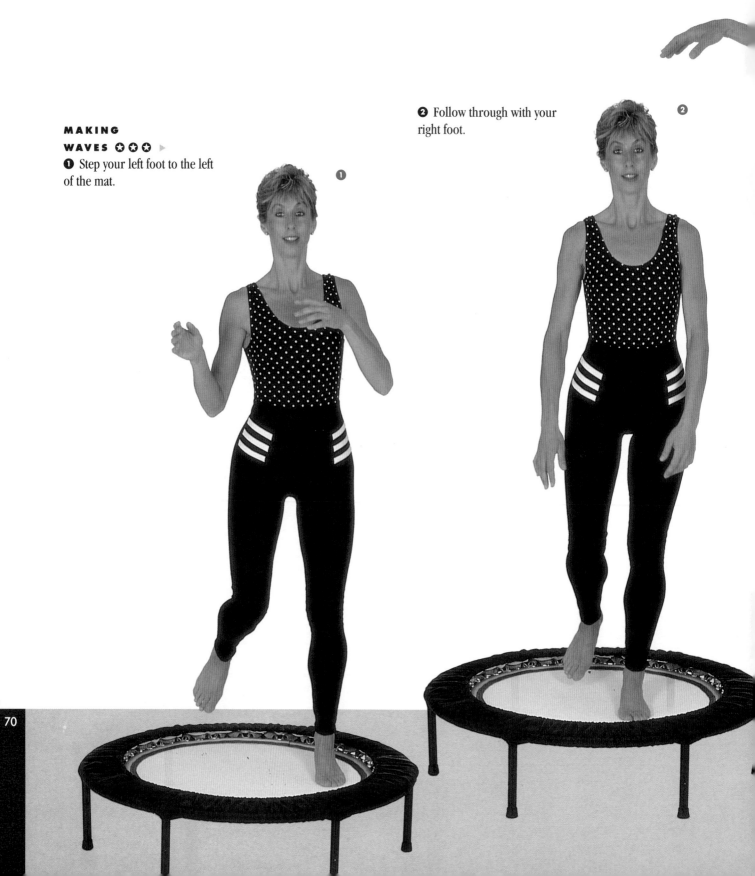

MAKING WAVES ✪✪✪ ▶

❶ Step your left foot to the left of the mat.

❷ Follow through with your right foot.

❸ Kick your left foot out to the side.

❹ Bring your left foot back in so feet are together.

● Repeat to the right. Step right, follow through with the left, kick right to the side, and repeat. Circle arms in front of your chest and reach in the opposite direction to the kick.

71

STEP-BY-STEP

● Practise each step by itself to build confidence. When you are ready combine the movements.

● When lifting your leg to the side don't raise it too high, taking care to clear the cover as you return your foot to the mat.

▼ **SPOTLIGHT** ✪ ✪ ✪

❶ Mark time in the Basic Bounce, and visualize a spotlight in line with your hip. Kick your right leg out to touch it as you bring your left hand toward your toes.

❷ Bounce back to both feet in the centre of the mat.

❸ Kick out with your left leg. Keep your toes pointed and knees soft.

● Remember as you land on the mat your foot strikes with a toe-ball-heel action.

● As you kick keep your back straight, abdomen gently contracted and buttocks tucked.

❶

❷

◄ **SOCCER** ✪✪ ►

❶ Bouncing on your left foot, kick your right leg out keeping it low.

❷ Bring it back to the mat lifting your left heel behind. Continue to repeat the sequence, then change sides.

73

Conditioning

Borg Scale: 8–11. Duration: 10–30 minutes.

GOLDEN OPPORTUNITIES

Once you've experienced the gentle cushioning your body is offered by your bouncer, you'll never want to perform conditioning routines from the floor again. As the punishment usually inflicted on your body during conditioning is removed, you'll enjoy every opportunity your bouncing programmes offer to slim-line and shape your body and strengthen your muscles.

Thanks to the raised surface of your bouncer mat, you can align your body properly in all positions. Knobbly knees and tender elbows are soothed, while your sacrum (the lower area of your back) will remain open throughout most sequences, remaining in alignment with the rest of your spine. The crunching around your shoulders, which usually creases you up on the floor, vanishes as you use the height of your bouncer to keep your body in a stress-free line.

GOLDEN RULES

To tone your muscles and slimline your body, you need to:

❶ Either, add resistance by using a resistance band or by holding each position for longer counts, so that you use your own body as resistance.

❷ Or, work with a lower resistance, but use a higher number of repetitions to progressively increase the workload of your muscles.

RESISTANCE BANDS

Bands add a bonus to many conditioning routines. You have to experiment to find the best means of attaching them for the most beneficial effects. Either tie them onto the leg of your bouncer and then attach them to the limb you are conditioning or use them to attach two limbs together.

LEGS, BUTTOCKS AND HIPS

1 DUSTY ROAD ▲

Lying back on the bouncer, resting on your elbows, grip the rim on either side, legs hip-width apart. Contract your abdomen, and curl your lower back into the mat. Lift your right leg from the knee until it is straight, pointing toes. Bend your knee and flex your foot as you lower leg to the floor controlling the movement. Repeat in sets × 8 with both legs.

2 PANTHER PRANCES ▼

From the same position as Dusty Road, open your right leg, bent at the knee, with your inner thigh facing the ceiling. Rest the outer edge of your foot on the floor. Lift your right leg, keeping your foot parallel to the floor. Pause and return to starting position. Repeat × 8.

COOL-DOWN REMINDER
● Plan for a gradual decrease in the intensity of your activity toward the end of your Conditioning techniques.

PIP SQUEAKS ▶
Lie flat on your bouncer, feet flat on the floor, hip-width apart. Grip the rim. Contract your abdomen, pressing your back into the mat, as you tilt your pelvis upward, squeezing your buttocks as you lift your hips slightly from the mat. Inhale as you relax your abdomen and release and lower your pelvis through to the mat. Repeat in sets × 8.

GRASSHOPPER ▲
❶ Flex your foot, slowly raise your right leg so it is in line with your left thigh.

❷ Point toes, bend and tuck your knee into your chest. Return to the starting position with your leg in line with your thigh. Repeat in sets with the right × 8 and left × 8.

◀ SAUSAGE ROLL
Raise your knees into your chest, in line with hips (feet and knees together). Roll legs towards your chest in a complete circle from right to left, keeping your back flat to the mat. Reverse direction.

KNEADING THE DOUGH ▶
With knees raised, grip the rim as you roll your knees together to the right and then to the left. As you roll tuck them slightly towards your shoulders.

◀ DOVETAIL TUCK-INS
Lie on the floor, feet raised to the bouncer rim hip-width apart and knees bent. Inhale fully. As you exhale, contract your abdomen, squeeze your buttocks, rolling your pelvis through, raising your hips slightly. Pause and hold for 3 seconds. Keep the upper body firmly pressed to the floor. Return to starting position.

GOLDEN ELEMENTS
● Arrange sequences so that the muscles you are conditioning get a chance to relax between routines.
● Nourish, never punish your body. Muscles in extreme discomfort are warning you to stop.

● Remember to release muscles to ease your joints at the end of each routine.
● After the cool-down from your bouncing, begin with techniques for your legs, buttocks and thighs.
● Gradually increase the repetitions you perform

with each set of muscles, by adding repeats in sets of eight, working on both sides of your body.
● Never load strain on your neck. Visualize your spine lengthening to the top of your neck, keeping your chin in toward your chest.

8 STOCKINGS ▶

● Kneel on the bouncer, and lower your trunk onto your elbows. With the sole of your foot facing the ceiling, hips square to the mat, point your toes and raise your right leg directly behind in line with your buttocks. Keep your back straight and neck in line with your spine, chin tucked in.

● Flex your foot and slowly lower your leg one inch from the floor. Slowly return to starting position and repeat.

● To intensify the routine, combine it with the following movement. Flex foot and hold your leg in line with your buttocks. Gently pulse, moving your leg no more than an inch to squeeze your buttocks. Repeat in sets × 8. Change legs and repeat both movements.

❶

9 ◀ STOCKING STITCH

❶ With your right knee resting on the bouncer, form a right angle at the knee and flex your foot.

❷ Lift your knee to form a line with your buttocks, holding firmly as you press the sole of your foot flat to the ceiling. Feel the squeeze in your buttocks as you lift. Return to starting position. Repeat × 8, pulse × 8 (as with Stockings) then change legs.

❷

STOCKING LADDERS
11
◀ **STOCKING LADDERS**

● From Stocking Stitch, hold your leg straight out in line with your hips, point toes.

● Bend your knee to form a right angle, as you flex your foot. Point your toes as you slowly extend, and flex your foot as you bring it slowly back to starting position to face the ceiling. Repeat with both legs in sets × 8.

10

CAT'S-EYES ▶

● Kneel on all fours, holding the rim with your arms straight. Check that your neck is aligned with your spine, chin facing downward. Point your toes, and tuck your right knee into your chest, bringing your forehead toward your knee at the same time.

● As you release your leg, flex your foot and extend your leg in a straight line with your spine. Don't arch your back. Slowly repeat in sets × 8 to both sides.

BACK IN LINE!

● Whatever routine you perform, always bear in mind the importance of maintaining a straight back.

● Contract your abdomen to help support your back.

● Keep your neck in line with your spine.

● Whenever you perform these leg raises bring your thigh up in line with your buttock. Keep both hips square to the mat.

● Avoid arching your back under all circumstances.

TUMMY, WAIST AND BACKS

HELPING HANDS ▶

❶ Lie back on the mat, knees bent, feet hip-width apart on the floor, small of your back firmly into your mat, with your head supported on the cover. Cross your arms in front of your chest. As you exhale slowly roll up, no further than a 45° angle. Contract your tummy as you raise your trunk. Keep your neck aligned with your spine, face looking at the ceiling.

UPSIDE DOWN ▼

This is an excellent position from which to perform any abdominal routines if you have any trouble with or tend to arch your back. Lie on your back on the floor, resting your feet on the rim of the bouncer. Perform any of the basic curls from this position. Working in this way ensures your back stays in complete contact with the floor.

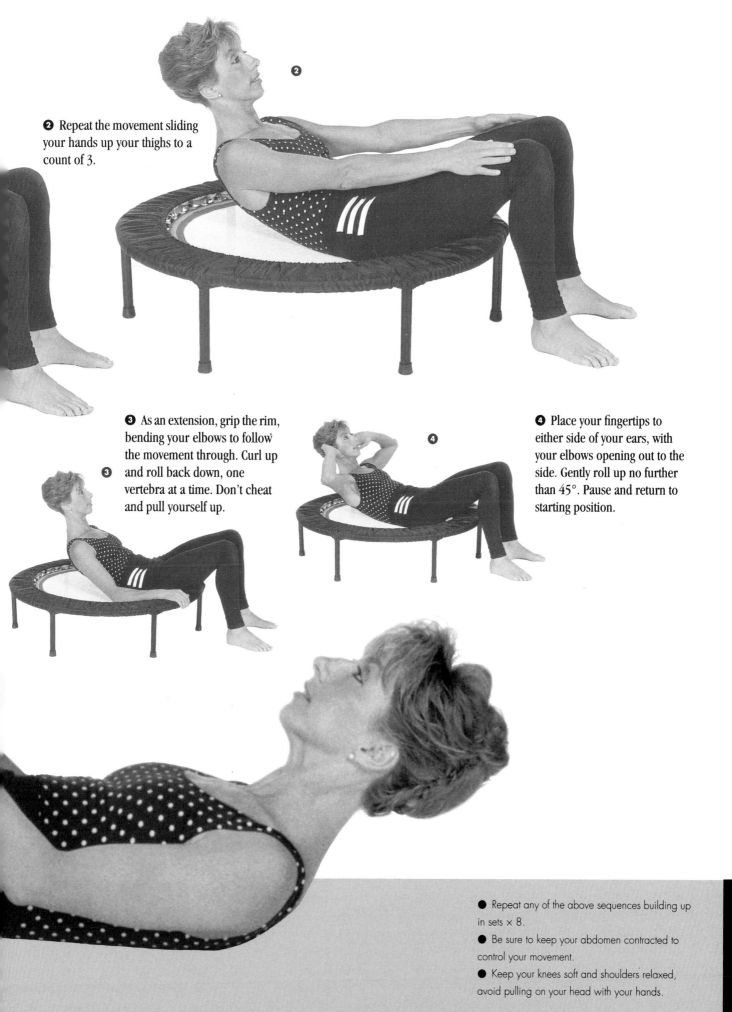

❷ Repeat the movement sliding your hands up your thighs to a count of 3.

❸ As an extension, grip the rim, bending your elbows to follow the movement through. Curl up and roll back down, one vertebra at a time. Don't cheat and pull yourself up.

❹ Place your fingertips to either side of your ears, with your elbows opening out to the side. Gently roll up no further than 45°. Pause and return to starting position.

● Repeat any of the above sequences building up in sets × 8.
● Be sure to keep your abdomen contracted to control your movement.
● Keep your knees soft and shoulders relaxed, avoid pulling on your head with your hands.

3 TIDDLYWINKS ▽

With legs raised, draw your right leg slightly into your chest as you raise your buttocks. Repeat × 8, then change legs. Contract your abdomen as you lift.

▲ 2 PORCUPINE

Lying flat on the mat, grip the rim beside your buttocks. Raise your legs into the air, bending them slightly toward your chest. As you slowly curl them inward, raise your buttocks from the mat a few inches, contracting your abdomen. Pause and release, controlling the movement.

HUNT THE THIMBLE ▶

❶ Place left foot on floor, and right foot on your left knee. As you curl up, reach through the gap between your legs with your left hand to touch your right hand.

❷ Release hands, pause and click your fingers before you slowly lower your body. Repeat × 8 and change legs.

▲ WATER PISTOLS 5

Raise your legs into the air, crossing your ankles, keeping your knees soft. Contract your abdomen, press your back into the mat and curl up reaching for alternate toes, exhaling as you lift. Pause at the top of the lift and slowly lower. Repeat × 8.

◀ MACHINE GUNS 6

● Lying back on the bouncer, feet on the floor, grip the rim with your right hand, elbows out to the side. Bring your left hand to your left ear. Contract your abdomen, pressing the small of your back into the mat. Raise your left elbow as you raise your right knee to touch. Return to starting position. Repeat × 8. Change sides.

● As an extension, raise your left elbow to touch right knee when raised. As you lower trunk, extend leg out in front. Repeat × 8, change sides.

81

DON'T CHEAT!
● Invite your stomach muscles to do the work.

LEGS, BUTTOCKS AND HIPS

PINS AND NEEDLES ▶

❶ Moving to the edge of the mat, relax your left thigh and knee into the mat, extending your right leg, with the foot flexed out to the side, aligned with your body. Grip the rim to support your trunk with your chest slightly forward.

❷ Slowly lower your right leg to the floor, pause and repeat the movement.

82

3 ◀ SIDELINER EXTRA

Lie on the bouncer on your left side, bending your left arm on the floor to support your upper body. Keep your elbow out from your shoulder. Hold the rim with your right hand in front of your chest. Align your hips. Check you don't roll back onto your buttocks. Bend your left leg back at right angles. In small movements, lift and lower your right leg, without touching down on your other leg. Repeat in sets × 8.

2 CHAIN GANGS ▶

❶ Lying on your side, bring your base leg forward, bending your knee to form a right angle with your body and between calf and thigh. Keeping your leg in line with your body bring your top knee towards your chest. As knee comes forward bend arm back with elbow bent at right angles.

❷ Extend upper arm forward, as you extend leg in line with body. Don't arch your back.

SIDE ON

● When you position yourself on your side, lean your upper body slightly forward to avoid rolling back onto your buttocks.

● If you need additional height place a firm cushion under your supporting arm.

● Combine these techniques as you learn to choreograph your routines.

JAM SANDWICH 4 ▶

❶ Lying on your side, grip the rim. Bend your knees forward with a right angle between trunk and thigh. Stack top knee about 6 inches above base knee.

❷ Lift your top leg to open toward the ceiling from the hip. Keep your knee and ankle aligned as you raise your leg, with your base leg firm. Only open as far as feels comfortable so as not to strain your back. Do not allow your legs to touch as you lower.

BONUS BANDS

● Remember bands are a great way to add resistance to help strengthen your muscles.

● Think about where you place the band to make it easier on your joints. For Jam Sandwiches, attach it to your thighs rather than calves (as shown).

6 STABLE DOORS ▽

Lying on your side, grip the rim of the bouncer, straightening your base leg. Bring the foot of the upper leg across to rest on the mat, knee bent. Flex the foot of your lower leg as you raise it firmly, aiming to squeeze your inner thigh as you pulse.

▽ JAM 5 DOUGHNUT

Lying on your side, with legs together, knees bent forward, raise your top leg toward the ceiling as in Jam Sandwich. Pause. Extend leg, flexing your foot towards the ceiling. Bend your knee and lower leg to starting position.

BEACH 7 BELLE ▲

Sit back on the bouncer with hands gripping the rim. Place a beach ball or cushion between your knees, keeping feet parallel and hip-width apart. Squeeze the ball, holding the tension for 3 seconds. Pause and repeat × 8.

85

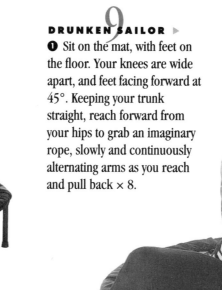

DRUNKEN SAILOR ▶

❶ Sit on the mat, with feet on the floor. Your knees are wide apart, and feet facing forward at 45°. Keeping your trunk straight, reach forward from your hips to grab an imaginary rope, slowly and continuously alternating arms as you reach and pull back × 8.

SHUFFLING ▲

Sitting on your bouncer mat, shuffle forward on your buttocks, with legs outstretched and knees relaxed. As knees reach the rim bend them forward and shuffle until your feet reach the floor. Shuffle back. Repeat × 8.

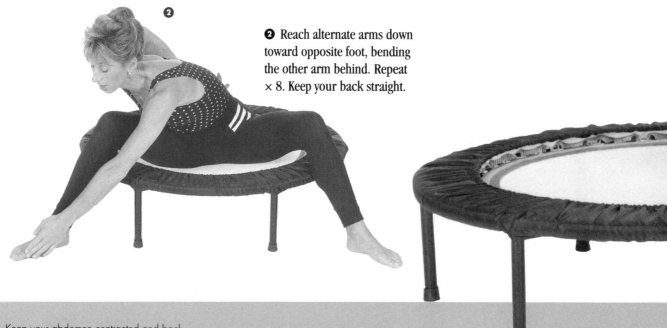

❷ Reach alternate arms down toward opposite foot, bending the other arm behind. Repeat × 8. Keep your back straight.

● Keep your abdomen contracted and back straight for all these techniques.

● When performing Hot Presses, as a rule, the wider your arms the more you will work your pectorals. A narrower position will work your triceps.

ARMS, CHEST AND SHOULDERS

1 TRICEP TRENDIES ▼

● Sit on the edge of the bouncer, knees hip-width apart, hands on the rim beside your hips fingers facing forward. Slide buttocks off the rim, keeping spine and neck straight. Begin to dip by bending and straightening your arms from the elbows, keeping arms parallel behind, with elbows soft. Check your arms are doing the work.

● As an alternative, as you dip, raise your left leg straight out in front, repeating × 8 dips with your right leg raised and × 8 dips with your left leg raised.

2 HOT PRESSES ▶

❶ Kneel on the mat, hands on rim, your face looking down. Keeping your back and neck straight, dip your upper body as you bend your elbows. Straighten and return to starting position. Repeat × 8.

❷ Move palms to the floor with knees on bouncer and repeat × 8.

87

By turning your bouncer on edge, balanced firmly on two legs, you have a perfect ballet barre. It offers numerous alternatives for stretch and conditioning techniques throughout your bounce programmes.

LOGGERHEADS ▶
● Face your bouncer, holding the legs. Balance on your right leg slightly rotated outward and bent. Bend left leg and cross your left ankle behind your right ankle, toes tipping the floor. Tilt your torso forward, tightening your tummy muscles.

● Keeping your left leg bent, lift it behind you. Use your buttocks to lift your leg back. Don't straighten your leg or arch your back. Move slowly to a count of 3, return to starting position and repeat in sets × 8.

RUBBER KNEES ▷
Face your bar with your legs hip-width apart, feet parallel. Bend your knees into a shallow squat, bringing your buttocks behind your heels, with back straight and keeping your feet flat. Pause. Squeeze your buttocks tightly together as you return to starting position. Keep your knees soft. Repeat in sets × 8.

DODGEMS ▷
Stand facing your bar. Bend your right knee, raising your heel behind to form a right angle at the knee. Lean forward slightly, keeping your back long. Your supporting knee is slightly bent. Dip your left supporting leg as you raise your right leg to your side, holding the leg position firmly. Straighten your supporting leg more as you lower your right leg to starting position. Repeat × 8 to both sides.

BACK UPS ▷
❶ Facing your bar, raise your right knee toward your chest, pointing toes.

❷ Flex your foot as you slowly swing the leg through and behind. Keep your back long and straight, hips facing forward, and abdomen contracted.

POSTURE STANCE
● Stand side on or facing the bouncer, outstretched arms gripping the legs or rim.
● Your feet should be in line and slightly wider than your hips, with knees soft and slightly bent.
● Gently contract your abdomen, buttocks tucked, tilting your pelvis slightly forward to flatten your back.
● Relax your shoulders, lengthen your spine from the base through the back of your neck, and release your facial muscles.

SQUAT ESSENTIALS
● Always keep your buttocks above knee level as you lower your trunk.
● As you bend your knees forward, keep them in line with your toes.

◄ SWISS ROLL

Placing your hands on the legs to maintain your balance, swing your hips in complete circles in both directions. Keep your knees bent and soft, and pelvis tucked under. Always move forward as you circle to prevent arching your back.

▲ BUMPERS

This is a perfect technique for toning that bump between your buttocks and hips that most women have real trouble shifting. Facing your bar, lean forward. Extend your right leg out to the side and slightly behind with toes pointed and knee slightly bent. Keep both knees soft. Slowly raise and lower your leg. Repeat × 8 and change legs.

BALANCE CONDITIONING

● Using a balance bar you can combine stepping routines with a variety of conditioning techniques.

● Keep your back straight. Don't over extend any limb position at the expense of your basic posture.

● Work within the limits of your own flexibility.

90

PENDULUM SWINGS ▷

❶ Standing side on to your
bouncer, extend your arm out
for support, knees soft, legs hip-
width apart, back flat. Gently
swing your outer leg to the
side. Pause.

❷ Return the leg inward, to
cross in front of your opposite
thigh. Squeeze thighs together,
bringing your toe to rest on the
floor, 9 inches to the outside of
your supporting leg, with the
toes of both feet aligned. Pull up
on your pelvic floor muscles as
you lower your free leg in front
of the other. Repeat in sets × 8.

Stretch and Relaxation

Borg Scale: 7–9. Duration: approximately 5–10 minutes.

COOL-DOWN INTO STRETCH

● You need to stretch out to re-establish a full range of motion within your muscles and joints.

● Hold these stretches for between 20 to 60 seconds, easing and breathing out any muscular tensions or spasms.

● Because your muscles are warmer at the end of a bounce session, they will become more flexible with less resistance.

● Either condition each muscle group, stretching at the very end of your session, or alternatively, stretch each muscle group thoroughly at the end of every conditioning routine.

● A full stretch is the perfect lead-up to a complete relaxation and meditation programme.

● You can combine your favourite stretches from the pre-bounce warm-up session along with a selection of the following to keep your sessions varied.

HAMSTRING CONCERTO 2 ▲
(Hamstrings, hips)
Lie back on the bouncer mat, knees bent, feet on the floor, facing forward. Raise and grasp your left leg, behind thigh, not knee, easing it in towards your chest, stretching through your hamstring. Keep your back flat to the mat. Intensify the stretch by straightening your leg. Repeat to the other side.

◀ 1 TAILORMADE
(Groin, hips, buttocks, upper back)
Sitting on your bouncer, draw your heels together, with your knees opening out to the side. Lean slightly forward with a straight trunk, to grip the rim of the bouncer. Ease into the stretch as far as possible.

VIOLIN STRINGS 3 ▲
(Hips, buttocks)
Following on from Hamstring Concerto, bend your left knee, opening it out to the side, to grip your foot with both hands. Slowly ease your foot toward your mouth as if trying to bite your big toe! Repeat to the other side.

KEY STRETCHING
● Adapt your stretch routines to include those stretches performed at the start of your workout. Always include Rubber Legs, Elastic Bands and Peg Legs (pp. 44–5) to stretch your calves and quadriceps.

● To develop your flexibility hold each stretch for about ten seconds, then take it a step further and hold for a further ten seconds.

SNAKES AND LADDERS 4 ▾
(Back and abdomen)
Lie back on the bouncer mat, with your hands behind your head, gripping the rim of the bouncer. Bring your knees up at a right angle, inhaling. Slowly roll your knees together over to the left, holding for 8 seconds, as you exhale. Roll back to the centre, inhaling. Continue to roll to alternate sides, repeating × 4 to each side.

PUPPET STRINGS 5 ▲
(Back, hips, abdomen)
Lie back on the mat, bending your knees at hip-width, feet on floor. Place your right heel to the outside of your left knee. Grip the bouncer rim with your right hand, placing your left hand to the outside of your thigh. Slowly roll your knee toward the mat, twisting through your spine. As you twist, gently turn and look in the opposite direction to your legs. Breathe fully into your belly, exhaling as you take your legs to the side. Hold the stretch for at least a count of 8, before changing sides.

◄ FENCING 6
(Side, waist, abdomen)
Kneel on your right knee, extending your left leg to the side, foot turned out, knee bent. With hands on hips, reach over your head with your left arm, aligned with your ear. Feel your chest opening toward the ceiling, breathing fully as you hold the stretch. As you extend, lean to the right, gripping your bouncer rim, in line with your body. Repeat to the other side.

❷ Release your grip, placing your right hand behind your back onto the outer edge of your opposite elbow, gently easing your arm into the stretch. Reverse sides.

● Roll your shoulders forward and back to a count of 8, to loosen and release any tension.

❸ Raise your right arm overhead, bending the elbow to allow the arm to fall behind your neck. Apply tension by pushing down with your opposite palm, breathing fully into the stretch.

▲ **STARLIGHT EXPRESS**
(Arms, shoulders, upper back)
❶ Sit comfortably, cross-legged, on your bouncer. Reach overhead, clasping your arms, stretching up through your trunk.

● Reach behind with your arms, clasping your hands together behind, keeping your back straight as you raise your arms upward from behind toward the ceiling.

● Perform these arm stretches from any sitting or standing position where you have a comfortable and straight back.

● A short bounce is a great way to prepare your body for a yoga session, and to spur the removal of toxins afterwards.

❹ Prayer position your palms in front of your chest, pushing in on the heel of your wrists. Hold for 3 counts.

● Repeat, prayer positioning your palms behind your back, feeling the stretch down the outer ridge of your lower arms.

● Release and circle your wrists, in both directions.

❺ Reach across your chest with your right arm, extended. With your opposite hand, press the arm closer in towards your body. Hold for a count of 8. Repeat with your other arm.

❻ Wrap both arms, criss-crossed, in front of your chest, pressing your fingers into alternate shoulderblades. Tuck your chin into your chest.

● Stand on your bouncer. Shake out any tension in your shoulders, shrugging them, completely vibrating your whole body.

95

8 LIZARD LOUNGER ▽
(Hips and buttocks)

Kneeling on both knees, lean forward and grip the front rim of your bouncer. Moving to one side of the mat, lift your right leg and extend it below your left buttock. As you lower your left buttock toward the mat turn your knee and foot inward, feeling the stretch through your buttocks and hips. If you sit to the back of the bouncer, your trailing right leg will bend to rest on the floor. Breathe fully into the stretch. As you become more flexible you can lean forward and ease your upper body onto the mat. Repeat with the other leg.

9 SITTING DUCKS ▲
(Hamstrings, lower back)

Sit on the floor facing your bouncer, with your back long and shoulders relaxed. Breathe deeply as you lift your left foot to rest on the rim of the bouncer frame, your right leg open to the side. Contract your abdomen and lean forward, with trunk straight, and neck aligned with spine. Grip the rim and ease your abdomen toward the front of your thigh.

10 SEAGULLS ▽
(Back)

● Lie on your back on your bouncer mat, hugging your right knee from under your thigh, into your chest, with your left knee bent and foot on the floor. Repeat with the other leg.

● Repeat the sequence hugging both knees in towards your chest together. Completely relax your back and wrap your arms, criss-crossed, in front of your chest. Lengthen your neck, breathe and relax.

11 PING PONG ▲
(Upper back, arms, shoulders)

● Curl into a ball on the floor, facing your bouncer. Lift your arms and place them shoulder-width, on the mat surface. Breathe fully as you extend your arms across your mat, releasing your head forward.

● As you become more flexible, raise your buttocks into the air at the same time, to extend the stretch.

LIZARD EGGS 12

(Back)

Curl into a small ball on your mat, knees and legs together, wrapping your hands forward in front of your scalp. Breathe fully releasing tension in your upper back. When you feel ready, bring your arms down to your sides, placing your fingertips on the soles of your feet. Curl your head further in towards your knees, into the tightest little ball you can possibly form. Breathe your tensions away in this pose, slowly unwinding.

KNEE BENDER 13

(Back)

Lie on your back on the floor, completely releasing tension in your upper back, and shoulders. Relax your arms to both sides, palms facing up. Bend your knees and place your calves on the mat. Lie in this position for as long as you are comfortable.

ICE CREAM SUNDAE 14

(Abdomen, hips, buttocks, back and side)

● Sitting cross-legged on your bouncer, tuck your right heel into your left thigh. Lengthen through the spine, as you lift your left leg to cross over the right, placing your foot on the mat. Turn to the left, easing your right arm down your thigh, aiming to touch your right heel, gently twisting as far as possible. Breathe deeply and grip the rim of your bouncer to help develop the stretch further. Repeat to the other side.

● If you are very stiff, simply sit on the front of the mat with knees crossed and stretch from this position, gripping the rim beside and behind to help develop your stretch.

GAINING REPOSE

Your body depends on the fact that it has homeostasis – an inbuilt ability to adapt and reset balance within a short time zone. To evoke this state you need to return to a completely restful state of calm and repose. Every system in your body needs time to redress the balance, particularly your organs, body fluids and glands, which reset your metabolism.

Plan for Time-Out (p. 128) to completely release and relax at the end of each full session. Enjoy a chance for complete rest and respite, away from the pace of the day. Choose a posture you find totally comfortable. Throughout this period your heart rate should return to normal (Borg Scale 6–8). Innerspaces (p. 132) offers the perfect routine to send you into relaxation. Incorporate it into your daily Starbound Workouts.

HEADING OUT

(Neck and shoulders)

Lie back on your mat, bending your knees, with feet flat at hip-width. Lower your chin into your chest, relaxing your shoulders. Gently roll your head to the left, moving your ear towards your shoulder, with your eyes looking upwards. Reverse direction. Look slowly from side to side, rolling your head softly across the mat, relaxing your facial muscles, breathing fully.

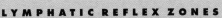

LYMPHATIC REFLEX ZONES

Now that you've worked your way through each of the five sections that form the complete Starbound Workout, you are refreshed and ready to head out into the world again! Before you go, take a step up onto your bouncer and gently recharge your energy in the Rhythm Bounce. Use your stroking techniques and bring your awareness back into your breathing patterns to loosen up any residual tension you may be feeling.

STARBOUND BULLETINS

Choreography

COMPOSING ROUTINES

If you want to be a creative bouncer the fun really starts when you begin to master the various skills and techniques, then create your own exciting routines to blend sequences together. You should vary your routines regularly, not performing more than eight of any one movement in a row. If any of your muscles or joints are under strain the more often you ring the changes the more they get to relax without any cumulative effects building up. There are numerous ways you can add variety to your sessions.

TAPPING THE BEAT

The first item on the list is music. Compared to exercising from the floor, the beat from your bouncer will be slower for the same routines. As a rule of thumb, the faster the music the lower and faster you bounce. A slower beat will encourage a higher bounce, which in turn requires additional effort. Jazz, rock and roll, instrumental, country and western, and even the blues will get your feet into bouncing mode. When you begin your Starbound programmes you'll start tuning into music that's been gathering dust on your shelves!

RINGING THE CHANGES

You can add variety to your routines with a few simple tricks:

● In whatever routine you are performing, move around the mat in a clockwise direction. Always change direction to weigh the balance.

● You can rotate the mat either with single routines or by combining routines to form sequences.

● Always lift your feet to turn your body. Jump the turns. If you lock either foot to the mat you will strain your knees.

● There are many ways you can move about the mat to create new routines. Experiment with fan patterns, diagonal v-shape patterns, back-to-front patterns, quarter and half turns. As a beginner start with quarter turns, and progress to half turns as your confidence and skills improve. Moving around the mat in quarter turns as you change techniques can be fun. For example:

> Twist × 4 to the front
> Jump and turn into the Shuffle × 4 to the right
> Jump and turn into the Twist × 4 to the back
> Jump and turn into the Shuffle × 4 to the right
> Jump to starting position and change direction

● It's easiest to work to music which breaks into sets of 8 beats. Vary the beat according to half, single or double time. As you develop skills, you'll discover you can bounce high and hard, or low and fast, regulating the intensity of your routines to suit the music.

● Your arms and legs act as levers. As a rule the longer the lever and the more levers involved in the routine, the more intense the activity will be.

CHOREOGRAPHY PATTERNS

The following are examples of the many formats that can be used to style different bounce routines.

❶ KEEP THE LEGS, CHANGE THE ARMS
Legs: Heel Flak × 4 each side
Arms: No arms, 1 arm, 2 arms, arms up
Legs stay on × 4; arms reduce × 4, × 2, × 1
Change legs to Crisscrosses: Keep arms × 1
Add leg out on one arm, then add side kick on arms up.

❷ INTERVAL PATTERN
Every verse: twist × 2, knees up × 4, toe twist × 4 right, then × 4 left.
Every Chorus: Soccer, diagonal right × 4, then left × 4,

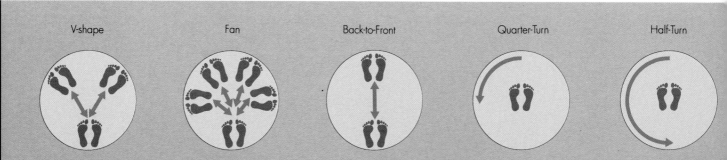

V-shape   Fan   Back-to-Front   Quarter-Turn   Half-Turn

Basic Bounce to front and back of mat × 8.
Instrumental breaks: Shuffle × 4, twist right × 4, shuffle
to centre × 4, twist left × 4.

❸ ADD ON PATTERNS
Side Sling right × 4, Basic Bounce to centre × 4, Side
Sling left × 4 (repeat sequence × 4)
Hopscotch × 2, Crisscrosses × 2, Knees Up Mother Brown
× 4 (repeat sequence × 4)
Repeat entire routine × 4 before adding a new routine.
See how long it is before you have forgotten your pattern.
It's a great way to exercise your memory.

◁ PECCY PRESSES
Bend your arms forming right
angles at the elbow, extending
them sideways at shoulder level.
Holding this position, squeeze
your arms in front of your chest
to touch each other at the
elbow, before returning to
starting position.

Armed Forces

The sky's the limit when it comes to combining arm
routines with bounce techniques. Experiment with
different combinations to add variety to your workout.

◁ PULLING ANCHOR
With both arms hanging loosely
at your side, clench your fists.
Lift your right arm up to
shoulder height, bending your
elbow as though you were
pulling a heavy anchor. Alternate
both arms.

WINDMILL ▷
Raise your right arm forward,
while lowering your left arm
down your left side to your
thigh. Keep your elbows soft
and alternate their position,
from above to below,
windmilling them as
you bounce.

◁ CURLYLOCKS
With your arms hanging loosely
at your sides, palms facing
forward, fingers outstretched,
raise both arms at the same
time, bending from your elbows
and clenching fists to your
shoulders. Open hands as
you release arms to your
thighs. Repeat.

99

MOSQUITOES ▷

❶ Extend both arms out to your sides at shoulder level, palms down.

❷ Bend your arms in from your elbows to touch your fingers to chin.

❸ Push both arms down toward each thigh. Pull arms up, bending them into your chin again.

TINKERBELL ▽

Release one arm out to the side as you swing the other up toward your chest. Immediately change, swinging through to the other side. Keep the extended arm slightly lower in front of your shoulder.

PARALLEL BARS ▷

❶ With your arms by your sides, bend them up and swing them to the right.

❷ Swing them back across your body to the left, keeping your forearms parallel.

❸ Click your fingers at the top of each swing. This works well with High Flier and other knee lifts.

100

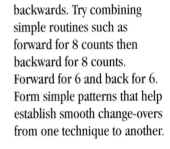

SWIVEL HINGE ▶

Extend both arms out to each side, with your palms facing downward. Hold your left hand stationary while you bend the elbow of your right arm. Swing your right hand back to starting position, at the same time pulling your left hand in towards your chest.

◀ BREASTSTROKE

Bring both hands in to touch your chest. Turn your wrists so that the backs of your hands press together. In a breaststroke action straighten your arms as you press them forward at shoulder height. Slowly separate your arms through to each side of your body. Return the arms to starting position.

HORSES IN THE STABLE ▼

Press each finger and the thumb of your left hand into the tip of each of the right. Spread your fingers as wide as you can as you push the tips together for 2 bounces. Release.

Bouncing Rope

Bouncing with a rope adds a definite flavour to your programmes as well as the chance to perfect some new skills. If you haven't skipped since childhood, expect to spend a few hours recapturing your basic skills. The combination of bouncing and skipping will certainly provide a challenge.

SKIP THE LOU

Hold the rope out to each side away from your body. Practise simple skipping forwards, establishing a rhythm that suits as you skip on the bouncer. Following the forward skip, reverse the rope and try backwards. Try combining simple routines such as forward for 8 counts then backward for 8 counts. Forward for 6 and back for 6. Form simple patterns that help establish smooth change-overs from one technique to another.

◀ NOUGHTS AND CROSSES

Establish a rhythm with the rope. Cross your arms in front of your chest as the rope comes over your head. Bounce through the loop and uncross your arms as the rope comes over again. Return arms to your sides and bounce through the loop from this position. Repeat the two movements to form the pattern.

JUMPING WAVES

Holding your rope out to each side, make small waves forward and backward. You have to jump the waves as the rope swings under your feet. This can be performed by double bouncing or hopping which is easier. Alternatively skip to the Basic Bounce combined with the Lift Off.

Have A Ball!

As long as you mind the chandeliers you can have a great time with a ball on your bouncer. Beach balls are perfect. They seem to float in time with your bouncing rhythm. A ball offers the perfect ploy for keeping the children occupied while you are bouncing. Throw the ball for them, creating simple games to keep them excited, and they'll spend a happy hour chasing ball while you bounce.

Play about and you'll soon find many ways in which you can include the use of balls into your sessions. Small tricks such as bouncing, clicking your fingers, catching the ball and clapping three times before you bounce again, will be challenging enough to keep you on your toes.

STAGE ONE:
Very low level of bouncing. One-star techniques such as the Rhythm Bounce. This is known as the Active Rest Stage. Duration: approximately 7 seconds. Borg Scale 8.

STAGE TWO:
Low impact bouncing; speeding up your action from Stage One. Use two-star techniques, such as Olympic Torch, bringing in arm movements, like the Swivel Hinge, to raise your pulse. Duration: approximately 7 seconds. Borg Scale 12.

Trimetric Bouncing

This method of training is also referred to as 'intensity switch training'. It offers a relatively new concept in aerobics training and is becoming more popular in class situations. Take the concept and apply it to training sessions from your bouncer. Based on interval training, where short bursts of intense activity are followed by periods of rest with minimal activity, it works extremely well, due to the short sharp burst of bouncing which ensures your heart rate doesn't decline in the resting period.

STAGE THREE:
High impact bouncing. Incorporate three-star Lift Off techniques, such as Zig-Zags, with high intensity arm and leg movements. Duration: approximately 15 seconds. Borg Scale 16 (maximum).

PLAN TO GAIN MAXIMUM BENEFIT FROM TRIMETRICS
❶ You need to follow the three stages for between 15 and 35 minutes.
❷ Repeat the three stages, staying with the same techniques (one set of three different steps for the three stages), for between 3 to 5 minutes, or less if you have a shorter piece of music to choreograph.

❸ Preferably the three stages should be repeated between 30 and 70 times.

❹ Stage One, where your body is in active rest, allows your body a chance to release wastes, repair damage to tissue, replenish your fuel supply and generally serve as an active recovery session. Don't neglect this phase of the training.

Bounce Plyometric Training

Recently, there has been a surge of interest in kangaroos under observation on treadmills. For their size and speed at which they move, they get by on less than half the energy that would be expected. Their secret for successful hopping lies in the fact that each time they land their tendons stretch elastically, snapping back and feeding the force to help their hop off rather like a pogo stick.

The part of your muscles that relates to speed lies within your tendons (which store up to 50% of energy from each running stride) and the elastic tissue of the muscle itself. Plyometrics is the method employed by athletic and sports coaches to train the tendon in the elastic tissue of your muscle. Many top coaches are now using bouncers in training sessions. They provide an ideal base for serious athletes to refine skills of coordination, agility, explosiveness, eye–brain development and strength.

PLYOMETRICS FROM YOUR BOUNCER

Either a build up or a full plyometric training programme can be carried out using your bouncer. This provides the optimum relationship between strength and speed which results in explosive power. Coaches concentrate on exercises containing bouncing at different levels, heights and speed. Hopping, skipping and a variety of your favourite bounce techniques can be included in your approach to plyometric training. The five categories include: coordination drills, single response jumps, bouncing, box drills and depth jumps. If using your bouncer for plyometric training you will not suffer nearly the intensity of muscle soreness for the same amount of work following a normal training session.

Circuit Bouncing

If you thrive on variety you'll enjoy creating a bounce circuit session combining techniques from bounce target zone and conditioning programmes. With a little imagination you can combine other simple activities into your circuit. Perhaps a couple of your favourite dance routines or even a little housework. Scrubbing the kitchen floor under the tick of your stop-watch can be an excellent circuit activity! Control studies show aerobic and muscular endurance is heightened when a circuit programme is interspersed with short sharp bursts of aerobic activity between conditioning stations. Bouncing is ideal because it brings your heart rate up quickly. The following may give you some ideas relating to your circuit planning.

❶ Plan your circuit to combine Bounce Target Zone, conditioning and stretch techniques.

❷ Time your Target Zone sequences and break conditioning routines into sets of 8 repeats.

❸ Jot the activities for your circuit down beforehand. A 45-minute outline for a beginner's circuit might be:

Warm-up, Mobility, Stretch: 10 minutes
Aerobic and Conditioning Circuit: 10 to 15 minutes
Cool-down: 5 minutes
Stretch and Relaxation: 10 minutes

❹ The following outline suggests the way in which you may combine your conditioning techniques: Begin with a 3 minute bounce routine, follow by 3 sets of 8 × Abdominal Prayers, follow by 3 minutes in a skipping routine, followed by 4 sets of Party Dips at the bouncer bar.

ELASTIC ENERGY
● The bouncer enables your body to reap the benefits of continuous eccentric contractions which occur as muscles lengthen. The release of elastic energy creates a greater input of power, generating mechanical energy which is stored in muscle cells.

Good Sports

Top sports personalities have impressed me with their interpretations of the way a bouncer can be used in their training sessions. Ice skaters, swimmers, wrestlers, golf enthusiasts, badminton, tennis and hockey players, even martial artists, are among those I have witnessed in training on their bouncers.

If you are suffering from injuries, and have to stop normal training sessions, Starbound programmes offer the perfect solutions to your problems. You can carry out a gentle maintenance programme which not only helps the recovery of your injury but will safeguard the stability of your fitness level.

I will use tennis and skiing to offer examples of how you can arrange your bouncing sessions to incorporate the training of specific sports skills.

TIME FOR TENNIS

Competent tennis skills often centre around strength, endurance and flexibility. When you play tennis you are concentrating your efforts mainly on one side of your body; for example, your right side if you are right-handed. Throughout your bouncing programmes you need to balance this factor by practising right/left movements in a balanced fashion. Techniques from Brainy Spotlights (p. 142) will help your brain and body coordination and techniques from Bright Eyes (p.146) will help your brain and eye functioning when you include them in your sessions. Use your tennis racket on your bouncer to really get you in the swing of things.

FOREHAND SWIPES

Moving in a variety of steps, prance around your bouncer holding your racket and concentrating on your forearm moves. Imagine you are hitting the ball from all angles. Visualize the ball aiming for a certain spot and bounce about as you hit the target. Bring yourself back into the Basic Bounce each time you hit the ball.

AT YOUR SERVICE

Practise your service exactly as if you were on court, marking time with the Rhythm Bounce. Immediately you have served await return, positioning your body for attack. Assume a forehand or backhand stance and position your body. Stay on the move in the Lift Off as you move about the mat. Every time you serve follow it through in this way. Concentrate on your arm action and keeping the opposite side of your body in balance. Change the height of your jumps as you respond to throw up for service.

BACKHAND GLORY

Starting from the Basic Bounce, visualize the ball coming at you from different directions calling for backhand angling. As you swing your racket perform quarter and half turns to hit the ball.

GAME, SET AND MATCH

● If you have a garden, you can place your bouncer in hitting distance of a racket-ball pole and start playing.

SKI THE SLOPES

If you are preparing for your winter jaunt to the mountains be wise and use your bouncer beforehand to prepare your body for action. Design your sessions utilizing techniques from all programmes to specifically strengthen and condition your legs, buttocks and back. Include the Slinky Skier, the Knock-Kneed Skier and Ski Corner. Here are a few more techniques to prepare you for days on the slopes.

SLALOM TIME

Imagine you are holding ski poles, knees slightly bent. Bounce rhythmically to both sides of the mat with your knees and feet together. Make a complete turn, once to the left and right, taking about 8 jumps to come full circle. Once you have mastered this technique, extend yourself further by angling your body 45° to the right below your hips as you jump left and 45° to the left as you jump to the right. Keep your upper body and head facing forward.

SLALOM SNAPPER

Bounce in the same way as in Slalom Time but every time you jump snap up your heels towards your thighs behind you. This will slow you down but intensify your coordination.

SPEEDY GONZALES

Stand with your feet flat to the mat, hip-width apart, with approximate right angles at your bent knees. Crouch down with your upper body. Keep your tummy contracted, buttocks tucked and back straight. You are preparing to ride the bumps. Bounce to raise your feet about 4 inches off the mat in quick succession. The faster you go the sooner you'll lose your breath! Try and hold your posture intact as you perform this technique. At the end of the routine perform the Mummy and the Shaker.

Chairbound!

If you have a disability that confines you to the spot, whether it be a wheelchair or even to bed, you still need to activate your body systems. With your bouncer close at hand ask a friend to bounce for you. As long as your feet are on the mat surface the vibration from the mat will work wonders, boosting your metabolism, strengthening your immune system, encouraging the circulation of all fluid throughout your body and tuning your elimination patterns.

● Roll your chair to the edge of the bouncer, placing your feet in the middle of the mat while someone bounces for you. Work with your friend telling them the intensity that feels most comfortable for you. This works well for your lower body from the hips down to your feet.

● If you can safely move from your chair to sit on the mat of your bouncer your friend can stand behind you and vibrate the mat.

● If possible, combine the two routines so that you get full stimulation from the bouncer. Try different positions for sitting on your mat. Crosslegged, supported squatting from the edge or with your legs outstretched over the mat.

● If your friend can help you through a stretch and mobility session before you are bounced you will benefit greatly. Synovial fluid is pumped around your joints, energy activated and niggling tensions and compressions relieved.

Bouncing Back For The Blind

Many people who are blind find it extremely difficult to weave safe exercise into their environment. They are finding the perfect solution with Starbound programmes, enjoying an aerobic component along with the chance to finally kick their heels up safely. The use of a balance bar is advisable at first, until confidence is instilled and skills are enhanced.

WALL OF SUPPORT

● Many people who are not so steady on their feet place their bouncer next to a wall which they use as a support while they develop skills.

A WHOLE NEW YOU

IN TRANSIT

TOXIC OVERLOAD

Over the twentieth century we've witnessed the use of drugs becoming a multi-million pound industry. We've all been bombarded in one form or another. If not with additives, colourings and preservatives in overprocessed foods, we've been overdosed with pesticide and insecticide residues in vegetables and fruit. We clean with chemicals, throw slug pellets laced with poison on our gardens and allow pollution of the environment to become so lethal that rain is labelled 'acid'. Medicine cabinets are filled to over-flowing with pills we are thoughtlessly urged to pop. Perhaps the biggest trap lies in our aimless addictions as we hang out for cups of tea and coffee, cigarettes and alcohol.

Your body deals with two types of toxins. Endo-toxins are naturally released as waste products from cellular metabolism, while exotoxins are absorbed into your body through your food, skin, breath and fluid intake.

Your liver has hundreds of duties to carry out, among them the breaking down and distribution of toxins. If it becomes overwhelmed, which is the case for many in the twentieth-century toxic hotpot, it simply stops dealing with all the toxins that come its way. Liver cells themselves die off adding to the toxic load. When toxins move through your liver without being broken down your body cells in general are bathed in blood that is toxically charged.

COLONY MATTERS

In the United Kingdom alone over fifty million pounds a year are spent on laxatives, indicating that the elimination of wastes is a problem for many. About 5 feet in length, and $2\frac{1}{2}$ inches wide, your colon is often referred to as the sewerage system of your body, quick to become a cesspool of pollution if you abuse it. When the food you have eaten is fully digested, your colon discharges wastes and toxins from your body. If congested, wastes accumulate layer upon layer. If poisons back up into your system they can cause autotoxaemia – literally self-poisoning.

Soluble wastes are reabsorbed into your blood-stream, placing a burden on your kidneys, skin and lungs. Digestion is hindered, natural bowel flora is disturbed and insufficient supplies of nutrients are absorbed into your bloodstream.

MARVELLOUS METABOLICS

Your metabolism consists of all the chemical processes that take place in your body, including the building up of new tissues from nutrients, as well as the destruction and breaking down of worn out cells when they've outlived their purpose. Metabolism is a continuous and complicated process, whereby every chemical change either uses or releases energy.

For top class metabolism, your first priority must be the complete and thorough digestion of food to sustain your body functions. Ingesting food saps about 10% of your total energy supply each day, while the energy required to fuel your physical activity shifts from between 15%, if you are relatively inactive, to 30%, if you bounce and get to grips with life enthusiastically.

The secret for activating your metabolism lies in shunting on wastes through your blood and lymph to be eliminated from your body, so they don't stockpile and block tissues. When you clear the way for fresh circulation necessary supplies can reach your cells.

REFINING DIGESTION

Digestion and congestion do not blend well. You simply can't digest your food properly, and absorb nutrients you need, if your colon is congested. From the time food enters your mouth, ideally it should exit the other end within twenty-four hours. In many Western countries the transit time takes over seventy-five hours, creating an invitation for the onslaught of disease. Irritable bowel syndrome, fissures, oedema, headaches, ulcers, appendicitis, acne and candida are prime examples of such ailments. Between two and four hundred varieties of micro-organisms co-exist in your intestinal tract, making it a potential channel for infection. The secret for striking a healthy balance in your bowel lies in maintaining a healthy balance in the colony of bacteria present. If undigested proteins reach your bowel, they can add fuel to an already toxic fire. When the contents of your intestines become putrefied, they can cause infections as far away as your teeth and tonsils.

THE HEALING CRISIS

As you bounce your body into balance, toxic residues will be released manifesting completely different symptoms for everyone.

Expect emotional and psychological reactions to surface as the physical debris shifts. Feelings of elation may see-saw with irritability.

Tingling skin is common in areas where energy or fluid is trapped. This is often a sign that blockages are moving, electrical switches are being turned back on and cleansing is taking place.

You may feel worse while you're getting better! Gently bounce and stroke zones for your elimination organs in the Rhythm Bounce. By keeping your supplies of oxygen charged you'll keep tensions and toxins that may be surfacing at bay.

Persevere! Your bouncer is the ongoing means for maintaining your immunity and energy levels. Often you will notice improvements around the six week mark as new patterns of body chemistry settle in.

BENEFITS AS YOU BOUNCE

● *The more you pump blood and lymph through your liver, the better it will operate. It is loaded with lymphatics, which transport fats and proteins, as well as carting off numerous wastes.*

● *Bouncing offers a natural laxative, decongesting your bowel, while stimulating digestion.*

● *You stimulate muscular reflexes, and strengthen the muscles of your alimentary tract and the movement of your colon.*

● *You speed the transit time of your food, and regulate bowel motions.*

● *Metabolism is stimulated to help your body deal with toxic loads more speedily.*

● *Nerve responses that set up natural peristaltic reactions, promoting the movement of food through your gut, are activated.*

● *Stagnating blood and lymph is stirred, which prevents toxic wastes and bacteria from stockpiling.*

● *The transportation of fats and proteins from your intestines in small lymph vessels known as lacteals is encouraged.*

RETURN TO SENDER

Although your heart finds it easy enough pumping blood around your body, by the time it has off-loaded supplies, the pressure of your heartbeat is not as strong for the return journey. This is one of the main reasons wastes accumulate. For the return journey of fluids to your heart you depend on your calf, thigh and abdominal muscles to stimulate flow and to control your valves. Nearly all Starbound techniques set up a rhythm in your calf muscles. They are your most important asset for directing the return flow. As blood and lymph continue upward, the contraction of your diaphragm, which controls your breathing, increases the pressure in your abdomen, easing your fluids forward on their journey.

CASTING WASTES

Waste products are flushed from around your body, due to the activation of your elimination systems, which off-load the rubbish picked up by your blood and lymph. Although they are naturally activated when you bounce, by massaging zones for your elimination organs while bouncing you empower all associated systems into action. At the beginning of your workouts massage these zones as part of your warm-up regime.

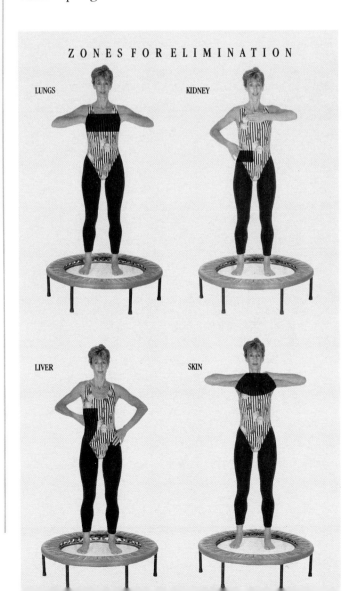

ZONES FOR ELIMINATION

LUNGS   KIDNEY

LIVER   SKIN

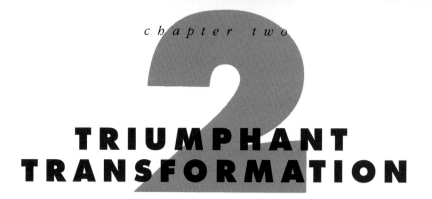

TRIUMPHANT TRANSFORMATION

FOOD, GLORIOUS FOOD!

Health cannot be purchased in a doctor's surgery, or thrown into a trolley at the supermarket. Your food should provide every cell with a selection of essential ingredients to secure your body's growth, maintenance and repair, provide you with energy and keep you warm. Rather than allowing indulgences to get the better of you, the fine line between using and misusing food is one that you must draw yourself by taking control.

The claim that we need to curb the growth of the population, because there are too many people for the world to feed, is blatantly untrue. There is simply too much food in the wrong places. How much went into your rubbish bin today? And did any rubbish go into your stomach?

The western definition of malnutrition suggests people are not able to obtain food they need to survive. The reality is that many people are in danger of not achieving genetic potential because they're overfed and undernourished.

Statistics constantly surface linking disease not only with a worrying lack of activity, but also to dreadful habits surrounding food intake. Food is often poorly used as we grab at it for oral gratification to satisfy various psychological needs. Moderation is the name of the game with a few treats saved for special occasions. Many problems relating food to ill-health occur because the treat has become the foundation of the diet, with essential nutrients provided as the exception rather than the rule.

QUALITY OR QUANTITY

The food you choose to eat and the way you choose to eat it has the power to kill, cure or nourish. Don't allow yourself to be sucked in by the media or the marketplace. There is a wicked amount of temptation to commercially lure taste buds. Salt, sugar and fat – the three musketeers responsible for the destruction of many lives – have been used to lace products to such an extent that millions of people are now addicted to these poisons.

Breaking habits of dependence on food can be as difficult as giving up alcohol or cigarettes. Because the quality of our food has diminished, in most cases,

we eat far too much. Many naturopaths and nutritionists now suggest the answer lies in increasing the quality and decreasing the quantity of food you eat.

Establishing a healthy lifestyle with a safe pattern of food input leaves few alternatives but to begin thinking organic. Many believe this may provide the only safe solution to the twentieth-century immune response to stress, toxic overload and poisons we are thoughtlessly and almost helplessly loading into our systems. Organic farming produces healthy, unadulterated food with no harmful side-effects to your health or the health of the planet.

TAKING STOCK

The following plan for action outlines bare necessities to ensure optimum health. The purpose is not for me to offer you a series of menus or a selection of recipes, but to help you reassess your present food habits and needs, so you can create choices which suit your lifestyle. I'll outline simple guidelines to help you survey the larder. Then you design your own plan to replace habits with a sensible approach you know you can follow. Your Starbound workout provides the perfect focus for preparing your body chemistry to adapt for optimum nourishment. Wave goodbye to the old food habits in your life, polluted tissue fluid and depleted energy levels. Consider the following two-fold approach.

① CLEANSE

Detox. Dimensions will provide the initial preparation your body needs. Plan to bounce away the cravings and stimulate the removal of wastes.

② REPLACE

Use the Five-Star Plan to investigate the areas of change you need to make. Draw up a list of objectives and goals if it helps you make a positive statement. When you are planning for change remember to assess which changes can be made in one strong sweep, and which you are going to have to implement slowly. For successful long-lasting transformation the secret lies in the fact that we don't give things up or change bad habits but rather replace them.

RESOLUTION PLAN

PHASE ONE
Cleanse:
Detox. Dimensions
~

WITH YOUR BOUNCER YOU CAN MAKE IT THROUGH
DETOXIFICATION SO MUCH MORE EASILY. DESIGN
YOUR PLAN CALLING ON STARBOUND
PROGRAMMES TO HELP REPLACE HABITS WHICH
SPELL TROUBLE.

BOUNCE BONUSES

Use your bouncer several times a day to help spur toxins and wastes out of your system. Because your liver will be working harder than usual stroke your reflexes regularly. Activate zones for elimination to speed the process. You'll be eliminating mainly through your breath, skin, urine and bowels. Your emotions reflect the cleansing that is taking place, so bounce to keep your energy in motion!

PLAN

● Make a note of everything you can think of which may regularly raise your toxicity. Consider foods, fluids (coffee, tea, alcohol), pollutants from the atmosphere, fabrics, cleaning detergents, cosmetic creams, stale air, cooking utensils, cigarettes and a host of other irritants.

● Decide which culprits top the list for elimination. Which items can be done away with 'en masse' and which things need finer attention? Certain foods can be easily dispensed with simultaneously, whereas cigarettes and other highly addictive substances need well-planned periods for successful transition.

● Set realistic time zones for each dimension of your detoxification programme.

● Plan to bounce as cravings appear. This will remove toxins and encourage the delivery of oxygen and nutrients to replace the pangs.

FOOD

Pay attention to your food intake.

● Eat plenty of fruit, to draw toxins from your cells, preferably twenty minutes before or after main meals to avoid fermentation in your stomach.

● Plan for a fresh vegetable and fruit foundation for food intake. Prepare food with at least 70% natural water content intact. Eat at least one fresh, raw fruit and vegetable salad daily.

● Keep fats to a minimum while detoxifying. Avoid saturated fats (see The Food File, p. 116).

● Always keep an apple on hand. Temptation may strike when your bouncer is nowhere in sight. Apples contain galacturonic acid, renowned for withdrawing toxins, as well as pectin, which inhibits proteins putrefying in your intestines. Apples stimulate your liver and the digestive secretions so essential for diffusing toxins.

● Water from fresh vegetables and fruit helps to flush out inorganic minerals, salts and toxins, which calcify in your body. Your cells require water: more than five million of your brain cells are over 70% water; muscle cells contain 75%; blood contains about 85%; and your bone cells about 25%. The best source of water is through foods which are rich in minerals and vitamins.

● Plan to slowly replace food in which you over indulge, breaking dependence on unnatural products.

FLUID INTAKE

● Begin the day with a 'Lemon Zinger' (p. 118). This will balance the acid in your system which naturally rises as you are detoxifying.

● Drink up to eight glasses of water a day, slightly warmed in the winter. You can spice it up with a slice of lemon.

● Dandelion coffee is an excellent substitute for activating your liver. Use it in the morning in place of regular coffee.

● Brew your own herb teas and drink fresh fruit and vegetable juices throughout the day, whenever possible, to flush and nourish your system.

REST

Establish clear patterns of rest, relaxation and activity. True healing takes place when you are in an absolute state of calm. Always work through a relaxation technique (p. 132) at the end of your bounce sessions. Utilize sound, facial and visual techniques throughout relaxation and meditation.

COSMETIC CONSIDERATIONS

● Massage your gums daily. Floss your teeth and clean the residue from your tongue every morning – using a separate toothbrush – before brushing your teeth.

● Use a deodorant rather than anti-perspirant. Your armpits are a major channel for the elimination of wastes from your skin. If you block these channels you create a backlog in your lymphatics. Any blockage in the lymph vessel and nodes in your armpits can also be dangerous for your breast zones.

● Speed elimination procedures by taking saunas and steam baths, and by using facial packs. Swimming in the salty sea is excellent, if the weather permits, and providing there is an ocean near by.

Holding Fast

If your health allows, set yourself into transition for your Detox. Dimensions with one of the optional cleansing regimes from the following selection. As you abstain from food, pent-up secretions and retained wastes are expelled from your body. Notable benefits emerge as harmful toxins and substances in your bloodstream and tissues are cleared quickly. Because your digestive system is allowed a holiday, your body is able to devote more energy to the process of detoxification.

Any fast has to be monitored very carefully. Anyone attempting to fast, especially when suffering from disease or disability, must consult their practitioner beforehand. You have to be psychologically and physically prepared to fast, even for a day on fruit. For each equivalent period of time that you intend to follow your fast, allow the same amount of time to ease your body into and off the plan.

Your bouncer is the most essential ingredient in any fast. Whether it is for a short fruit fast of a day, or over a longer period, bouncing will help speed the elimination of toxins from your system, preventing them from stockpiling and triggering cravings. I follow a day or two of fruit or fluid fasting each month to perk up my energy and cleanse my system.

FLUID ISSUES

● Keep your fluid intake high in order to prevent dehydration. Flush your tissues and help off-load toxins and cravings.

● Herb teas are excellent as you fast. Alpine tea acts as a mild laxative. Stay away from regular tea and coffee.

● If you are monofasting, allow twenty minutes between food and fluid intake.

● Aloe vera juice acts as a mild purgative.

● Drink distilled rather than mineral water.

TOPICAL TIPS

FAST PROSPECTS

❶ As you fast your emotional and mental preoccupations become clearer. If you have a problem the solution often comes to light. Suppressed emotions may surface as memories are triggered. Plan time-out and meditation each day, following your bouncing session.

❷ In the beginning, irregular bowel motions may occur as you throw off wastes and the debris layering your bowel is lifted. Bounce regularly.

❸ Massage your abdomen in small circular motions for a minute in a clockwise rotation and then anticlockwise while moving in the Rhythm Bounce (p. 29).

❹ Discharges you experience when you bounce are often signalling the removal of wastes.

❺ Headaches are often a sign that toxins are stirring in and around your brain. Activate your neurovascular reflex points in the Rhythm Bounce.

❻ Plan periods of abstinence so they don't coincide with social activity which revolves around food. Plan in advance how you intend to resist temptation where people, food or drink may entice you to fall short of your goals.

DAY-IN-CLEANSE
Periodically, fast from all food for twenty-four hours.
PREPARATION
The day before, prepare by eating salads, fruit and yoghurt in small meals. Bounce several times and drink a Lemon Zinger before retiring.
THROUGHOUT THE DAY
● Start the day with the Lemon Zinger.
● Follow up every hour with fluid, either herb tea, freshly squeezed fruit juice or distilled water.
● Between fluid intake bounce for a few minutes.
THE DAY AFTER
● Start the day with the Lemon Zinger. Mid-morning eat a piece of fruit and at lunchtime enjoy fruit salad with a helping of yoghurt.
● Snack on fresh vegetables in mid-afternoon. Carrot, celery, pepper and cucumber sticks dipped in yoghurt are excellent combinations.
● In the evening prepare a light vegetable meal.

THE APPLE AND CELERY WONDER
This plan is a firm favourite for many because it allows you to eat while still reaping fast benefits.

PREPARATION

The day before, eat salad and fruit that is in season. Gather a stock of fresh and delicious apples and a bunch of celery. An hour before retiring, munch away on an apple followed by a piece of celery.

THROUGHOUT THE DAY

● Start the day with the Lemon Zinger.

● During the day eat as many apples and pieces of celery as you wish. Apples provide an excellent cleanser for your system and a perfect liver stimulant. Peel them, slice them into cubes or try them grated and sprinkled with cinnamon.

● I find it best to eat at regular intervals with five good apple meals a day. However, eat when you feel hungry.

● This is a great plan to follow if you need to learn to chew your food more slowly. After a couple of days on the apple and celery muncher you'll be enjoying every last crunch.

THE DAY AFTER

When you are ready to come off the plan, gradually introduce some salad vegetables and sprouts to your lunch. Follow the principles for breaking fast as with the Day-in-Cleanse.

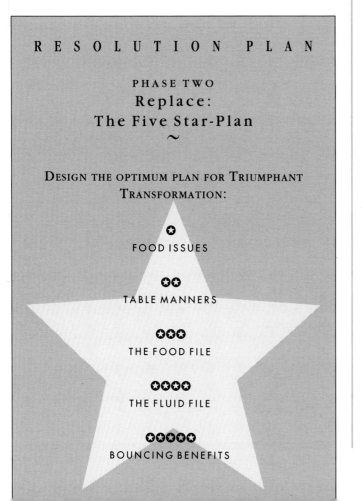

R E S O L U T I O N   P L A N

PHASE TWO
Replace:
The Five Star-Plan
~

DESIGN THE OPTIMUM PLAN FOR TRIUMPHANT TRANSFORMATION:

✪
FOOD ISSUES

✪✪
TABLE MANNERS

✪✪✪
THE FOOD FILE

✪✪✪✪
THE FLUID FILE

✪✪✪✪✪
BOUNCING BENEFITS

Food Issues

THAT FAT

Fat has become such an issue that it's sometimes hard to decipher the basic facts. It will pay to keep these few pointers in mind.

SATURATED FATS: Mainly those fats that are hard or harden when cold; saturated fats are found in dairy and animal produce, such as whole milk, butter, cream, cheese, eggs, lard and meat and some vegetable oils, including coconut and palm, and those that have been hydrogenated. These fats are thought of as the 'Baddies' from which you should steer clear. They tend to raise your blood cholesterol levels and to make matters worse they often contain large amounts of dietary cholesterol as well.

UNSATURATED FATS: These fats are thought of more as the 'Goodies'. They can be divided into two categories: polyunsaturated fats in seafood, vegetables and in such oils as soya bean, safflower and sunflower; and monounsaturated fats, especially from olive oil, peanut oil and avocados. These are thought of as 'Exceptional Goodies' in the fat family.

We have to mention Omega-3 fatty acids which are 'Favourite Fats' found in fish, seafood and certain vegetables. Fish such as herring, mackerel, trout and salmon are excellent sources of these fats.

You need a certain supply of essential fatty acids in your food every day, which should come from your natural food supplies. There is no need to add refined fats to your menu at all. Your body must have supplies of linoleic and linolenic acid which are two essential fatty acids found in green leafy vegetables, seeds, nuts, sprouts and wholegrains. These cannot be stored by your body so you have to eat them daily. If you eat enough of these, your body can manufacture all the other fats you need. Be warned: benefits from essential fatty acids are often cancelled out in the presence of saturated fats for which your body has no real need. Lie low on saturated fats!

CHOLESTEROL

Cholesterol is vital to your functioning and body chemistry. Troubles with cholesterol surface as your levels rise surplus to requirements and remain in the circulation.

Simply removing cholesterol from your diet won't spell the balance between health and disease. Cholesterol is a soft, fatty substance found in animal and human cells. It is actually manufactured by your body in large amounts, appearing as white wax-like material in your vessels. Although it is mostly water, it doesn't melt in water or blood. So it is carried about your body in special carriages called lipoproteins, consisting of fat (lipo) and protein. These carriages are referred to as high density lipoproteins (HDL) and low density lipoproteins (LDL). Although cholesterol is the same in both of these carriers, the way it is metabolized creates the difference as they transport fats through your bloodstream.

❶ LDL carry cholesterol from the liver to your cells. Excess cholesterol sticks to your arteries. Plaque gradually builds-up, narrowing the artery and hampering the flow of blood. LDL are kept to a minimum if you wipe saturated fats from your plan, increasing the amount of unrefined carbohydrate in your diet.

❷ HDL scavenge through your tissues, carting away surplus cholesterol back to your liver where it is used or disposed of. The best way to help raise levels of HDL is through exercise, losing weight and quitting smoking.

Your blood cholesterol levels rise as you eat foods high in dietary cholesterol, particularly those high in saturated fats. They cause your liver to go overboard, producing additional cholesterol to add fuel to your fire. Fruit, oats, barley, vegetables and sweet potatoes often help decrease your levels because of the soluble fibre they contain.

PROTEIN POINTERS

Between only 10% and 15% of your daily calorie intake should be obtained from proteins. If they are not chewed and digested properly they putrefy, in the presence of bacteria, in your large intestines.

Every cell requires protein to enhance numerous body functions. You need to include a variety of quality proteins from grains, fruits and beans to form the nine essential amino acids, out of a total of twenty-three, which your body doesn't manufacture independently. Beware, animal protein has a high fat content! A steak is about 70% fat and 30% protein.

CARBOHYDRATES

Unrefined, complex carbohydrates are your best sources of energy and should make up to 75% of your total food intake.

They offer your body excellent steady supplies of energy, nutrients, essential fatty acids, protein and fibre. The less refined the carbohydrate the more steadily glucose is released into your blood, keeping your blood sugar levels stable.

FRUIT AND VEGETABLES

A wide selection of nutrients are provided as you munch away on fresh fruit and vegetables.

Fruit, which contains its own digestive enzymes, digests in your stomach in about half an hour. So that it doesn't ferment with other food in your stomach, try and eat it fresh and by itself. Both fruit and vegetables provide high fibre, cleanse tissues, help removal of toxic residue and provide a natural source of fluid, vitamins and minerals. Try to be creative, finding ways to prepare fruit and vegetables that won't remove their natural fluid or nutrient content.

SPROUTS

What better way to keep your kitchen alive than by taking pride in your own little patch of sprouts?

You can sprout seeds, nuts, grains and beans. In sprouted form they prove to be the most nutritious form of food you can obtain. Not only are they delicious, but will provide an excellent source of protein and natural water content, to aid your digestion and nourish your tissues.

FAITHFUL FIBRE

All the fibre you need can be obtained from a variety of natural unprocessed foods.

Fibre is any part of food that cannot be broken down into smaller enzymes, or molecules, in your digestive tract. Insoluble fibre is found in all wholegrains, some fruit, beans and vegetables. Soluble fibre is found in carrots, yams, fruits, oat brans and other such produce. You need a healthy balance of both types of fibre. Insoluble fibre helps the movement of food through your colon and is considered important for the prevention of cancer of the bowel. Soluble fibre helps to lower your LDL, stabilizing your blood sugar levels and insulin swings and helps to prevent the development of gallstones.

SALT

As salt creeps into your diet balance is usually thrown out. High blood pressure is triggered, the sodium/potassium pump of your cells is upset and as fluid is drawn to your cells fluid retention often sets in.

Just as salty foods make you want to drink, in the same way they make your cells thirsty. Over three-quarters of the salt in your food is added by manufacturers. If your body required this amount nature would provide. Many diseases involving inflammation, skin and kidney disorders and hypertension might be prevented if food was not laced with salt.

SUGAR REFINING

Although small amounts of refined sugar won't damage your health, ongoing indulgences definitely stockpile, poisoning your tissues.

When glucose is released into your bloodstream too quickly your sugar levels become too high. As your body steps into action to remove the excess it usually takes away too much, swinging your blood sugar levels down too low, resulting in hypo-glycaemia. Give thought to the hidden sugar content in many foods. 'Go low on sugar', obtaining it from natural sources. Leave highly processed sugars on the shelf where they belong.

THE BUTTER BATTLE

False implications from advertising confuse many about whether to use butter or margarine.

The only bonus in favour of margarine is that it takes less time to spread on your bread if your butter has gone cold on you. The final crunch may be felt in your arteries, as neither product does you any great favours. When supplies of butter became short in the war years, margarine was artificially designed to take its place. Although it is formulated from polyun-saturated oils, don't let the term 'polyunsaturated' fool you. From a liquid state, oils are hydrogenated – heated and bubbled – until they turn solid. In the process margarine becomes a totally saturated fat, which means your body is unable to utilize essential fatty acid supplies. Because of this artificial pro-cessing, margarine floats about in your tissues like bubble gum, interfering with your digestion. If you have to choose one or the other my guess is that butter is best! But why not create healthier alternatives to spread on your bread, like nut or avocado butter?

TEA AND COFFEE

Are you among the masses who rely on cups of tea and coffee, not only when your energy is flagging, but as a social coat-hanger?

Although caffeine may temporarily influence your blood sugar levels, offering a brief boost in energy, it actually stimulates the reverse reaction. Caffeine also causes twice the amount of calcium to be leached from your body, depleting your supplies. The average cup of coffee contains about four times more caffeine than the average cup of tea.

UNREFINED COMBINATIONS

The way you combine your food can make a huge difference to your digestive capacities.

Your body uses acids to help digest proteins and alkalis to help digest starches. Undigested proteins putrefy. If starches are not completely digested they ferment, creating conditions for stomach acidity, gas, heartburn and chronic digestion problems. Because everything causes a reaction in your stomach, mixing protein with starches in the same meal is not con-sidered the best way to encourage thorough digestion. The rules are simple: if you want to refine your digestion eat mainly unrefined foods!

❶ Helpings of proteins and starch should be the side portion of each meal, never the mainstay.

❷ Allow about four to five hours between meals.

❸ Salads, fruit and vegetables will form the major part of your menus. Take care when you prepare them to retain as much of their natural fluid, vitamin and mineral content as possible.

❹ All fruit should be eaten by itself, or in a com-bination fruit salad, leaving at least fifteen minutes between courses.

❺ When you consider your meals, think in terms of four pointers of alkaline foods to one pointer of acid food.

Alkaline Food Sources
80% of your food intake
Sample guide: mainly unrefined carbohydrates
Potatoes, carrots, beetroot, spinach, dandelion coffee, tomatoes, root vegetables, celery, cucumber, onions, melons, pineapples, bananas, currants.

Acid Food Sources
20% of your food intake
Sample guide: mainly protein
Meat, eggs, poultry, lentils, peas, milk, ice cream, prunes, fried foods, tea, asparagus, dried beans, walnuts, honey, hazelnuts, rhubarb.

A QUICK REFERENCE

● Vegetables, salads and fleshy fruits are mainly alka-line in base.

● Meat, fish, eggs, cheese and grains are pre-dominantly acid in base.

● Milk and yoghurt combine well with most foods except meat.

● Raisins, nuts, seeds, unrefined unsaturated fats, salads and vegetables combine with all meals.

ARRANGING YOUR MENUS

You may want to adopt the following combining pattern. It is a simple guideline towards better digestion but not one you have to cling to religiously!

Arrange meals as usual but never combine your main starch or protein in the same meal. They are both eaten once a day but not together. You may choose to have rice and vegetables for lunch which provides your starch component. For dinner you may choose chicken and salad to fulfil your requirements for protein. The beauty of this planning is that you can make the most of your digestive juices to prevent them from cancelling each other out. Acids and alkalis tend to neutralize each other making the complete digestion of your food an almost impossible task.

Fruit is the best breakfast food and can be well combined with yoghurt. Your liver is still working at its peak until midday and fruit provides an excellent liver stimulant and detoxifier. For top digestion combine acid fruit, such as apples, apricots, prunes and cherries, with proteins. A starch meal, with an unrefined pasta base for example, is best followed by sugars. These include figs, bananas, dates and honey.

When you master the basics of your transformation guidelines, food will become a creative pursuit again. This is a 'whole' new beginning based on 'whole' new foods for a 'whole' new you. Forget any thoughts of deprivation. You are planning to achieve an optimum state of health with the least fuss and bother. Food can be delicious and nutritious with minimum time spent in preparation. Once you stop over-processing and refining your food, you'll have more time to relax and savour the flavour.

Table Manners

Many chronic illnesses have their roots not in what we eat, but rather in how we eat. Cancer of the colon, stomach ulcers and irritable bowel syndrome are a few of the complaints that will gradually worsen with digestive stress. If you swallow 'dis-ease' with your food your body has to digest the strain. Relax and take your meal slowly.

THE GOLDEN RULES

● **ONLY EAT WHEN YOU ARE COMPLETELY RELAXED:**
If stressed you lock and inhibit your nerve reflexes. Combined with release of adrenaline, this makes complete digestion of your food impossible. Anything that makes you feel even slightly uncomfortable while you eat will create these reactions. Blood is diverted to your brain, heart, lungs and muscles away from your digestive organs. Nourishment is impossible under these conditions.

● **CHEW FOOD INTO A PASTE BEFORE SWALLOWING:**
This gives your digestive acids a helping hand to ensure they have plenty of surface area to efface your food and break it down further.

● **DON'T DRINK FLUIDS WHILE YOU EAT:**
You need an abundant supply of stomach acids in your stomach to break down and digest food.

● **PACE YOUR MEALS:**
It takes about twenty minutes for the 'feeding centre' in your brain to register that nutrients have been well supplied. This is the approximate time you should aim to spread your main course.

● **TUNING YOUR FEEDING CENTRE:**
Even though you think of your stomach as needing to be satisfied by a meal, the real control centre is deep in your brain. Two small pairs of nerve centres control your eating behaviour. Your feeding centre signals the message urging you to eat. This is dampened by your satisfaction centre when the urge has been fulfilled. If your cells begin to sense that nutrient supplies are running low, your brain centres swing onto 'all alert'.

The Food File

THOUGHTFUL CHOICES

Within a healthy lifestyle there are many 'right ways' to eat! Your food file will serve as a reminder and reference for main considerations you need to bear in mind to create optimum conditions for your health. Different claims are put forward by different nutritionists. One group says 'raw, raw, raw', yet on the other hand, macrobiotics, which claims many great and healthy influences, says 'nothing raw at all'.

If you decide you need to devise a plan to improve the quality of the food you consume, aim to find food patterns that are just right for you. This will evolve as you become more in touch with what you really need. Thoughtful menu planning should enable an adequate supply of nutrients over a weekly spread of food. However, this is based on the premise that your food is fresh and prepared with minimum processing and leaching of nutrients.

● Set the meal patterns that suit your needs and lifestyle. You may choose five smaller meals or three fuller meals daily.

● Think carefully about the way you prepare your food. Raw, casseroled, steamed, stir-fried, grilled and baked vegetables all preserve essential nutrients.

● Even a little organic produce is better than none.

● Consider your cookware and the toxic residue it may leach into your food. Glassware is excellent, stainless steel is preferable to aluminium, which is absolutely out. Use non-stick pans so you never have to fry in fat.

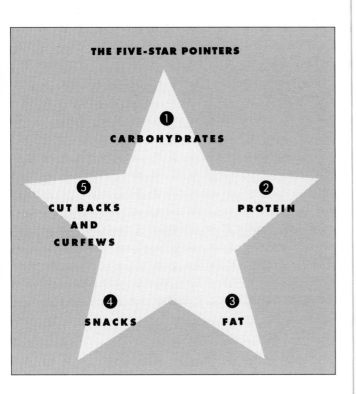

THE FIVE-STAR POINTERS

❶ CARBOHYDRATES

❺ CUT BACKS AND CURFEWS

❷ PROTEIN

❹ SNACKS

❸ FAT

❶ CARBOHYDRATES

Plan to eat about 75% of your food from unrefined carbohydrate sources. Avoid refined carbohydrates which are devoid of fibre while often loaded with salt, sugar and fats.

GOOD FOOD SOURCES

Vegetables ● Fruit ● Wholegrains: rice, millet, rye etc ● Whole cereals: oats, wheat, bran etc ● Beans, legumes ● Peas

❷ PROTEIN

Over the course of your day, protein should make up between 10% and 15% of your food plan. Restrict the intake of red meat to twice weekly at a maximum. Rotate your proteins throughout the week.

GOOD FOOD SOURCES

Beans ● Wholegrains ● Vegetables ● Yoghurts ● Non-fat dairy products ● Beans ● Nuts ● Sprouts ● Lean meat ● Chicken ● Eggs

❸ FAT

You need no more than 10% to 15% of your total daily food intake to come from unsaturated fat supplies. Nearly 70% of your fat supply should come from vegetables, fruit and grains in your menu. Around 25% should come from fish, poultry and lean meat. Less than 10% should be obtained from animal fats.

GOOD FOOD SOURCES

Fish ● Seafood ● Green leafy vegetables ● Olive oil ● Peanut oil ● Polyunsaturated, unrefined oils: corn, safflower, sunflower, soya bean ● Nuts ● Sprouts

❹ SNACKS

Snacks in between meals should be natural.

GOOD FOOD SOURCES

Vegetables, carrots, celery, pepper ● Yoghurt dips with nut butter flavourings ● Fruit ● Freshly pressed vegetable and fruit juices ● Nuts ● Seeds

❺ CUT BACKS AND CURFEWS

Saturated fats, such as full-fat milk, yoghurts, butter, cheese and ice cream, need to be brought right down. Hydrogenated fats, such as those found in refined manufactured products, cakes, biscuits and pastries, need to be kept to the bare minimum. Eventually wipe these products from the slate.

BAD FOOD SOURCES

All refined white flour products ● White bread ● Crisps ● Manufactured snack foods ● Tinned foods containing preservatives, colourings and additives ● Alcohol ● Artificial sweeteners ● Refined breakfast cereals ● Soft drinks ● Fried foods ● Sugar products ● Confectionary ● Processed man-made meat products

THE FIVE POINTER CHECK
Use this simple check to ensure you plan meals to keep your system in an alkaline balance.

VEGETABLES AND RAW FRUIT

VEGETABLES AND RAW FRUIT

VEGETABLES AND RAW FRUIT

WHOLEGRAINS
(Whole pasta, brown rice etc)

PROTEIN   NATURAL SUGARS
UNSATURATED FATS

The Fluid File

SUSTAINING LIQUIDS

● Work towards replacing tea and coffee, all but for one cup a day.

● Fresh fruit and vegetable juices make excellent drinks throughout the day, as well as nutritious snack-fillers.

● Natural distilled water is your best source of liquid. Drink up to eight glasses a day. If you eat mainly raw vegetables, with their natural water content intact, simply drink when you are thirsty.

● You can concoct delicious fruit cocktails on ice!

● Herb tea, dandelion coffee and a wide variety of malted barley and chicory-based coffee substitutes are better than the real thing.

● Warmed fruit punch, spiced up with cloves and cinnamon, is wonderful in the middle of winter.

THE LEMON ZINGER

This is an excellent recipe for balancing the acid–alkaline levels in your tissues.

The juice of a fresh lemon

2 dessertspoons of pure maple syrup
or 1 teaspoon of pure honey

$\frac{1}{4}$ teaspoon of cayenne pepper
(for cleansing)

16 fluid ounces of warm or cool water

Blend the ingredients together in a tumbler.

Bouncing Benefits

● Plan to bounce between or before meals. An hour of relatively relaxed activity should always follow a meal. Your abdominal and pelvic muscles are known as your 'pelvic shunt'. A large percentage of blood to these regions is cut off when you exercise so your main working muscles can obtain the oxygen and nutrients they need for work. Apart from the diminished blood supply, your intestinal wall relaxes along with your gastrointestinal sphincters which close down your digestive processes. Never exercise on a full stomach.

● Bouncing helps to stimulate waves of peristaltic contraction in your gut, which enhances digestive processes, as well as the necessary stimulation of blood and lymph throughout your intestines.

● Your stomach, which is just below and to the left of your breastbone, is an amazing centre of activity. It ranges in size from about a pint when empty, to hold about ten pints of food when full. Among the helpers in your stomach to digest your food, you have some strong corrosive chemicals, including hydrochloric acid, which have the power to eat away at strong fibres like those found in meat. These substances are so strong that if they touch your skin they can burn holes in your flesh, creating ulcers. Jelly-like mucus protects the lining of your stomach from these acids. If these linings become inflamed you will be susceptible to ulcers. While you bounce you help to reduce inflammation of these linings which are also aggravated through stress and nervous tension.

● As you bounce regularly your body chemistry will change, helping all systems related to digestion, absorption and elimination function more efficiently.

● As body chemistry improves you will have a measurable increase in energy.

● Bounce your way through cravings until your body no longer requires, and eventually rejects, foods it previously thrived on.

WORDS OF WISDOM

Are you eating because you are hungry?
Are you hungry when you eat?
If in doubt, bounce for a few minutes and assess the hunger pangs. Are they real or is your brain playing tricks on you? Think before you eat by putting your craving to the test.

WEIGHTY ISSUES

SHEDDING THE POUNDS

The amount of energy most people take into their body is far greater than they need compared to the amount of physical exercise they are getting. If you are carrying extra weight, your concerns should wisely centre around the possible development of high blood pressure, the metabolism of your blood sugar levels and the possibility of chronic heart disease or strokes striking you down. Obesity is known to accelerate the development of osteoarthritis in your weight-bearing joints, eventually restricting your mobility. Diabetes, hypertension and a trail of complaints may well lie dormant in your fatty cells.

Many ingredients combine to produce the slope down which a sluggish metabolism will slide, hand in hand with stagnating circulation. Intercellular wastes can stockpile to such an extent that even if your menu is not deficient in nutrients, their chances of reaching your cells might be as slim as your dream of losing weight.

Dieting is probably the most common pursuit of women in the Western world. Problems arise as fad dieting is followed by periods of relapse into the problems that set off the weight gain in the first place. A series of diets, followed by relapse, invites a slower loss of weight the next time around. In fact, to make matters worse, you are more likely to put weight on more quickly again with each successive cycle.

Overall, 70% of people express disappointment and discomfort surrounding their present weight and body shape. Whatever your size and shape, you have got to learn to love and appreciate your basic structure before you can make really positive developments, bouncing your body back into balance, lumps, bumps and all.

ADAM AND EVE

Men are designed to carry the heavy loads through life in short sharp bursts, and are endowed with more muscle tissue than women. Women, not to be outdone, can boast they have 50% more fat cells than their male counterparts, with the bulk of additional cells primed to hang about their thighs and buttocks. It is just the way God made us!

During pregnancy these 'milkmaid thighs' become accentuated to provide mothers with a feeding reservoir for their newborn baby. The additional fat supplies provide the energy requirements for lactation. But men have their magic belts for fat as well. They wear them around their middles which are ripe for fat cells geared for releasing and storing triglycerides.

Compared to other cells in your body, fat cells have a reputation for being notoriously slothful. They provide the perfect warehouses for thousands of toxic substances which float about in sluggish circulation seeking accommodation.

Bouncing will help to change the pattern of your energy output. While you bounce away those extra supplies of fat, you need to reset your foodlines to suit your needs and become more conscious of what you are eating. Different people use energy at different rates so there is no point in following the system of 'counting calories'. The fitter you become the more energy you will use up over the same period of time.

SWITCHING FIBRES

You have two types of muscle fibres. Slow-twitch fibres, usually red in colour, are used for sustained aerobic activity that requires endurance. For a source of fuel your slow-twitch fibres use glycogen from carbohydrates at first, but then quickly switch to supplies of free fatty acids stored in your fat cells or from your bloodstream. Warning! Your slow-twitch fibres degenerate if they are not used, losing their ability to call upon fat as a fuel, slowing your metabolic rate down even further.

Fast-twitch fibres, usually white in colour, are used when your muscles require immediate and swift reaction. The fuel for these fibres comes mainly from carbohydrates in your diet which are broken down into glycogen and stored in your muscles and liver.

If you are prone to lazing about and are already overweight, you are likely to gain fat while eating just moderate supplies of food. Because your slow-twitch fibres are wasting away, your chances of burning fat as a supply of energy are more limited.

Plan your Starbound workout to gently retrain your muscles, to develop slow-twitch fibres and get your metabolic engines revving again. The conditions your body needs to readily use your fat supplies as your main source of energy will be recreated. You have to be prepared to set aside at least thirty minutes a day, three times a week, to get the wheels turning.

RESOLUTION PLAN

Bouncing Back to Square One
~

BOUNCING BACK TO SQUARE ONE MEANS
BOUNCING YOUR WEIGHT BACK TO WHERE IT
SHOULD BE. YOU SHOULD NEVER HAVE TO SPEAK
OR THINK OF DIETS EVER AGAIN!
● THE PROGRAMME FOLLOWS A NATURAL
PROGRESSION FROM THE CLEANSING OF DETOX.
DIMENSIONS (P. 111). REFER TO FOOD
REPLACEMENT IN THE FOOD FILE (P. 116) TO
PROVIDE THE FOUNDATION FOR YOUR FOOD AND
FLUID PLANS.
● THERE IS NO POINT TRYING TO BUST YOUR
BOILER OR STRAIN YOUR BODY BACK INTO SHAPE.
TAKE TIME TO CREATE A PLAN WHICH IS GENTLE
TO YOUR BODY AND EASY ON YOUR MIND.
● BECAUSE BOUNCING BACK TO SQUARE ONE
PROVIDES A TRANSITION PERIOD TO ACTIVATE
YOUR BODY'S FURNACES TO METABOLIZE YOUR
FOOD, PLEASE PUT COMPLETE DIGESTION AT THE
TOP OF YOUR LIST! REMEMBER YOUR METABOLIC
RATE IS THE SPEED AT WHICH YOU BURN ENERGY
IN THE PRESENCE OF NUTRIENTS AND OXYGEN,
WHICH COMBINE TO STOKE YOUR BODY'S FIRES.
● YOU NEED TO CONSIDER A TWO-FOLD
APPROACH TO FACILITATE WEIGHT LOSS
❶ BOUNCE-BURNERS
❷ RESETTING YOUR FOODLINES

BOUNCE-BURNERS

Throughout your resolution plan you need to stimulate your metabolism by working in your target zones, by bouncing at least every second day for between twenty and forty minutes. In a Bounce-Burner session your heart rate must fall to between 60% and 75% of your maximum. Fat is a major fuel for energy required to maintain steady aerobic bouncing within your target zones (p. 48).

● Include at least four conditioning periods a week at the end of your bouncing session.

● Bounce thirty minutes before your main meal for a few minutes to stimulate your digestive system.

● Never bounce until at least an hour after your meal or your energy becomes divided in purpose.

RESETTING YOUR FOODLINES

You need to bounce away surplus supplies of fat while gently resetting your foodlines. Your body has to become comfortable with the idea that it is carrying less fat and it is likely it will feel cheated for a while.

● Gradually reduce the amount you eat to reset your balance.

● Spend longer chewing your food.

● At a regular interval, perhaps once a week or fortnight, follow the Day-in-Cleanse (p. 112). This will help drop your weight that little bit more while encouraging your body to adapt to the new weight.

● Vitamins B1, B2, B3 and B6 are essential to adequate metabolism. They are water soluble, so include daily allowances into your food plan. Wholegrains, beans, yeast, milk, green leafy vegetables, eggs, bananas, oranges and cheese are good sources.

● Pure, distilled water is one of the best aids for releasing fat. Add lemon juice for flavour and to reduce the acid in your tissues. Any fluids suggested in your Fluid File (p. 118) can be used for variety and will help speed weight loss. Drink as often as you need to quench your thirst with at least one glass between each meal.

CONTROLLING CRAVINGS

The essence of success lies in your positive ability to reclaim control, not just over what you are eating, but regarding the quality of your energy and how you utilize it. From this point on, direct your tastes so they serve you rather than you catering to them. Learn to distinguish between real and learned hunger. Your mind reaches for food if hunger is learned. Your body reaches for food if it needs nourishment. Since they are either chemically or habitually orientated, you need to assess cravings as they arise.

❶ If your bouncer is at hand, bounce. Boost your oxygen supply, clear away toxins and enjoy some light-hearted activity. The chances are by the time you are off your bouncer and have enjoyed a refreshing glass of water, cravings will have vanished.

❷ If your bouncer is not at hand, try some breathing techniques (p. 135).

❸ Activate your Lymphatic Reflex Zones for your pancreas, liver and kidneys (p. 33).

❹ If you need a snack, choose wisely. Don't eat on the run, sit down, prepare your food and enjoy.

❺ Munch an apple to activate your liver to withdraw the toxins as well as the cravings.

❻ Enjoy a refreshing drink of herb tea, freshly squeezed juice or a liquid of your choice.

BENEFITS AS YOU BOUNCE

● *Nutrients are distributed more efficiently which will help cravings disappear and will also balance your appetite.*

● *Increased oxygen supplies from your lungs to your tissues kindle the metabolic fires to burn your fat stores.*

● *Fatty tissue is replaced by welcome supplies of lean muscle tissue, which is far more active metabolically.*

● *Dieting without exercise slows your metabolic rate down, whereas your bouncing programmes will speed it up.*

● *If you are sluggish the feeding centre in your brain senses the need for nutrients and oxygen. When you reach for the wrong foods they rob your cells of oxygen in the process of digestion. Your blood sugar levels may swing, throwing your metabolism further out of kilter. Instead of reaching for food BOUNCE!*

● *Because you are overweight your Starbound programmes offer a superb foundation for exercise, which is safe for your skeletal structure while cushioning impact on your weight-bearing joints.*

SHOPPING LISTS

Prepare yourself to overcome temptations when you shop. Decide on an initial food plan for shopping. Throughout transition aim for less quantity and better quality foods – preferably organic. Choose a sensible shopping venue, identify problem foods and leave them on the shelf. Shopping on an empty stomach can be disastrous. Children or friends may try to sway you so prepare your reactions in advance.

CRASH CAUTIONS

Your body can't store fitness nearly as well as it can fat! If you stop bouncing for prolonged periods you're likely to lose your fitness and gain fat back. Crash bouncing won't do you many more favours than crash dieting. Build your programmes gradually so they become part of your daily routine to preserve and enhance your health. Initially you may lose fat and gain muscle which may weigh more. Allow a full three months to ring the changes. This is not a race against time. As you gain more muscle tissue, your metabolism will speed up accordingly. Beware dieting without the appropriate exercise regime. You may

lose muscle tissue as well as fatty tissue. Any regain in weight will be as fat and not as muscle. This will slow your metabolism even further.

Your tummy muscles corset your internal organs, including your stomach, bowel and womb so, quite apart from the fact that a firm tummy flatters your figure, it needs to be strong and toned to hold these organs in place. Practise Abdominal Doming, Diaphragm Doming and Granny's Corset (p. 137). To flatten and tone your abdomen, cleanse your digestive and eliminative organs and help contract your stomach so you feel less inclined to gorge on food.

EMOTIONAL TRIP-UPS

If you eat as a comforter for depression, bouncing will overcome the blues for you. If you are bored, head for your bouncer and choreograph some new routines. If you are angry bounce the aggressions away. If you are anxious take yourself into Innerspaces (p. 132) and arrive at a state of calm. Consider what factors have caused you to gain your excess weight. Then you'll eliminate the causes, not just the symptoms, of your weight problems.

Eternal Cellulite?

How many times have you stood on your bathroom scales, satisfied with your weight, but unhappy with what you see? The structure of your tissues is completely unique. You may have a loose cellular structure and find that a small amount of fluid will make you balloon. With a tight cellular structure, although less water is pulled from your bloodstream, you may still suffer the consequences. Size has nothing to do with the state of the fluid in your body.

With roots in poor circulation, cellulite develops over a series of phases. Soft heaps of wastes and toxins slowly become imprisoned in your tissues, setting in to crystallize, creating circulation blockages.

Constipation is a common complaint for people with cellulite. If wastes are not being removed from your system efficiently they have no choice but to hang about within. Poor lymphatic drainage will also lead to the build up of wastes and toxins in your intercellular fluid, inviting cellulite to spread.

WATER YOUR TISSUES

When you bounce not only are you shunting lymph forward but you are raising the amount of fluid in your tissues which becomes lymph obligatory. For this reason you must never overexert when exercising.

If your lymphatics can't pick up the quantity of fluid rising in your tissues to maintain the balance, it will show up as oedema.

Quite the opposite to waterlogging your tissues you need to water them daily to cleanse your internal waterways and flush wastes and toxins from your system.

If your body is deprived of the water it requires it will intuitively hold on to current supplies. When you increase your intake of fluid your body will let go of the water it is retaining and reset the natural balance. Drink water fifteen minutes before you bounce and immediately after your sessions to help flush your system.

RESOLUTION PLAN

The Cellulite Stripper

~

COMBINING REGULAR BOUNCING WITH OTHER SENSIBLE ROUTINES IS BY FAR THE BEST WAY TO ACTIVATE YOUR BODY FLUIDS. AS WELL AS SETTING THE SCENE FOR THE SWIFT DISPOSAL OF WASTES, YOU STRENGTHEN THE WALLS OF YOUR CAPILLARY VESSELS, BALANCING THE AMOUNT OF PLASMA THAT SEEPS THROUGH INTO THE SPACES BETWEEN YOUR CELLS.

IF YOU ARE SERIOUS ABOUT REMOVING THE LUMPS YOU HAVE TO PLAN TO PAVE THE WAY FOR A NEW FOUNDATION FROM WHICH YOUR BODY WILL FLOURISH. CELLULITE APPEARS GRADUALLY OVER A PERIOD OF TIME, PRIMARILY DUE TO A LACK OF OXYGEN AT A CELLULAR LEVEL, POOR CIRCULATION AND BAD FOOD HABITS.

DESIGN YOUR PLAN TO STRIP CELLULITE IN THREE PHASES OVER A PERIOD OF ABOUT A YEAR. CHANGES OCCUR SLOWLY BUT SURELY. YOU NEED TO INCORPORATE THE FOLLOWING CONSIDERATIONS INTO YOUR LIFESTYLE:

❶ DETOXIFICATION TO 'CLEANSE' AND A FIVE-STAR PLAN TO REPLACE FOOD HABITS (P. 110).

❷ COSMETIC BOOSTERS TO IMPROVE YOUR CIRCULATION.

❸ STARBOUND WORKOUTS. AT LEAST THREE TIMES A WEEK INCLUDE THE CELLULITE STRIPPER FOUR-PHASE ATTACK INTO THE CONDITIONING PHASE OF YOUR WORKOUT.

HELP TO DETOXIFY

● Follow Detox. Dimensions (p. 111) to get yourself started.

● Your food choices are essential. I finally stripped my cellulite by combining my bounce programmes with an 80% raw intake. Within six weeks I could see the difference. Within six months it was gone!

● Follow Triumphant Transformation resolution plans. Absolutely no foods spiced up with salt, sugar or refined products. Stay with whole foods, choosing wholegrains and meals high in fibre.

● Under all conditions remember 'FRESH IS BEST'.

● Stroke reflex zones for your liver and thyroid. An underactive thyroid and cellulite often go together.

● Limit yourself to one cup of tea and coffee a day.

COSMETIC CIRCULATION BOOSTERS

● Use only natural products on your face and body so that chemicals, additives and preservatives do not linger in your tissues.

● Use essential oils every day (p. 133). Oregano, thyme, lemon, grapefruit, celery, cinnamon leaf, black pepper and cypress are great for cellulite. Massage your body daily with a pure vegetable base and essential oil. For severe cellulite apply one compress a day to the area. Add six drops of one or a combination of the above to half a pint of warm water dipped in a towel or lint. Place the concoction on your skin, with another towel over the damp compress to keep it as warm as possible. Leave the compress on for about ten minutes.

● Give your skin a brush. Use either a hand glove or a long-handled bristle brush on your body when it is dry. Start from the area around your shoulders and collarbone, to clear any build up of congested lymph, before brushing your entire body in long even strokes. Brush from your fingertips, up your arms, then brush your back and abdomen. Whisk the brush around your buttocks clockwise and anticlockwise. Although the back of your neck and throat will thrive on a gentle downward sweep, never brush your face.

● Following the brush up, bounce gently to make the most of your activated skin tissue as a source for elimination.

● When you're ready for your shower, make use of the time to massage your body with your favourite oil, pinching your skin with your fingertips in short sharp movements.

● When you shower, begin with warm water to loosen your tissues, cooling it down toward the end to pep up your circulation.

STARBOUND WORKOUTS

The Cellulite Stripper four-phase attack is a conditioning and cleansing sequence. It is designed to help soften crystallized tissue, invite oxygen in, free fluids and finally flush them from your system.

When you have become familiar with the programme combine other conditioning and stretch routines into Phases Three and Four.

Always warm up thoroughly beforehand.

Phase One: Gently bounce for 30 seconds in the Rhythm Bounce. Set your breathing pattern. For example, inhale, inhale, exhale, exhale, exhale.

Phase Two: Intensify your bouncing for 60 seconds in the Lift Off.

Phase Three: Repeat two different conditioning techniques, gradually increasing the repeats.

Phase Four: Choose a stretch technique, to release the muscles you have just conditioned.

ROUND ONE

PHASE ONE	**PHASE TWO**	**PHASE THREE**	**PHASE FOUR**
Rhythm Bounce	Lift Off	Helping Hands. 2 sets × 8 Machine Guns. 2 sets × 8	Lazy Lizzies Hold for 30 seconds

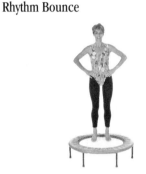

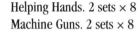

ROUND TWO

PHASE ONE	**PHASE TWO**	**PHASE THREE**	**PHASE FOUR**
Rhythm Bounce	Lift Off	Sitting Shuffle. 2 sets × 8 Loggerheads. 2 sets × 8 each side	Jingles Hold for 30 seconds

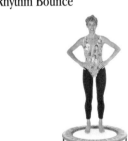
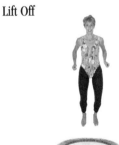

ROUND THREE

PHASE ONE	**PHASE TWO**	**PHASE THREE**	**PHASE FOUR**
Rhythm Bounce	Lift Off	Beach Belle. 2 sets × 8 Sausage Rolls. 2 sets × 8	Tailormade Hold for 30 seconds.

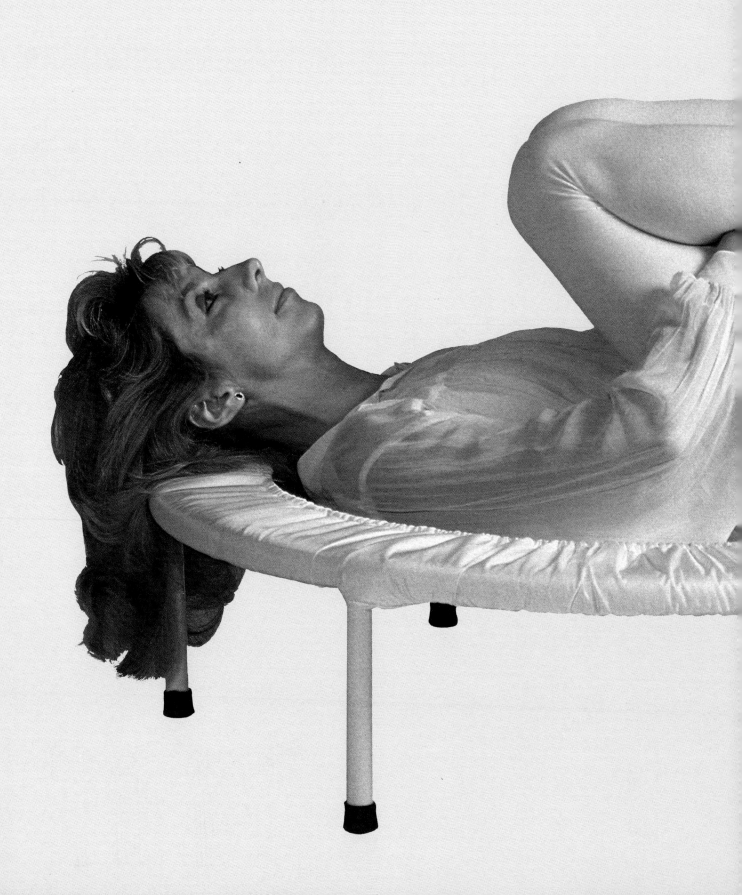

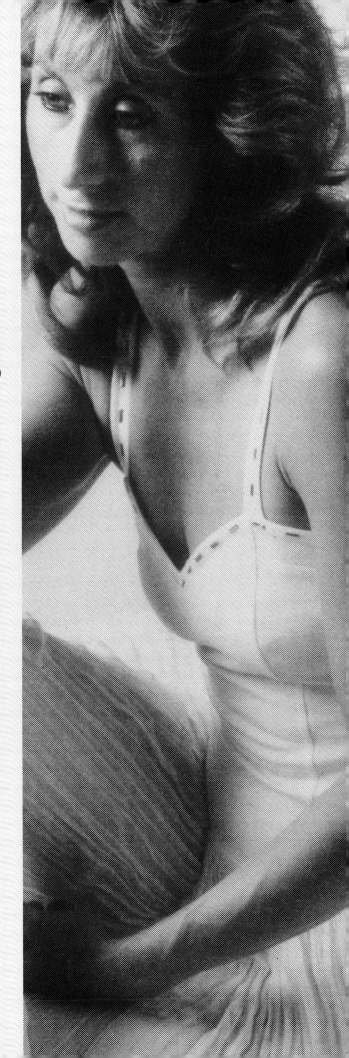

1

ALARM BELLS! STRESS!

THE STRESS TRAP

Sifting through statistics, you'll find one in four people suffer from chronic stress. Their days roll by through a filter of fatigue, aggression, worry or anxiety. Combined with a lack of activity and poor food habits, reactions to stress are responsible for the onset of many chronic illnesses.

Destructive stress covers a multitude of sins, including everything in your environment that you either inwardly or outwardly shrug your shoulders at. Even the smallest feelings of discomfort and aggravation will prime your body to react to stress.

When primitive man lived close to nature, response to stress offered a life-saving device, enabling spontaneous reactions in dangerous situations. Although cavemen had the same instinctive impulses as we do today, they could either fight in defence, or prepare to flee, depending on the size of the dinosaur. Modern-day society makes it virtually impossible to follow instinctive reactions to restore a natural balance following a stress impact.

FIGHT OR FLIGHT?

Whenever you react to anything stressful, your body is primed to fight or flee as part of your internal survival kit. When your brain receives a threatening signal, a series of reactions occur in your body:

- Heart and circulation speed up, with a rise in your blood pressure.
- Blood is sent to your working muscles to prepare for action.
- Fats and glucose pour into your bloodstream to provide energy.
- Glands are stimulated into immediate overload to release various hormones.
- Brain waves change rapidly, stimulating your nervous system.
- Digestion is completely interrupted, as blood is diverted away from digestive and eliminative organs.

- Emotional response becomes vulnerable.
- Thinking capacity may switch between 'all alert' to 'blocked and blurred', depending on the stress.

These are among the reactions stimulated so you can fight to defend yourself or speed off into the sunset! However, let's remember a certain amount of stress is essential to inject your energy levels.

EXHAUSTION PLAYS HAVOC

Dr Hans Seyle, at the University of Montreal in the 1920s, described the three stages of ongoing stress as the alarm reaction, resistance stage and exhaustion. If you reach the point of exhaustion a condition known as hypoadrenia sets in. As tranquillizers are dished out, your condition takes a downward slide.

Exhaustion is not an unusual complaint, nor are the symptoms that plague our lives because of it. If stress takes a grip, negative habits often step in. Mood swings, aggression, failed friendships, frustration, gloom, defeat, despair and depression knock on the door. Marriages are doomed to failure. Family relationships suffer needlessly. Communication breaks down. Instead of taking positive steps to redress the balance, the opposite often happens. Common patterns of insomnia, excessive nervous energy and drained nervous responses, catapult lives into confusion.

We have to be able to maintain our balance, when pressure surfaces from many directions. Have you noticed that you are most prone to falling ill, or prey to a virus, when emotionally or mentally drained of energy? Flagging spirits, negative thoughts and emotional upsets all serve to weaken your resilience.

WIPING STRESS OUT

Within fifteen minutes of adrenaline hitting your bloodstream the smallest dose challenges your immune system to release lymphocytes. Adrenaline inhibits the ability of your white blood cells to fight off antigens. Corticosteroids also suppress your immune

RELAX YOUR BODY, SMOOTH YOUR MIND

- Gravity not only threatens to compress your body, but influences all aspects of your being.
- The negative aspect of gravity physically compresses, emotionally suppresses, mentally

depresses and spiritually oppresses.
- You overcome these forces by disengaging with gravity for a split second every time you bounce.

response, leaving another door open for invasion. If stress is heavy over a prolonged period, an overdose of corticosteroids can cause the withering away of your lymphoid tissue altogether. Positive responses and attitudes offer the best foundation for a healthy immune system. Your bouncer offers the perfect focus for establishing such attitudes and developing techniques to counteract stress.

TELL TALE SIGNS

If you are bored, you owe it to yourself to seek challenges. If you are heading for exhaustion through excessive stress, you have to learn to discern the signs and retreat for a quieter pace. You can harness the energizing power of stress to become its master, or fall into the trap to become its slave.

Many people use their bouncing programmes purely for relaxation and to release stress and tensions as they arise. The moment you sense tension in your muscles, or tight fixed mental patterns settling in as you work or worry, jump on your bouncer and set yourself free. A few minutes will bring blood to your brain, and balance to your energy levels.

SOLDIERING STRESS

Wilhelm Reich was the first doctor to explain how we use our body as an armour to defend against the onslaught and effects of stress. If unexpressed emotions and blocked energy become trapped, muscles and tissues become the perfect sites to house tensions.

Many forms of therapy are now connecting the relationship between the mind and emotions with the body. Biodynamic Psychotherapy and Psychology refers to the principle of the natural and spontaneous flow of energy. Therapists are concerned with balancing the movement of fluid and energy in your body so health can blossom. The link between your tissue and the muscular armour that you build up is paramount. Locked tension in your muscles causes adrenaline and other waste products to remain in your tissues, creating a fluid distension pressure. Biodynamic therapists work from the premise that fluid carries the energy as energy revitalizes the fluid.

Therapists utilize many methods to encourage the movement of energy in the deep organs and systems in your body. They use a stethoscope to listen to the unique range of sounds they are able to identify, which lead them to the part of your body requiring attention. Psychoperistalsis is the name given to the process of dissolving tensions to free trapped energy and fluid.

The movement of energy through your bloodstream introduces an electrical charge which is tapped by rhythmical pulsating activity when you bounce. This sets up a mechanical tension which in turn creates a bioelectrical charge. According to Biodynamic theory this builds up to a point of fullness, until a discharge occurs, which in turn stimulates relaxation.

BENEFITS AS YOU BOUNCE

❶ *Under stress, adrenocorticotropic (ACTH) is released to enable your body to adapt to the stress. The production of this hormone is inhibited by a lack of exercise as well as poor nutrition.*

❷ *Gentle vibration work on your bouncer helps to free muscular holding patterns.*

❸ *Momentary changes in muscle tone and breathing, encourage the release of tension in your abdominal muscles. Tension in your jaw, chest and back dissipates within minutes of gentle bouncing.*

❹ *Over a period of time, you'll experience a decrease in your heart rate and blood pressure, and a balance in hormonal output, blood lactate and cortisol levels.*

❺ *Brainwave frequencies balance out, to induce a state of relaxation.*

❻ *By combining techniques from your Starbound programmes, you can learn to off-load your problems one at a time, rather than letting them pile up and swamp you.*

❼ *Hormonal secretions are released, which invite feelings of tranquillity, while helping to ensure a positive outlook. Wave the tranquillizers goodbye!*

SUPPLEMENTARY BULLETINS

● Vitamins A and D, and the minerals calcium, phosphorous and magnesium, stimulate your pituitary gland. This in turn issues your adrenal gland with the instruction to fight or flee, and also issues the hormone adrenaline.

● A deficiency in these nutrients implies your body won't be supplied with sufficient ACTH to activate your adrenals. Check your supplies as you plan to Space Stress Out.

RESOLUTION PLAN

Spacing Stress Out
~

YOU CAN USE YOUR BOUNCER WITH A TWO-FOLD APPROACH TO STRESS.

❶ THROUGH YOUR BOUNCE PROGRAMMES AIM TO BUILD UP YOUR RESILIENCE, LEARNING TO REACT MORE POSITIVELY TO STRESSFUL INFLUENCES.

❷ ONCE PRIMED FOR STRESS, USE YOUR BOUNCE PROGRAMMES TO RELEASE TENSIONS, ANXIETIES OR AGGRESSIONS, BOUNCING YOUR BODY BACK TO A STATE OF CALM AND REPOSE. YOU WILL BE ABLE TO INCORPORATE CERTAIN TECHNIQUES FROM SPACING STRESS OUT INTO YOUR STARBOUND WORKOUT. ALTERNATIVELY, YOU MAY CHOOSE TO USE TIME-OUT SESSIONS.

TIME-OUT

However busy your schedule, you need time each day for reflection, relaxation and problem solving. You can use the Pulse Base to ease into relaxation, or alternatively take time following your Starbound Workout. This is time to positively call your own, to reinforce your resolution plans, and practise visualizations, affirmations, prayer, meditation and other support techniques.

THE PULSE BASE

This is the perfect technique to start your Time-Out session. The magic of pulsing from your bouncer emerges with two shared rhythms becoming one. As you pulsate with your bouncer, you undo blockages, and help to recreate a flow that you probably haven't allowed yourself for some time. The rocking motion helps to release long- and short-term tensions as you tune in and flow with the movement of your tissues from within.

● From the Rhythm Bounce, with your feet completely flat to the mat, release your shoulders, loosen your knees and let your arms hang loosely to your sides. Release and relax any tension in your face and jaw, with simple release techniques (p. 139).

● Gently pulsate your body, completely releasing all tension from your shoulders and upper back, by shrugging the entire area in time with the rhythm of your bouncing.

● As you pulsate, exhale through your mouth, utilizing breathing techniques (p. 135).

● Work through your whole body from top to toe, releasing tension in your face, throat, neck, shoulder blades, upper back, chest, lower back, abdomen, knees and feet.

● As your body is pulsating, visualize the point of pulsation through your abdomen to help open your breath and expand your chest.

● When you have worked through your entire body for a minute or two, bring your awareness back to any muscles that still feel tense or locked. Gently pulse your tensions away.

128

● Try placing a sheepskin or rug over your bouncer and stretching into Time-Out, slowly winding down and calming your mind.

● Set the scene to suit your mood. You can always burn some essential oils, light a candle and enjoy soothing music.

PROBLEM SOLVING

Hardly a day goes by, when we don't have to deal with an issue which requires a clear channel of thought. Problems need to be dealt with one at a time. The following Five Steps for Problem Solving are often used by Bahá'í's around the world, whose faith encompasses all religions. Whatever your faith may be, you'll find this an extremely positive approach for solving problems; coupled with the calming influence of meditation, contemplation or prayer.

❶ Pray and meditate about your problem, before remaining in the silence of contemplation for a few minutes.

❷ During contemplation arrive at a decision and hold it. Even if it seems almost impossible to accomplish, accept it as an answer for your situation, then immediately take the next step.

❸ Muster determination to carry the decision through. Many of us fail here. The decision is blighted, and instead becomes a wish or vague longing. When determination is born, then take the next step.

❹ Have the confidence and faith that the power will flow through you, the right door will open, the right thought or message will be given to you. As you finish contemplation, take the fifth step.

❺ Act as though everything has been solved, operating with tireless, ceaseless energy.

JAWS!

Over 50% of your nervous signals flow to your brain via your jaw, which is one of the most powerful muscles in your body. Blockages of tension and emotions are often locked in this area of your face.

● Bounce in the Pulse Base.
● Clench your back teeth together, then stretch your mouth as wide as possible.
● Wiggle your jaw from side to side, with your mouth open.
● Imitate a shivering vibration from your jaw to stimulate the release of nervous tension.
● Practise some of the jaw and facial techniques from your facial programme (p. 139).

CLIFF HANGER

A perfect technique to balance the nervous system, release tension in your shoulders, chest and lungs, release gas and stimulate digestion.

❶ Limber up your shoulders, rotating in all directions as you bounce. When you feel completely loosened, place your bouncer on the rim. Turn to face the opposite direction. Reach behind to grasp a leg at either side. Keeping your back erect, begin by moving into a gentle squat. As you lower your trunk bend your arms. Keep knees aligned over your toes. Your trunk is straight as buttocks move behind your heels. Keep your feet flat on the floor. Straighten your arms as you open your chest outward, inhaling as you stand erect.

❷ Exhale as you relax and bend your knees and elbows, letting your arms take the weight. As you slowly lower your body relax your neck, tilting your head forward. Sound HAAA as you go down. Inhale as you bring your body up. Repeat the sequence × 8.

Sounding Off!

Sound physically vibrates, influencing all body cells, muscles and nervous tissue. Although you may be unaware of its subtle influence, sound continually has an immense effect on your well-being.

Because it is carried in waves, coming at you from all directions, your brain has to decipher messages from each ear independently. Apparatus in your ears contain tiny hair cells, which waver as they float in fluid, reacting like the keys and chords in a piano. Each of them relates to a certain pitch, from which signals are transmitted to your brain. Every time you make a noise, sound waves boom through your being. Muscles dampen down the vibrations in your ear bones to stop you from becoming deafened.

Children naturally use sound to recharge their batteries. The spontaneity of early childhood allows for the use of sound as an immediate form of communication and to release tensions. Natural reactions through sound are necessary to express and deal with frustrations, and to communicate needs and desires.

The release of sound stimulates the release of natural pain relievers in the form of hormonal secretions. When giving birth, for example, women naturally release these hormones as they release the very natural primal cries that surface throughout labour. The connection between your throat, mouth, voice and sexual organs is very strong.

BODY ECHOES

When molecules throughout your body are struck by sound waves close to their own frequency, they resonate. You can include techniques utilizing sounds that have a positively recharging effect throughout your Starbound workouts.

Your diaphragm acts like an amplifier from the bouncer. The combination of your voice and the vibration as you bounce, harnesses energies in your body. There is no end to the sound work you can perform exploring your voice in numerous ways. Don't save your singing for the shower!

SOUND WAVES

HAAA ▷

Squatting from the edge of your bouncer, sound HAAA. Take the pitch as low as you can. You will probably start with a throat sound, then deepen it through your abdomen, increasing the resonance of the sound as you visualize it moving lower through your body. Repeat × 4.

◁ THE BOUNCE VIBRATION . . .

Sound III as in it

Moving in the Rhythm Bounce, sound III as in it. Place your hands around your scalp, squeezing your head as you sound III. Follow your breath and repeat for a few seconds. You should feel as if a swarm of mosquitoes are buzzing around in your head! Repeat × 4.

HAIR RAISERS . . . ▷

Sound UUU as in you

❶ Lie on your back on the floor. Raise your feet onto the mat of your bouncer, loosen your hips to open your knees to each side. Turn your palms upward. Relax your breath.

❷ Inhale as you draw your feet in towards your groin. Exhale, releasing the sound UUU as in you, returning your legs to starting position. Keep your leg movements slow and continuous, in tune with your breath. Repeat × 8.

◀ SCARY SPIDERS . . .

Sound AAAH as in far

❶ From the rim of the bouncer sit in a wide squat, clasping your hands behind the back of your head. As you exhale, relax your arm weight and release your head downward. Sound AAAH as in far.

❷ Raise your head, and open your chest wide, inhaling. Repeat × 8.

◀ MISS MUFFET . . .

Sound EEEE as in see

Sit cross-legged on the bouncer, with your wrists crossed in your lap. Joints should be touching in alternating left–right sequence. Keep your spine straight, with your eyes looking at the floor about a metre in front of you. Take a slow deep inhalation. Sound EEEE as in see, as you exhale completely, focussing your attention on your throat area. Repeat × 4.

STICKY WEBS . . . ▷

Sound OOO as in go

❶ Lie back on your bouncer, placing hands behind your knees. Inhale as you draw your knees into your chest. As you exhale, hold the rim on each side, tuck your chin in to your chest, sound OOO as in go.

❷ Rock gently from the lumbar region of your spine to a sitting

position, with your feet flat to the floor. As you rock back, contract your abdomen and roll through your spine to create a massaging effect. Keep your chin tucked in. Roll only as far as your upper back. Don't take any weight on shoulders or neck. Rock × 8 forward and back. Repeat entire sequence × 4.

WISE DERVISH

This routine brings you back to your centre core. It closes off the seven facial openings, allowing your body energy to flow, balance and harmonize after bouncing.

❶ Place thumbs and fingers over the following areas of your face:
THUMBS over and in your ear canals, INDEX FINGERS softly over your eyelids, MIDDLE FINGERS over the tip of your nose, RING FINGERS over your

closed lips, SMALL FINGERS over your chin.

❷ Hold the position for about 30 seconds, breathing fully. When you release from this position, gently vibrate in the Rhythm Bounce.

131

Innerspaces

You can move into full relaxation from any of your sessions, or after a simple Pulse Base. To ensure you are going to be warm enough throughout the relaxation keep a blanket or warm sweatshirt close by. Lie flat on your back, heels together, toes falling apart. Your arms are relaxed to your sides, palms facing upward, shoulders relaxed. Keep the back of your neck flat, with your chin slightly in. You are preparing to completely relax your body, moving from your feet, up through your body to your head. Every time you concentrate awareness on another body part, instruct yourself to 'release, relax and fall away'. Direct your breath to the associated area and imagine you are breathing away lingering tensions.

❶ Bring your attention to your feet. Release and relax your big toes, imagining they are falling away from your body. Follow with your second, third, fourth and fifth toes. Move to the soles of your feet, heels and bridge of the foot. 'Release, relax and fall away'.

❷ Move up through your ankles. Repeat the instruction 'release, relax and fall away'. Move up through your legs, releasing your shins, calves, knees and thighs (front and back).

❸ Visualize, release and relax your hips. Squeeze your buttocks really tight, exhaling. Release and relax your abdomen, inhaling to fill your abdomen with air.

❹ In the same way, visualize, release and relax the rest of your body. Lower back, upper back, shoulder blades, ribs, chest, breasts and shoulders.

❺ Come down into your fingers. Continue your instruction to release and relax your thumbs, first, second, third and fourth fingers. Move through the palms of your hands, wrists, elbows, upper arms and shoulders.

❻ By now, your body is completely released and relaxed. Move through the back of your neck, release your throat, chin, jaw and cheeks. Feel the back of your head releasing further into the floor. Release and relax your ears, lips (teeth apart, lips together), eyes, eyebrow bones, upper eyelids, forehead and scalp.

❼ Move over the back of your head into your scalp, and bring your attention to the area between your eyebrows (often called your third eye). From this point you can either completely still your mind, and when you are ready come out of the relaxation, or alternatively, if you want to, move further into deeper relaxation and meditation.

RETURN FROM RELAXATION . . .

● When you are ready to emerge from relaxation, ease your body back into a wide awake state.
● Keeping your eyes closed, stretch your arms over your head. Breathing deeply, visualize a ribbon of energy moving up and down your spine. Feel a stretch through your whole body from your fingertips to your toes. Open your mouth and stretch your jaw area. Feel the strength of your back and softness of the front of your body.
● Push up to rest on your elbows, slowly straightening your back. Before opening your eyes, take a few deep breaths.
● From the end of any meditation or relaxation session, move onto your bouncer into either the Rhythm Bounce or Pulse Base. A few minutes will leave you fully alert and revitalized.

Flower Power

RESOLUTION PLAN

BELLA AROMA

The powerful aroma of essential oils, collected from the petals of flowers, herbs and wood, has been used for centuries, to relieve stress and to enhance general well-being. They contain next-to-magic properties for rejuvenation and regeneration and I am never without them.

The essence comes from within the cells of plants, which account for why they offer such a powerful healing stimulant and renowned beauty aid. Research shows that the molecules of the plant cells lodge themselves in the limbic portion, the emotional centre, of your brain. Simply by sniffing oils you can alter your mood, emotional framework and mental state.

Essential oils will provide a natural bonus to any of your bouncing programmes. Keep a variety on the shelf and become familiar with their properties.

FRESHLY FRAGRANT

Once you have decided how to use essential oils, they do the work while you reap the benefits. There are many ways that you can use your oils while you bounce.

MASSAGE: Mix one drop of essential oil to a few drops of unrefined vegetable oil. Almond, grape and walnut make excellent base massage or facial oils.

CANDLE: Add essential oil to the melted wax of a candle, avoiding the wick or flame.

DIFFUSERS: Work with candles or electricity. Add the oil to the top bowl, preferably in a base of water so that the essence diffuses without any toxic chemicals from the burn-off. The molecules rise into the atmosphere of your room. This is also an excellent remedy for relief from colds, flu and other ailments.

LIGHT BULB RINGS: Add a couple of drops of oil to the ring which you place on top of the light bulb of a table lamp.

ROOM SPRAY: Add about six drops of oil to half a pint of warm water in an indoor plant water spray. Avoid the furniture as you spray the mixture evenly around the room.

HUMIDIFIER: Place the oil in the water mixture of the humidifier next to your radiator in the winter.

SCENTED SELECTIONS

The possible choice of oils is so vast that I have simply selected a few of my favourites. These are oils I can personally vouch for, having used them consistently for nearly ten years. As you bounce, plan to use oils in your programmes.

GERANIUM: Refreshing and relaxing. Combats depression, congestion, obesity, fluid retention, sore throats, mouth ulcers and infections of the skin. Astringent qualities clear and heal any skin conditions.

ROSE: Good for nerves, reducing stress and depression; aids and tones digestion. Excellent as a hangover remedy. Great for dry and mature skins.

CLARY SAGE: A pick-me-up at any time. If you feel depleted at the end of the day and need a second wind before facing the evening, treat yourself to a few drops in the bath. Boosts your mood, as well as regulating blood pressure, and relieving menstrual problems.

LAVENDER: Relaxing, calming and generally therapeutic. A nerve sedative, it also lowers blood pressure, helps catarrhal complaints, sprains, rheumatism, indigestion and nausea. It is a must whenever infection is lurking, as it encourages the multiplication of antibodies at the scene of the infection.

SAFEGUARDING SELECTIONS

● There are many imitation oils stacked on shelves that will not serve any therapeutic purpose. The molecular structure of the oil must be genuine to influence your brain and to exert a healing effect.

● Test the difference between a fake and pure oil by placing a small drop of essence on a piece of blotting paper. Pure essences will evaporate and disperse, leaving no residue, whilst mineral oil and spirit-based essences will leave an oily patch on the paper.

2

THE KISS OF LIFE

ALIVE ALIVE O$_2$

Oxygen is not only your lifeline, but proves essential to the healthy functioning of every cell and tissue in your body. When cells are unable to absorb essential quantities of oxygen, electrical conduction, growth, repair, maintenance and other simple life processes are unable to take place. More dangerous than a lack of oxygen, is the load of internal pollution that rises quickly if carbon dioxide remains in your tissues.

DECLINING SUPPLIES

Your ability to extract and use oxygen declines at a steady rate of about 1% a year. Unfortunately, your metabolic rate decreases hand in hand, so that:

● You tend to gain weight more easily.

● The strength of your muscle tone, bone and skin tissue deteriorates.

● Your muscles have to work harder to activate their fuel supplies.

● Your organs are unable to perform the same amount of work.

● Every cell is deprived as your body's ability to extract and deliver oxygen is diminished.

● The metabolic fires that fuel the building, maintenance and repair of your tissues diminish.

BETTER LATE THAN NEVER

Although the air surrounding us contains about one fifth oxygen, we differ in our ability to absorb it. The size of your lungs, the speed at which oxygen enters your blood and the speed at which your blood carries it to your muscles, determine the rate at which it can be delivered to your cells. These factors all depend, in turn, on the speed at which your cells can get rid of their waste products. By the time you are eighty, your oxygen flow is expected to have degenerated to about 66% of your potential maximum. Obviously, the less oxygen you absorb, the greater the chances of your health crumbling.

BENEFITS AS YOU BOUNCE

● *Your heart and lungs are strengthened, welcoming a healthier supply of oxygen to your cells.*

● *As your heart becomes stronger, you extract more oxygen for the same amount of blood.*

● *Your breathing capacity is expanded when you breathe more deeply and fully.*

● *Fluid circulation improves, carrying more wastes from your tissue spaces, enabling more efficient absorption of oxygen at a cellular level.*

● *Lymphatics are activated by the additional respiratory pressure.*

● *Activity of your red bone marrow, which produces red blood cells for carrying oxygen, nutrients and wastes, is stimulated. Five million red blood cells are released into your bloodstream every minute, and bouncing enhances their function.*

● *Your lungs are cleansed, so are able to perform more efficiently.*

● *As you become fitter, you develop more blood capillaries which enable quicker transport of oxygen to your cells, and ensure the swift removal of carbon dioxide and wastes from your tissues.*

● *Enzymes throughout your body are able to make better use of oxygen.*

● *Improved patterns will overflow into the rest of your life as you reclaim the natural rhythm of your breath, letting go of tensions and patterns that have been restricting your breathing capacity.*

● *A full spontaneous flow of breath is the best natural tranquilliser you will find. As you calm and nourish your nerves and revitalize your energy reserves, you'll find sleep patterns restored to a natural balance and tension levels in your life diminishing.*

BETTER LATE THAN NEVER

● Combined with breathing techniques, your Starbound programmes help restore and return your supplies of oxygen to a level that was your potential years ago.

● Disturbed breathing patterns, stemming from childhood, are often associated with emotional responses to fear and worry, coupled with restricted clothing and poor posture.

R E S O L U T I O N   P L A N

Totally Breathtaking
~

TAKE EVERY OPPORTUNITY THROUGHOUT YOUR
PROGRAMMES TO CENTRE YOUR AWARENESS
THROUGH YOUR BREATH.

❶ DURING THE WARM-UP AND COOL-DOWN
PHASES, OPEN YOUR BREATH POWERFULLY,
TAPPING IT TO HELP RELEASE RESIDUAL TENSIONS
AND BRING SPIRIT TO YOUR ACTIVITY.

❷ THROUGHOUT ALL STRETCH ROUTINES YOU
HAVE THE PERFECT OPPORTUNITY TO USE BREATH
TO EASE AWAY KNOTS OF TENSION.

❸ YOU'LL PROBABLY FEEL MORE COMFORTABLE
USING NASAL BREATHING DURING SLOWER, MORE
MEDITATIVE ROUTINES. DURING FASTER
ACTIVITIES IT IS NATURAL TO BREATHE THROUGH
YOUR MOUTH, WHICH TENDS TO KEEP YOU
GROUNDED, WITH ENERGY CENTRED IN YOUR
LOWER BODY.

❹ WHEN YOU BRING YOUR AWARENESS TO YOUR
BREATH, TRY A VARIETY OF RHYTHMS AND
ROUTINES. AS YOU BECOME A MORE EXPERIENCED
BOUNCER, YOU WILL FIND IT EASIER TO
COORDINATE A VARIETY OF BREATHING
TECHNIQUES.

YAWWWN

Yawning is nature's way of inviting you to open your
door to take a fuller burst of life-giving oxygen, which
is especially famous for livening up a listless brain. A
good yawn helps release tension in your abdominal
muscles and encourages stagnating fluids and energy
on their way. Digestive processes thank you for the
helping hand, while the masseter muscles around
your jaw are able to release tension. Brain power is
refreshed and your eyes are bathed in fresh supplies
of cleansing fluid.

● Stand on your bouncer and allow yourself the luxury of a good yawn. Then another and another. Bouncing in the Rhythm Bounce, begin to shrug your shoulders, further releasing tension from your trapezius muscles. Keep on yawning!

● Blink your eyes, making the most of the additional fluid, bathing and cleansing your cornea, rolling your eyes in a full swing to the left and then to the right.

● As you yawn, sound off at the same time – AAHHHH, OORRRR, HAAAA – letting go of the tension in and around your throat and shoulders. This vibrates beautifully as you bounce. As a new world of yawning opens up for you, invite your friends to join the fun. Yawning is very catchy!

HUMMM

I call this my didgeridoo bounce dance, and you'll soon see why!

● In the Rhythm Bounce, or Walk, inhale through your nose. As you exhale, through your nose, find a pitch and let go a long HUMMM. As you continue, move the pitch of your hum higher and lower.

● Enjoy experimenting as you change melodies.

● Calm the hum into a purr, then intensify it so that you are humming very loudly.

● Change your hum, inhaling through your mouth and exhaling to the sound of AAAHH.

● After a time, combine the two sounds, HUMMM then change to AAAHH, and then back to HUMMM.

● Experiment with different pitches and patterns as you bounce. The combination of humming and bouncing offers a perfect opportunity to loosen your belly and deepen and free your breath.

BELLY FLOPS

This simple technique will serve as a reminder of the natural release that should occur when you breathe fully into your belly. This implies that your upper body should be released so your abdomen can serve as the seat of your breath.

● Lie flat on the ground, with your legs raised onto your bouncer mat, bent at the knees. Check your body is aligned and relaxed.

● Focus your attention on your breathing rhythms as your breath flows naturally and subtly, in and out.

● Gently raise your head a couple of inches from the floor.

Hold it for a moment as you breathe into your belly. Register the sensation of your abdomen completing housing the breath. When your upper body is called upon to support your head in this fashion, your abdomen has to take the full capacity of your breath. This is what is meant by 'true belly breathing'.

ALTERNATE NOSTRIL BREATHING

Yogis have practised alternate nostril breathing for years to stimulate the nerves in each nostril which correspond to centres in your brain. The following technique helps to rebalance the right side of your brain, which reflects your creativity, with your left brain, which is more analytical.

● From the Rhythm Bounce, gently press the thumb of your right hand over your right nostril. Touch your index fingers to your forehead, bringing your middle fingers down towards your left nostril.

● With your thumb blocking off the right nostril, inhale deeply through your left nostril. Pause briefly.

● Lifting your thumb, press your middle finger over the left nostril, exhale through your right nostril.

● Repeat the pattern, inhaling through your right, and exhaling through your left, and then inhaling through your left and exhaling through your right.

● Repeat × 8 with each nostril.

PATTERNING

Try a variety of breathing combinations. The following are simple examples:

● Inhale through your nose to a count of 3 bounces. Exhale through your nose to a count of 6 bounces.

● Inhale through your nose to a count of 2 bounces. Exhale through your mouth to a count of 4 bounces.

● Inhale through your mouth to a count of 3 bounces. Exhale through your mouth to a count of 3 bounces.

NASAL PRESSES

● With your mouth and jaw relaxed, inhale through your nose to fill your abdomen and chest cavity to full capacity.

● Exhale through your nose, pressing in from your ribs, in several short bursts, contracting your abdomen until your lungs are completely emptied.

● Pause at the end of each outbreath, before continuing.

● Repeat sequence × 4 or × 3.

MOUTHER!

● Completely relax any tension from your jaw, breathing in and out through your mouth, finding rhythms that suit your capacity.

● Count and expand over a period of time.

RESOLUTION PLAN

TRAIN CHOOS

● Inhale through your nose, or mouth to full capacity.
● As you exhale, make a CHHH sound, pressing your tongue hard on the roof of your mouth. Continue the sound in short sharp bursts, until you need to inhale again.
● As an alternative, instead of several small CHHH sounds, make one longer CHHHH sound as you contract your abdomen.

DIAPHRAGM DOMING

If your belly feels bloated or blocked, your breathing capacity will be restricted, along with the associated return of blood and lymph from the limbs to your heart. Your diaphragm, the dome-shaped muscle forming the floor of your ribcage, activates your breathing.

● The deeper you inhale, the lower it flattens, allowing your lungs to descend and fill with air. As it descends, your diaphragm presses your organs down, helping to stimulate digestion and elimination.
● By breathing deeply and fully as you bounce you stimulate your thoracic cavity to move blood and lymph back toward your heart.
● The activity also applies a powerful suction effect on the large veins passing through your abdomen. Organs below your diaphragm are massaged, particularly your large intestine.
● Deep belly breathing is the best digestive aid and natural laxative you can possibly find.

❶ In the Rhythm Bounce, with hands on hips, inhale through your nose. Fill your belly with air and open your chest.
❷ Exhale, contracting your abdomen, slowly pressing all the air from your lungs until they feel completely empty.

❸ When you think all is empty, press your abdomen that much further. Pause before the next inhalation, repeating the cycle × 8.

ABDOMINAL DOMING

This technique has numerous regenerative and rejuvenative qualities. It will also help establish correct breathing patterns.

● Always exhale as you contract your abdomen. Inhale as you release your abdomen and open your ribcage.
● Hold your breath until it can't be held any longer, then inhale.
● Abdominal Doming removes the blockages that have contracted the muscles of your chest and diaphragm, preventing deep breathing from taking place. It also helps overcome constipation, negative thought patterns and prevents tension from developing. It cleanses and purifies your intestines, stimulates digestion and removes that dreadful 'bloated belly' feeling that plagues so many women.

❶ Place your bouncer on the rim. Stand about three feet away, holding the rim with arms outstretched. Bend forward slightly to hump your upper back, knees loose and bent, head tilting forward. Open your mouth. Exhale, pressing as much air as possible from your lungs. Without further inhalation, draw your diaphragm upward under your ribcage pulling your tummy back toward your spine. Hold the suction for as long as comfortable, gradually extending the time as you become familiar with the technique.

❷ Inhale, as you release your abdomen, and relax your back. Repeat the entire routine several times, in the morning and evening.

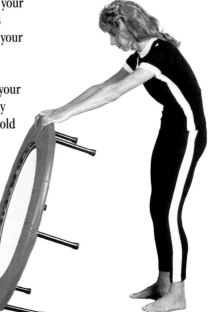

GRANNY'S CORSET

● This technique requires the isolation of your straight abdominal muscles. Perform for a couple of minutes in the morning and evening as an excellent tonic for your entire abdominal region, tightening your pelvic floor muscles and toning the position of your uterus.
● Kneel on the floor on all fours, then raise your hands to the bouncer rim. Let your head hang forward and hump your back slightly.
● Practise Abdominal Doming. Open your mouth exhaling as far as possible. Without further exhalation, contract your abdomen to draw your diaphragm up under your ribcage. Slowly push the centre of your abdomen forward.
● Inhale as you release your belly.

LET'S FACE IT!

BEAUTY AND THE BEAST

True beauty evolves in life as you age and discover who you are, moving forward with confidence and conviction, able to express your self-worth. If the emotional charge infiltrating your psyche is not expressing a positive outlook, no amount of facial or body conditioning will mirror your beauty.

Cosmetic sculpturing cannot release tensions that destroy your appreciation and zest for life, or rebuild a positive sense of self-value and purpose. As you face facts, you can use your bouncing programmes to apply techniques that not only influence the rejuvenation of your connective tissue and physical appearance, but also patterns related to your breath, meditation and relaxation, to help you rediscover a radiance that will set you aglow.

There's a story to be told for every stubborn line that appears on your face. We become so accustomed to the mask we are wearing, we seldom notice our expressions, let alone feel the underlying emotions. Over ninety muscles hold the complex bony structures of your shoulders, neck and face in place, combining to mould a form that reflects in you!

SKIN DEEP

Your skin, which is the largest organ in your body, covering between 15 and 20 square feet, serves as a mirror, to reflect the condition of your inner health. With numerous functions to perform for your preservation and well-being, it consists of two major layers of living cells. The outer is known as the epidermis, while the inner and deeper layer, which consists of connective tissue, is referred to as your dermis.

Small blood capillaries nourish every cell in both layers of your skin, with lymph capillaries filtering throughout to pick up debris. Sweat glands and nerves also infiltrate your skin, which is connected by elastic attachments to the tissues of muscles that underline it, keeping it firm, padded and flexible.

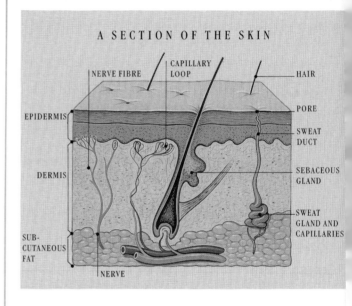

A SECTION OF THE SKIN

CONNECTING TISSUES

Blood capillaries carry essential supplies of oxygen and nutrients to the cells in your connective tissue. If tension builds up in your tissue spaces, restricting the flow of these tiny capillaries, your skin cells become imprisoned and malnourished. Trapped in their own waste products, they are unable to receive essential supplies of nutrients and oxygen. Their life force is cut off.

Connective tissue consists of cells that secrete collagen fibres, woven together to form a net-like structure, rather like a spider's web. They also secrete a jelly-like substance, which fills the spaces between the collagen fibres.

Although it is said that your skin loses natural padding and resilience with age, in fact it is nothing more than a stiffening of the jelly-like matter that binds the chains of molecules together. Skin simply becomes less flexible as the gelatin stiffens, with wrinkles settling in, as the layers of connective tissue stick together.

BENEFITS AS YOU BOUNCE

● *You tap the additional bonus of up to three times the force of gravity at the bottom of each bounce. Your skin cells respond to the additional G-Force and become stronger.*

● *Connective tissue encasing the facial muscles is stimulated, which creates space for your muscles to lengthen and relax.*

● *Muscle tone is balanced as tense muscles become poised, and lazy muscles bounce back to life.*

● *Lymphatic vessels are stimulated to cart away debris, bacteria and toxins.*

● *Expressions of tension begin to disappear. Emotional strains are eased from armoured tissues.*

● *Because you look and feel better, your face is able to reflect your positive outlook.*

● *Your vision and hearing will improve, breathing deepen and relax, and frequent headaches and stiffness around your shoulders will melt away.*

● *The ability of your tissues to utilize oxygen is greatly improved, stimulating conditions for cellular functioning.*

● *Acne and blemishes will clear as glands are balanced and wastes eliminated.*

● *Regular use of your bouncer prevents facial armouring patterns from settling in.*

● *Eyes regain their lustre, bags disappear and manifold benefits surface with regard to improved vision (p. 148).*

● *Crystalline deposits break down from around your jaw, neck and shoulders.*

● *As underlying connective tissue is stimulated, wrinkles deform and your facial contour will become firmer.*

● *You'll find yourself smiling more often, which relaxes every muscle in your face, helping to restore and animate your energy.*

RESOLUTION PLAN

Face Savers
~

THE MUSCLES AND TISSUES IN YOUR FACE NEED THE BOOST STARBOUND PROGRAMMES HAVE TO OFFER. MOST FACIAL EXERCISE PROGRAMMES ARE PERFORMED STATICALLY, WITH LITTLE THOUGHT GIVEN TO THE REMOVAL OF WASTES OR THE STIMULATION OF CONNECTIVE TISSUE AND FLUID. AS YOU BOUNCE INTO FACIAL REJUVENATION, THE MUSCLES THAT GIVE YOUR FACE SHAPE AND FORM WILL BECOME TONED AND FIRM WITHIN SIX WEEKS.

FABULOUS FACADES

The following techniques form the Fabulous Facades rejuvenation exercise programme for your face, neck and shoulder area.

● Either include your facial techniques into your bouncing sessions, or create a separate programme for facial rejuvenation.

● Perform routines in the Rhythm Bounce or Rhythm Walk, until you have the skills mastered, then use them to accompany other bounce routines. If you practise a selection of these sequences regularly, you will soon notice visible improvements.

LOCK-JAW!

Tension thrives in your jaw, which can clench over 500 pounds in weight.

❶ Locate your jaw, by placing your thumbs to either side of your ears, while you open and close your mouth. Open your jaw as wide as you can, breathing in and out through

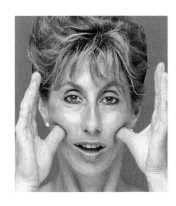

● Don't waste a moment: spice up your Starbound Workout with these facial exercises for rejuvenation. Combine them with any of your programmes as you bounce.

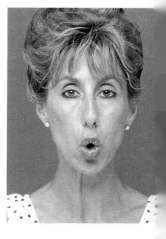

your nose. With your mouth closed, teeth apart and jaw relaxed, press your thumbs from either side of your ears, under your cheekbones, to your lips, in a downward movement. Repeat × 8.

❷ With your mouth slightly open, twist your lips to the left, and then to the right, breathing through your nose, holding each position to a count of 4 bounces.

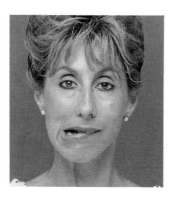

❸ Imitate a chewing motion, opening your mouth as wide as possible, forming your lips into a thin tunnel as you protrude your jaw forward.

FACE SHAKER

Stimulates circulation and releases tension.

❶ Open your mouth and eyes as wide as possible for 2 bounces.

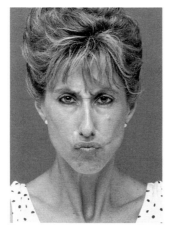

❷ Squash and tighten your face with your lips and eyebrows pressing together for 2 bounces. Repeat × 3.

CHINSTOPPERS

Stimulates circulation of connective tissue around your jaw, preventing a double chin from surfacing.

Clench both fists, gripping the flesh between your thumbs and index fingers of both hands, pinching the flesh along the jawline, under your chin, up to your ears. Work gradually along, back and forward. Repeat × 4.

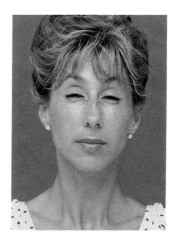

EYESHINER

Reduces puffiness around eyes, strengthens lower eyelids.

Raise your eyebrows × 8. Holding your upper lids down as firmly as possible, try very hard to raise your lower lashes, looking through slit eyes. Repeat × 8.

WINKER

Strengthens eye area and upper and lower lids.

Wink one eye at a time × 8. Alternate × 8 winks to the left, then × 8 winks to the right. Wink deeply × 8 to either side.

JAW-STRINGS

Strengthens jaw, throat muscles, smooths mouth, defines lips.

Say OOOOOOOO, then EEEEEEEE, exaggerating the movements as strongly as possible. Repeat × 8.

HOOK, LINE AND SINKER

For lip lines, neck and double chin.

Hook the tops of your index fingers into either side of your mouth. Do not clench your teeth. Smile aiming for your ears, while resisting with your mouth. Hold × 2 bounces. Repeat × 8.

STEAMROLLERS

Stimulates circulation, removing blocked tensions.

Vibrating your lips together, begin to create a vibratory sound as a child might make, pretending you are playing train engines!

You can carry on like this for a couple of minutes, remembering to take a break for breath.

Activate your Reflexes

The reflex points in this programme are known as your 'neurovascular holding points'. They improve the nerve and blood circulation to both the associated muscle and the related organ.

❶ Activate these reflexes while moving in the Rhythm Bounce or Rhythm Walk.

❷ Stand quietly to begin. Place the pads of your fingers gently on the reflexes shown. In a few seconds you may feel a pulsation, which is thought to connect to the blood capillaries in your skin.

❸ Begin to vibrate in the Rhythm Bounce, while firmly holding your hands on the points for between 30 to 60 seconds.

NEUROVASCULAR REFLEX POINTS

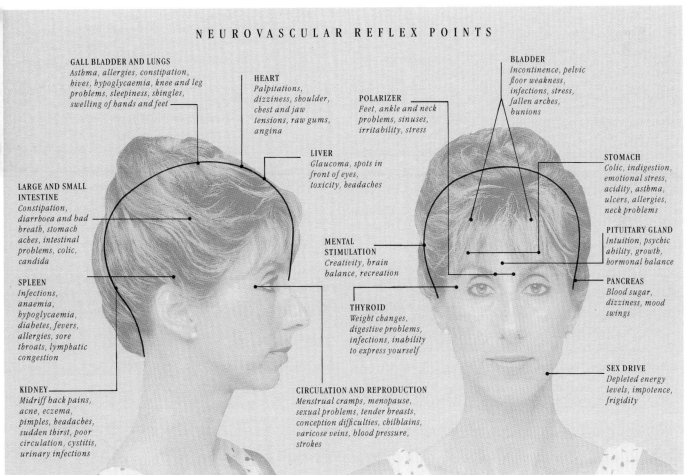

GALL BLADDER AND LUNGS
Asthma, allergies, constipation, hives, hypoglycaemia, knee and leg problems, sleepiness, shingles, swelling of hands and feet

HEART
Palpitations, dizziness, shoulder, chest and jaw tensions, raw gums, angina

POLARIZER
Feet, ankle and neck problems, sinuses, irritability, stress

BLADDER
Incontinence, pelvic floor weakness, infections, stress, fallen arches, bunions

LIVER
Glaucoma, spots in front of eyes, toxicity, headaches

STOMACH
Colic, indigestion, emotional stress, acidity, asthma, ulcers, allergies, neck problems

LARGE AND SMALL INTESTINE
Constipation, diarrhoea and bad breath, stomach aches, intestinal problems, colic, candida

MENTAL STIMULATION
Creativity, brain balance, recreation

PITUITARY GLAND
Intuition, psychic ability, growth, hormonal balance

SPLEEN
Infections, anaemia, hypoglycaemia, diabetes, fevers, allergies, sore throats, lymphatic congestion

PANCREAS
Blood sugar, dizziness, mood swings

THYROID
Weight changes, digestive problems, infections, inability to express yourself

KIDNEY
Midriff back pains, acne, eczema, pimples, headaches, sudden thirst, poor circulation, cystitis, urinary infections

CIRCULATION AND REPRODUCTION
Menstrual cramps, menopause, sexual problems, tender breasts, conception difficulties, chilblains, varicose veins, blood pressure, strokes

SEX DRIVE
Depleted energy levels, impotence, frigidity

HEAD SPINNER

● If you want to clear your head, or wake yourself up in a hurry, a few moments on your bouncer practising this technique is all you need. It also loosens your face, shoulders and neck for facial exercise and massage.

● In the Rhythm Bounce, use your facial exercises to loosen your jaw, eyes, nose, forehead and lips. Separate your fingers, (placing them on top of your scalp. Massage the entire area with brisk movements, as if you were furiously scrubbing your head. Spend about five bounces in each spot,

before shifting your fingertips.

● When your coordination improves, you'll have no trouble bouncing and massaging at the same time. Try adding some breathing and sound techniques.

4
BRAINY SPOTLIGHTS

BRAIN OR BRAWN

With a bit of enthusiasm any old brain can bounce back to life. Brainy matter is seething with electrical and chemical activity, providing important links for feelings, thoughts and actions. Your brain thrives on fresh supplies of oxygen, which you provide in abundance as you bounce.

Clear transmission between your brain and spine determine the communication throughout the rest of your body. Many of the tiny vessels that lead into your brain are finer than the hairs on your head. If toxic residue accumulates in these vessels, it dampens the supply of power transmitted along your lines. As you bounce you experience clarity as brainy tissue is cleared of toxic wastes and permeated with fresh supplies of nutrients and life-giving oxygen.

EUREKA!

Rhythm, established as you bounce, is transmitted via pulsing waves, falling in line with the on/off sine wave of your autonomic nervous system. Bilateral co-ordination of the cerebral hemispheres in your brain is stimulated, creating impulses which can be read as synchronized coherent brain wave activity. This induces a state often labelled the 'Eureka Experience'.

Inside your brain you have chambers, filled with cerebro spinal fluid, which circulates and protects your spinal cord and brain, acting as a carrier of electrical ions. This fluid is powerfully stimulated as you bounce, creating a more efficient transport system for the electrical messages relayed to your brain. Stagnation of this fluid affects the control relationship between your brain and the rest of your body. The stimulation of this fluid is one of the main reasons you feel such an immediate lift on all levels when you bounce.

Little is spoken about the importance of this fluid. Exaggeration of your normal range of movement increases its flow, and it is powerfully stimulated if you perform cross-crawl movements, due to the greater flexion of your sacrum. Although chambers in your brain house this fluid, it is secreted by special vessels, seeping out all over your body, influencing the quality of your electrical signals.

BRAINY LESIONS

Well-tuned connections between your brain and body are linked most efficiently when the left hemisphere of your brain controls the right side of your body and the right portion of your brain controls the left.

Each half of your brain is associated with clear and definite functions and processes.

LEFT BRAIN	RIGHT BRAIN
Male Qualities	*Female Qualities*
Controls right side of body	Controls left side of body
Introversion	Emotional
Objectivity	Philosophical
Hearing	Creative
Thinking	Intuitive
Learning new things	Initiating
Achieving	Relaxation
Materialistic	Spatial
Organizing	
Mathematical	

CEREBRAL HEMISPHERES
OF THE BRAIN

MOOD

MOTOR CONTROL
(Movement)

TOUCH

TASTE

SIGHT

SPEECH
(Broca's area)

AUDITORY
(Hearing)

SPEECH
(Wernicke's area)

HOMOLATERAL SWITCHING

Although your brain looks like two halves of a walnut, it acts like a sponge. Processes delegated to either side are not all that cut and dried, due to information that passes between nerve fibres.

Many factors may cause you to switch to a homolateral pattern, where one side of the brain is dominant in terms of behaviour. Emotional stress, illness, birth trauma, conflict, fear, anxieties and even fatigue may throw your brain out of kilter. Homolateral movements, relating the same side of your brain to your body, were important before you started to crawl, when the necessary cross-over takes place. (When a baby explores space by crawling, a free flow of knowledge enters the brain centres to trigger healthy cross-lateral patterns.) This is a preparation time for activities such as reading and writing, where eyes, mind and hands rely on the integration of both sides of the brain. If there has been insufficient stimulation for the change to take place, some people never make the necessary transitions, and may experience poor brain-body patterns throughout life.

WHEN LEARNING IS NO FUN

Under many disguises, more children suffer learning difficulties than you might imagine. Discrepancies often exist in the connection of one side of their body and the corresponding hemisphere in their brain. Poor coordination and balance are often signs of such difficulties. Simple weaknesses between a right hand and left foot offer evidence that the brain and body are not synchronized. Difficulties can even begin in the womb, where poor nutrition, emotional traumas of the mother and even environmental contamination may stamp their influence.

BRAINY CONNECTIONS

Many children are institutionalized, and ignored by society, simply because they are plagued by neuromuscular disfunctioning, not with diminished intelligence. Even though they store complete information within their cells, brain patterns and nervous circuits simply don't allow the vital connections. Numerous therapists are now performing an 'about turn' in methods of treatment. As they train the body to work with the brain, so the brain's demand to move a muscle corresponds with the movement.

Simple skills can be applied on the bouncer to benefit brain-damaged children. Combined with muscle testing treatments and massage, response is partly due to the stimulation of nerve cells and the cleansing of the brainy tissue itself.

You might spot a therapist at work with a child on a bouncer, playing ball and clapping games and monitoring simple 'call out' instructions. Hand–eye coordination, balance, attention span, spatial awareness and self-confidence are among the skills enlisted to refine brain power.

Many learning disabilities, stemming from physical imbalances, are projected in the guise of personality, and emotional and mental conflicts. If more emphasis was placed on physical education programmes for children, from an early age, numerous problems that manifest as behavioural difficulties or learning traumas would simply never arise, or at least be rectified as soon as they did.

BENEFITS AS YOU BOUNCE

- *If nothing else, a good bounce will bring you to your senses.*
- *Channels of hearing, taste, sight and touch all interact with your brain, sharpening sensual awareness.*
- *Natural chemicals are released into your bloodstream which provide the perfect antidote for depression and pain. As depression is naturally lifted, the portion of your brain that rises to creativity will emerge.*
- *Your emotional responses are centred and stabilized as your nervous system is activated.*
- *Regular cross-crawling from your bouncer will:*
  Balance the hemispheres of your brain.
  Improve your learning ability.
  Offer clearer thinking.
  Aid brain damage recovery.
  Aid medical recovery from strokes.
  Help overcome dyslexia.
  Improve cerebro-spinal circulation.
  Balance your energy levels.
  Bring clarity from confusion.
  Aid your emotional balance.
  Help your coordination, memory and thought processes.

- We all tend to have a leaning toward being right brain dominant (the dreamer) or left-brain dominant (the thinker).

143

RESOLUTION PLAN

Brainy Blitz
~

YOUR BOUNCER PROVIDES THE PERFECT FOUNDATION FOR ACTIVATING BOTH HEMISPHERES OF YOUR BRAIN. THE MOVEMENTS IN THIS SIMPLE PROGRAMME ARE CALLED CROSS-CRAWL. THERE ARE AN ENDLESS RANGE OF COMBINATIONS YOU CAN PRACTISE, OFFERING FUN AND BRAINY STIMULATION AT THE SAME TIME. WHEN YOU BECOME AWARE OF THE POSSIBILITIES FOR FITTING CROSS-CRAWLING INTO YOUR DAILY SESSIONS, YOU CAN BEGIN TO CHOREOGRAPH YOUR ROUTINES TO BALANCE YOUR BRAIN.

❶ USE THE ONE-STAR RHYTHM BOUNCE OR TWO-STAR BASIC BOUNCE AS A CENTRE BOUNCE FOR THE TECHNIQUES IN THIS PROGRAMME.

❷ ANY MOVEMENTS REQUIRING OPPOSITE ARM TO LEG MOVEMENTS SIMULTANEOUSLY, WILL ACTIVATE BOTH HEMISPHERES OF YOUR BRAIN TO WORK HARMONIOUSLY.

❸ USE THESE CROSS-CRAWL TECHNIQUES IF YOU'RE FEELING TIRED, BLURRY, CONFUSED, ANGRY, UNINSPIRED, OR JUST PLAIN 'OUT OF SORTS'. EVEN A MINUTE ON YOUR BOUNCER, CROSS-CRAWLING, WILL WORK WONDERS IN HELPING TO PIECE YOUR BRAIN TOGETHER AGAIN.

❹ ONCE YOUR SKILLS HAVE DEVELOPED, SPEED YOUR MOVEMENTS UP TO ADD VARIETY TO YOUR ROUTINES, BY MISSING THE CENTRE BOUNCE FROM BETWEEN EACH SIDE OF THE MOVEMENT.

❺ WHEN POSSIBLE, CHOREOGRAPH YOUR STAR-BOUND WORKOUT WITH CROSS-CRAWL PRINCIPLES IN MIND, SO YOU REAP THE BENEFITS OF IMPROVED BRAIN AND BODY COORDINATION.

TRAFFIC DIRECTEUR ▲

❶ From a base bounce, kick your right leg and left arm forward. Bounce back to base.

❷ Repeat with your left leg an right arm forward. Bounce back to base.

❸ Change the position of your right leg, to swing it across in front of your body, while you swing the left arm to cross in the opposite direction in front of your abdomen. Bounce back to base.

❹ Repeat the pattern alternating right and left sides.

RESOLUTION PLAN

JERKY JUGGLERS

❶ From base position, bend your right knee, raising it toward your waist, as you bend your left arm to shoulder level, with your right arm swinging down to your side. Bounce back to base.

❷ Reverse sides. Bounce back to base.

KITE FLYING ▲

❶ From the base, kick your left leg out to the side, as you raise your right arm away from your shoulder.

❷ Bounce back to base, reverse sides and repeat.

❸ Open your right arm and left leg out to each side. Bounce back to base.

❹ Reverse sides and repeat the sequence.

SKID ROW ▶

❶ From base, slide your left leg forward, while punching with your right arm.

❷ Change position with no base bounce in between, gliding your feet across the mat. Swing opposite arm back behind your body, bent at the elbow.

HOPSCROSS ▲

❶ Bend your right knee raising your heel behind, toward your buttock. Reach behind with your left hand to touch your right heel.

❷ Bounce back to base, reverse sides and then repeat.

◀ THE NUTCRACKER

❶ From a wide-legged base, cross your left leg in front of your right, crossing your right arm in front of your abdomen and your left arm behind your back.

❷ Bounce back to base, reverse sides and then repeat.

BRIGHT EYES

LIGHT WAVES

You receive what you see through waves of light, which have to be processed and interpreted by your brain, in terms such as brightness, shape and colour, before the image can be of any use to you. Tiny vibrations of light energy called 'saccades' constantly flicker and dance about you, enlightening the process of vision. Although saccades move incredibly quickly, if the energy flow through your eyes diminishes, saccadic vibrations become dim, inviting visual blur.

Light energy is converted to chemical signals that carry information to your brain, via your optic nerves. For perfect vision, these rays of light must all focus clearly as they are processed. When this happens, according to the experts, you are seeing 20/20.

MIRROR OF YOUR SOUL

Your eyes also mirror your health and soul, projecting an entire reflection of your personality and character. Simply by reading your iris, an iridologist can glean all necessary information regarding your health. As an embryo in the womb, your iris was actually a part of your brain, expanding as you developed, onto your iris stalk, from where thousands of nerve transmissions throughout your body are coordinated.

BRAINWAVES OF LIGHT

Because your eyes are set apart from each other, they perceive any scene uniquely, forcing your brain to compare the two pictures. Messages are signalled to a separate part of your brain, as muscles shift your eyes about, to process your view of the world in three-dimensional form. Your right eye, corresponding to the right side of your body, is controlled by the left side of your brain. Your left eye, corresponding to the left side of your body, is controlled by the right side of your brain. Healthy vision depends on quality integration between both sides of your brain.

LEARNING TO SEE

Learning to see clearly involves:
- Learning to coordinate direction and movement.
- Understanding where you are in relation to other objects.
- Memory comes into play, as you recall familiar shapes, speeds, locations, distances and depths.
- Your relationship with gravity in terms of spatial orientation.
- Muscles that operate your eyes have to be coordinated and cooperating.

It's never too late to set about improving your eyesight. International pioneers in the field of optometry and visual improvement believe that seeing is not just an isolated function, dependent on eyes alone. It is an integrated process, calling upon intelligence, posture, personality, nutrition and among other things, exercise.

RHYTHMICAL VISION

Your vision pulsates, clouding and clearing in response to your experiences, emotional states, energy levels and purpose in life. But to accept it naturally deteriorates is admitting defeat. The percentage of spectacles prescribed annually is growing, with people accepting their refractive errors as fate. Myopia, astigmatism and squint are among a few of the conditions that you do have the power to improve. You have the means for natural vision and the capacity to sharpen your focus. If you are prepared to work for your sight, your bouncer will provide the perfect foundation from which to practise techniques for visual improvement.

20/20

Dr R. M. Kaplin, an international authority in the field of vision training, outlines the new directions for dealing with the visual blur in his book, *Seeing Beyond 20/20*. From his experience as a professor in Schools of Optometry, in Texas and Oregon, Dr Kaplin observed that the approach of optometrists was to provide glasses or contact lenses. The traditional viewpoint is that a defective eyeball needs a corrective device to compensate for the imperfection. Corrective tools, like lenses, should eventually be removed once the therapy is complete. On the contrary, prescriptions typically become stronger leading to a greater dependency. In 1976, he was introduced to the idea of working with clients on a trampoline, which revealed how tensions such as fear and anger may restrict the quality of vision. He discovered that bouncing offered a 'process orientated therapy', and tended to move a person more quickly through their learning and re-enlightenment. He believes bouncing to be an excellent way to increase blood flow and brain integration for improved vision and eye fitness.

BOUNCE TO IMPROVE VISION

① VISUAL CODING

Visual disturbances result from confused messages. To train your automatic learning response, chaotic visual information is supplied, which forces you to sharpen your perception. As you bounce, everything is moving in your field of vision, so your brain has to constantly update what it sees. Your eyes tend to be fixed on one particular spot, and they have to compensate by using internal muscles that focus as well as extrinsic muscles which move from side to side. Throughout your programmes you apply techniques for focus and attention, requesting your eyes to stabilize.

② SPATIAL ORIENTATION

You use your muscles with agility and speed, while your mind is freed to experience a total awareness of where you are in space.

③ VISUALLY-GUIDED BODY MOVEMENT

In tune with your hand and eye coordination, relationships between visual size, space, form and direction, visual-auditory integration, visualization and memory integration are all encouraged in your programmes.

④ DIRECTIONAL AWARENESS

Left and right orientation is developed.

⑤ NEUROMUSCULAR COORDINATION

Skills relate to steady, consistent rhythm and timing as your body receives instant feedback regarding its orientation in space. Transition techniques help your eyes establish accurate information through your optic nerves to your brain. As you bounce, your arms, legs, brain, eyes, hands and ears, all work together to form this orientation.

⑥ MEMORY BANKS

While every thought, feeling and perception is coordinated in your brain, the actual site of memory is in the cell. Your learning centres are contained within every cell of your body, where complex blueprints are recorded of every stimulation you've received in your lifetime.

⑦ CLEANSING FLUIDS

Debris settle around the tissues in your eyes. The aqueous solution bathing your cornea, iris and lens is refreshed as you bounce, cleansing, nourishing and providing your tissues with oxygen.

⑧ SEEING YOUR FEELING

Try to focus your awareness on how your thoughts and feelings affect your eyesight. As you monitor the variables, while you're bouncing, you'll probably notice that there is no time to think of anything but the present. Under these conditions, if you start to think about the past, or worry about the future, your present state of being will break down, as will your performance. Your response to these breakdowns enables you to 'see' your inner fears.

⑨ THE BEING STATE

When you relax your 'mind's eye thinking', as well as your body and eye muscles, you will be more with the present, aware of where you've been, aware of where you're going. This helps to improve your vision, encouraging far better use of both eyes, increasing your seeing, reading, and memory in general.

⑩ ENERGY IN MOTION

Bouncing takes you out of your 'head' thinking mode, and puts you into a dynamic experience of energy in motion. You have to feel, because you are constantly moving. You are stimulating areas of your brain that you are not using when sitting in a chair.

THE TRAMPOLINE CONNECTION

● Since 1930, vision therapists have been tapping bounce techniques as a tool for retraining vision. Improved balance, rhythm, visually-guided direction and movement, spatial awareness, tactile and kinesthetic awareness, attention span and improved breathing patterns are among the skills nurtured in their programmes.

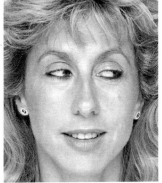
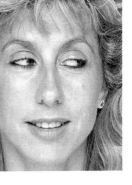

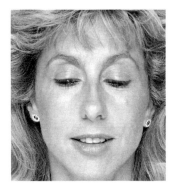

RESOLUTION PLAN

Delightful Eyes
~

BY PRACTISING A SELECTION OF THESE TECHNIQUES WHEN YOU BOUNCE, YOU WILL BE ENCOURAGING CRYSTAL CLARITY, INCREASED CONCENTRATION AND A SENSE OF WELL-BEING. THIS PROGRAMME IS DESIGNED TO ENCOURAGE A HEALTHY BALANCE BETWEEN 'LOOKING' AND 'SEEING', AND THE STATE OF 'DOING' AND 'BEING'.
YOU CAN COMBINE THIS PROGRAMME WITH YOUR MAIN STARBOUND WORKOUT, OR SET TIME ASIDE EACH DAY TO FOCUS ON EXERCISING YOUR EYES. SELECT ONE-STAR, TWO-STAR OR THREE-STAR TECHNIQUES REMEMBERING TO VARY YOUR MOVEMENTS. WHILE YOU ARE BOUNCING SIMPLY INTEGRATE A SELECTION OF THE FOLLOWING TECHNIQUES INTO YOUR WORKOUT.

CRYSTAL GAZING
Suspend a lead crystal from a doorway or ceiling. As you bounce, focus on the different facets, finding the colours of the rainbow, and tuning in to them. Focus on three different cuts on the crystal. Subtly shift your eye from one cut to the next, holding each cut for 2 bounces, and then 3 bounces and then for 4 bounces, up to 10. Swing the crystal like a pendulum. Focus as it moves, to and fro. This is excellent for getting your eyes moving.

PEEP PO
❶ As you begin to bounce, move your eyes in all six directions, to tone your eye muscles.
   Visualize the six muscles attaching to the white of your eyes, as they move your eyeballs.

Completely relax your shoulders, neck, facial muscles and breathing.
   On every second downward bounce, change the direction of your eyes. Focus on a point to the left and then to the right. Repeat × 8.

STRUNG UP
● If you don't have a crystal then try the following technique instead.
● Suspend a string from the ceiling, or light fixture, between 8 to 16 inches in front of your eyes. Focus attention on the string while you bounce. Continue for a few minutes.
● Ever other bounce, focus your attention from the string to a distant point.
● Aim your eyes from the string to the left visual field, back to the string and to the right visual field. Continue in this manner until you feel tired or disorientated.

On every third upward bounce, change the direction of your eyes to focus on a spot on the ceiling. Change to a spot on the floor. Keep your head still, but relaxed, concentrating on moving your eyes.

❷ Holding your index finger about 18 inches in front of your nose, focus on the tip with both eyes. On every second bounce, focus on a point in the distance, before returning to your

fingertip. Repeat × 8. Change time periods so that you vary the number of bounces between refocussing.

Focus on the tip. Circle your eyes to the right, down and around the side to the floor, up and around to the left, and finally back to focus on your fingertip. Relax your eyes for 4 bounces and then reverse direction. Repeat each circuit × 4.

Focus on the tip of your nose, crossing your eyes for 2 bounces, swing both eyes to the left for 2 bounces, return to focus on the tip of your nose for 2 bounces, and repeat to the other side. Repeat the entire sequence × 4.

In the Rhythm Bounce take a deep breath, looking up, then a deep breath looking down. Take a deep breath looking to either side. Finishing by rolling your eyes in full circles to the left, then to the right.

NEWSREADING

Mount a newspaper on the wall, at about eye level. Shift the position of the bouncer every few minutes, so you can focus on reading different sizes of print types.

As an alternative, hold a book as if you were sitting reading. Recite a paragraph out loud, forcing yourself to focus on the print.

HEADLINERS

As you bounce, turn and draw a line with your eyes, tracing the angle where the ceiling meets the wall, all the way around the room. Move your head, not just your eyes. Then draw a line around the edge of the floor.

BLINKERS ON

Blinking is absolutely vital to healthy eyesight. Problems with blinking set in when you begin to stare! Watching television, working computers, sitting at typewriters, all change your blinking patterns. On average you should blink about once every three seconds. Itching, blur, burning eyes and cold stares are really all begging you to blink more often. Blinking is nature's way of insisting that your eyes are constantly bathed in cleansing fluids.

● As you bounce, breathe through your mouth. On every fourth bounce, exhale and blink. Exaggerate the blink as you depress the mat. Repeat × 8.
● In the Rhythm Bounce, turn your head to the left, and then to the right. Come back to central focus, blinking each time. This is a speed technique, and you may prefer to set 2 small bounces for each turn before blinking. Repeat in both directions × 8.

MAGIC PAINTING

In the Rhythm Bounce, massage the tip of your nose, attaching a magic paintbrush to the end. Moving your entire head, start painting the outlines of objects, beginning with large items and then painting smaller, more delicate outlines. Bring your attention to shapes, colours and light. Breath deeply.

TWIN TOMMIES

In the Rhythm Bounce, hold your thumb about 10 inches from your eyes. Relax your breathing and blink regularly while you focus on your thumb. Expand your focus into the distance, still gently bouncing. You should now see a double image. If you suffer with a lazy eye your brain may cut one image off.

6
BETTER BACKS

About eight out of ten people are expected to suffer back pain sometime in their lives. Most injury and pain can be prevented and cured if you accept fuller responsibility for your health. When you regularly follow your bouncing programmes pain, caused by spinal problems, tensions, kidney and abdominal problems, and especially from emotional undertones, should become a thing of the past.

Your spine has to be strong, supportive and flexible to fulfil its purpose. For such a delicate structure, it is quite remarkable that it can support your trunk, bear the weight of your upper body and head, and protect your spinal cord. Without a doubt it is well worth your effort to give it a little love and attention.

The little bones called vertebrae are different in each part of your spine, so they can cope with loads and movement in different parts of your back.

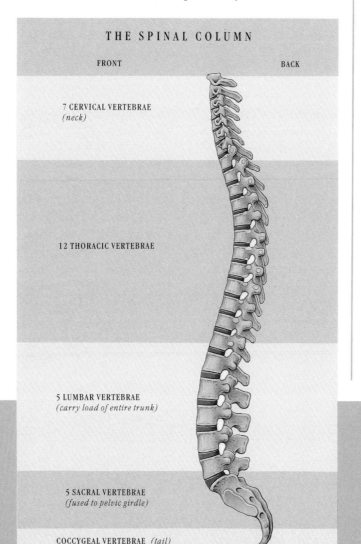

THE SPINAL COLUMN

FRONT   BACK

7 CERVICAL VERTEBRAE
(neck)

12 THORACIC VERTEBRAE

5 LUMBAR VERTEBRAE
(carry load of entire trunk)

5 SACRAL VERTEBRAE
(fused to pelvic girdle)

COCCYGEAL VERTEBRAE *(tail)*

BENEFITS AS YOU BOUNCE

Many people who have had problems with their back find gentle bouncing programmes offer the only form of exercise – other than swimming – they can participate in. Numerous back problems are attributed to people being overweight and underfit. Your programmes are designed to provide the remedy for both ailments.

● *To avoid increasing stress on your lower back as you bounce, keep your posture in check, avoiding any arching of your back. Your spine should be lengthened, your chin slightly in, knees loose and relaxed. Abdomen contracted and buttocks tucked under to keep your lower back flat.*

● *Control movements that involve kicking your heels up behind, bending from the knee rather than your hips.*

● *Always include abdominal sequences in your conditioning routines.*

● *The stimulation of fluid around your vertebrae should help ease calcification from between your vertebrae, cartilage is nourished more readily and armourings, that may cause pinched nerves and congestion, are released.*

● *Damaged discs often result from carrying unacceptable loads. Your discs, which consist of mainly protein and water, depend on the exchange of oxygen and nutrients from surrounding tissue to nourish them. As you bounce, the weight of your body creates hydrostatic pressure, with muscular pressure and your body weight squeezing fluid from the disc. Osmotic pressure sucks fluid into your discs, helping to create a balance of the pressures at work.*

● *Inflammation in the small joints and ligaments in your spine is gently eased as you bounce, encouraging mobility and restricting pain from settling in.*

WEAR AND TEAR

The cushioning substances between your spinal discs lose their ability to operate, due to wear and tear, particularly in the lower back, because they are forced to carry more weight. Poor postural habits, calcification building up around your vertebrae, armoured muscles, inflammation and poor nutrition all lend a hand to create conditions that invite pain.

R E S O L U T I O N   P L A N

Backing Up
~

ABOUT 15% OF ALL BLOOD THAT LEAVES YOUR HEART EACH MINUTE FLOWS TO YOUR BRAIN, CARRYING OXYGEN AND ESSENTIAL NUTRIENTS WITH IT. TO REACH YOUR BRAIN, BLOOD VESSELS PASS THROUGH A SMALL PASSAGE VIA YOUR NECK BONES. YOUR NECK PROVIDES AN IMPORTANT BRIDGE BETWEEN YOUR HEAD AND BODY AND MUST BE RELEASED AND RELAXED FOR YOUR SPINE TO PERFORM ITS PURPOSE. PAY ATTENTION EACH DAY TO RELEASING ANY TENSION THAT BUILDS UP IN YOUR NECK (P. 139).

The lowest compressional forces on your spine are measured when you are lying down, flat on your back. When momentum is added, if you have back problems, you may be wise to adopt this posture for conditioning; flexing, extending, and rotating your muscles and joints to increase your mobility.

● If you have suffered back or neck problems in the past, begin your bouncing programmes gradually, a few minutes at a time, using One-Star techniques.

● You'll be more comfortable with those requiring single-foot strikes, such as the Rhythm Walk.

● Practise a variety of techniques to stretch and condition the muscles of your back, from the mobility, conditioning and stretch programmes.

● Use Spacing Stress Out (p. 128) as often as you can to counteract tensions. These techniques both help to release and prevent pain in your back.

● Essential oils of black pepper, camphor, juniper, lemon and rosemary will all be of benefit if you are suffering pain in your back.

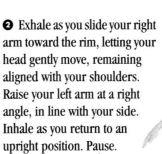

HORIZONTAL BARS

● Stand the bouncer on the rim. Place your outstretched arms on the rim for support at shoulder-width.

● Lean forward so that your arms and upper body are horizontal, your neck long and aligned with your spine.

SEESAW

❶ Kneel on the bouncer on your right knee, with left leg bent to the side. Keep spine aligned, with abdomen contracted and buttocks tucked under. Press your palms together in front of your chest as if praying. Inhale.

● Press down through your heels, breathing deeply into your belly.

● Visualize, release and relax any points of tension, slowly dissolving them with your breath.

❷ Exhale as you slide your right arm toward the rim, letting your head gently move, remaining aligned with your shoulders. Raise your left arm at a right angle, in line with your side. Inhale as you return to an upright position. Pause.

▲ SWISS ROLL (p. 90)

▲ STARLIGHT EXPRESS (p. 94)

▲ STEAMROLLER (p. 35)

▲ LAZY LIZZIES (p. 47)

▲ PEG LEGS (p. 45)

▲ PIP SQUEAKS (p. 75)

▲ HELPING HANDS (p. 78)

▲ SEAGULLS (p. 96)

▲ HAMSTRING CONCERTO (p. 92)

FLAPJACKS (p. 158) ▶

▲ INNERSPACES (p. 132)

BACKING UP

● The above techniques can be adapted for use in your Starbound programmes to stretch and condition, and to alleviate tensions in your back. Also include Flutter Legs (p. 164).

7

FABULOUS FEET

When a reflexologist works the reflexes in your feet, points are stimulated to convey impulses to corresponding organs, muscles, glands and systems in your body. When the point is pressed, the stimulus creates an electrochemical impulse, which travels in pathways on the same side of your body, to recharge your body circuits. Nerve cells carry the impulse to a cluster of cells, known as ganglia, near your spinal cord. From there, the message is transferred to other nerve cells, which carry the impulse to the associated organ, creating the 'reflex response'.

If the delicate nerve endings, related to your various organs and body systems, become trapped in a deposit of wastes, calcium deposits or polluted tissue fluid, the energy flow of these pathways will also be hindered. You have about 72,000 nerve endings in your feet, which are connected to every area in your body. Treat your feet to the attention they deserve.

R E S O L U T I O N   P L A N

Treat Your Feet
~

TWENTY-SIX BONES, ARRANGED IN A SERIES OF
ARCHES, SUPPORTED BY LIGAMENTS, MUSCLES
AND TENDONS, AND INTERWOVEN WITH A
COMPLEX NETWORK OF BLOOD AND LYMPHATIC
VESSELS, CANNOT BE EXPECTED TO PERFORM
WITHOUT SOME CARE AND ATTENTION.

ON YOUR BOUNCER

If your feet feel swollen, walk barefoot on your bouncer, completely rolling through the ball of your foot. Use a foot roller daily as part of your warm-up to your Starbound Workout.

● It's wise to buy shoes at least half-an-inch longer than your feet. If you have to wear heels vary the heights daily.

● Stimulate circulation in your feet by bathing them in warm and then cold water. Or give them a footbath using five drops of peppermint oil.

A STRONG FOOTING

Following your bounce session, treat your feet at least once a week, to keep you on a firm footing.

● Press the reflexes on your feet with your fingertips, not with your thumbs. Start at the top of the foot, which corresponds to the top of your body.

● Your hands will probably run intuitively to the points on your feet which may be the points of your problems. Any tenderness or pain often indicates you have touched on an imbalance. Work that area thoroughly.

● Breathe fully throughout the massage.

● When you have finished the reflexes on both of your feet, then you may want to treat yourself to an oil massage.

THE LEGSHAKER

Sitting on the rim of your bouncer, take your left leg in both hands. With thumbs and fingers gripping the top of your leg, grip your shin and shake your leg loosely. Completely release all tension in your feet, which should flop about as you shake your leg. Continue to shake your leg for about 30 seconds. Repeat with your other leg.

OIL MASSAGE

Rotate your toes clockwise and then anticlockwise. Grip all of your toes and swivel them in both directions together. Stroke and massage the soles of your feet. Follow the lines of your feet, feeling for any areas of residual tension or blocked tissue, kneading and easing your skin as you massage. Massage up and round your ankles, finally stroking the tension away from your calves and shins.

THE LIFE CYCLE

MIRACULOUS CONCEPTIONS

TRANSFORMING POWERS

Pregnancy provides an ideal transition period; not only for growth of a baby, but to heal yourself on numerous levels. Outstanding issues, old griefs and the unravelling of deeper emotions are often spontaneously resolved. Anything that tends to block the flow of energy between a mother and her baby naturally surfaces, offering the perfect opportunity for transformation, healing and empowerment.

BIRTHDAY ISSUES

Giving birth in a recumbent position is both illogical and possibly detrimental to mother and child. Preparation for birth, during pregnancy, offers a valuable foundation to ensure the chances of the safe and natural delivery of your baby.

Many believe that you face serious disadvantages if you recline on your back throughout labour, compressing the base of your spine, restricting your main abdominal vessels and organs, blocking the large artery of your heart, inhibiting circulation to your uterus and placenta, inviting distress for your baby.

You need to work with gravity to give birth, not against it, which will occur if you lie back, immobilizing your sacrum and blocking your coccyx. Your pelvis is designed so it can work for you during birth, in a pivotal action, backward and forward. The upright positions of kneeling and squatting are ideal. They enable your sacrum to adjust to the position of your baby's head as it descends through your birth canal. The area around the base of your spine is also related to your reproductive organs and the quality of energy needed to give birth.

BOUNCING PARAMETERS

Throughout pregnancy you need to sink your roots down into gravity, through your feet, allowing your mother earth instincts to move through you in a free and uninhibited manner. This means turning your bouncing programmes around, so you use the base of the bouncer to sink into and to stretch from, but not to bounce off!

RELATING RESEARCH

The way you exercise influences the blood flow, heart rate and temperature of your developing baby. Although the effects are difficult to assess, the birth weight of your baby may also suffer if you exercise in excess. The American College of Obstetricians and Gynecologists have presented internationally accepted guidelines for safe exercise parameters during pregnancy.

❶ Your heart rate should always remain lower than 140 beats per minute.

❷ Avoid overheating.

❸ Avoid heavy exercise that will last more than fifteen minutes.

❹ Drink plenty of fluids as you exercise to prevent dehydration.

❺ Stay out of jacuzzis, saunas and hot temperatures.

❻ Warm-up and cool-down periods need to be more gradual with no rapid and jerky movements.

TURNING GRAVITY AROUND

Light mobility exercising and yoga-based stretching are the best possible means for stimulating your health and fitness when you are pregnant. You can practise in a passive or profound way, stimulating any part of your body, or the systems of your body as a whole, without any stressing or straining. You need to rediscover your organic, natural positions and body habits, during pregnancy, and for childbirth. When you come into contact with your inner centre you are more aware of the presence of your baby inside you. In many older matriarchal societies, such as traditional Japan, the mother was encouraged to spend as much time and space in meditative harmony with her developing child as possible.

WARNING

● Many women do continue to bounce throughout their pregnancy. I do not recommend it.

● At most you might walk on the mat and stimulate very gentle vibration.

● Turn your bouncing sessions around. Tune into your breathing, stretching, mobility and relaxation techniques.

RESOLUTION PLAN

Safety Pins
~

THERE IS NO OTHER WAY TO WALK THE MATERNAL PATH, BUT WITH PRACTICAL FEET, FIRMLY PLANTED ON THE GROUND. NOW IS THE TIME TO MAKE THE MOST OF THE DIFFERENT LEVELS THAT THE BOUNCER PROVIDES FOR STRETCHING FROM. MAKE YOURSELF COMFORTABLE, PLACING A SHEEPSKIN OR RUG OVER THE SURFACE OF THE MAT, AND SNUGGLE UP FOR THE MONTHS AHEAD, PREPARING TO NOURISH YOURSELF AND YOUR BABY. ENJOY THIS CHANCE TO EXPLORE THE USE OF THE BOUNCER AS YOU MOBILIZE, STRETCH, MEDITATE, RELEASE AND RELAX.

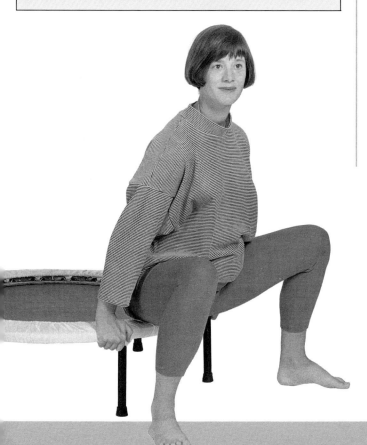

❶ The same rule applies to stretching in pregnancy that applies at any other time. Always loosen and limber your body beforehand. Remember a cold muscle is an invitation to injury.

❷ Adapt any stationary warm-up and limbering routines from other programmes. Use the Starbound Workout Warm-Up (p. 34) as a guide.

❸ Make the most of the mat during pregnancy to protect your knees and back. Use the rim to develop your flexibility further throughout your stretching routines.

SQUAT

Squatting is an ideal position for preparing for and giving birth. As you squat the benefits are numerous.

● Elimination channels are internally massaged.

● Lymph and blood circulation is quickened as internal pressure is applied to your vessels.

● Your immune system is activated.

● Your belly is naturally released for a full flow of breath.

● Energy centres are naturally shifted closer together, with less effort for energy to flow from one station to the next.

● Blocked and armoured muscles are spontaneously released and relaxed.

● It allows the front of your body to soften, stretching your back.

You can choose from the following selection to create a safe transition through pregnancy.

◀ **SQUATTING DUCKS**

● Sit on the bouncer rim, bend your knees and spread your legs comfortably.

● Keep your feet flat to the floor, aiming to keep them parallel, with the weight falling on the outer edge. Relax your shoulders and belly.

● Be aware of extending up through your spine, to the crown of your head through the back of your neck.

● When you become comfortable in this position, you can gradually take your pelvic weight lower. Bring your hands onto the rim to support you from behind, using your hands to take more weight as you lower your pelvis into the floor.

● When you are flexible enough, simply remove support from your hands, bringing them forward from your shoulders.

PRAYING MANTIS ▽
● Sit on your shins with your knees opening out to either side, your heels tucked under your buttocks, toes facing inward.
● Lean forward with your hands gripping the rim. When you feel supple enough, bend your elbows to lower your upper body so that your forehead is resting on the mat.
● Breathe fully, concentrating on the release in your pelvis as you exhale.

TAILOR-MADE ▲
● Sit on the bouncer, bring the soles of your feet together, placing a cushion beneath your knees for comfort if you prefer.
● Breathe deeply into your belly, opening up as you breathe in.

● Place your hands on either side of the bouncer rim for support and gently ease yourself forward into a deeper stretch on your exhalation.

FLAPJACKS ▽
● Sit on the floor between 12 to 15 inches from the bouncer with your legs spread as far apart as comfortable.
● Relax the back of your thighs and soften your knees.
● Place your hands on the bouncer mat.
● Keep your legs flat and groin tight to the floor at all times, your spine and neck long, with your chin tucked slightly in.
● Breathing fully into your belly, when your hips feel loose enough, ease yourself forward, sliding your arms over the mat.
● Eventually as you become more supple, you will be able to bring your head to rest on the mat.

CAMEL HUMPS ▽
● Kneel on the bouncer, come forward onto all fours, gripping the front rim with both hands.
● Tuck your chin into your chest, lengthen your lower back, humping your upper back slightly.
● Release and repeat × 4.

SWISS ROLL ▲
● As you release from Camel Humps, relax your back, and roll your hips to the right in a full circle. Repeat × 8 to the right and then × 8 to the left.

● You can bring your hands forward onto the floor, so that your back is gently elevated as you roll. Repeat in both directions.
● Stand the bouncer on the rim, gripping the edge for support, as you roll your hips × 8 to the left and × 8 to the right.
● Press your left hip outward for 8 counts, and alternate with your right.
● Gently tilt your pelvis through, squeezing your buttocks and releasing for a count of 8.

AROUND THE BEND ▲
● Lying on the bouncer mat, place your right heel on your left knee.

● Place your left hand on the outside of your knee, with your right hand gripping the edge of your bouncer.
● Gently ease your knee across toward the left side of your bouncer, turning your head in the opposite direction. Pause.
● Reverse sides and repeat.

THE STORK WALK ▷
● Stand the bouncer on the rim, turn your back, grasping it from behind.
● Grip your hands over the rim, arms shoulder-width apart.
● Stretch out your arms, feeling the release of tension through your shoulder blades.
● With your knees softly bent, walk a few inches away from your bouncer, stretching your arms a little further. Keep your buttocks tucked under.
● Release all tension in your belly and breathe fully. Hold for about 4 full breaths.

THE MAGIC OF TOUCH
When your baby is first born, much of your initial communication will be in terms of touch rather than speech. Having a relationship with a partner or friend allows you to explore touch and develop trust, offering an excellent preparation for the new relationship with your baby.

You'll gain tremendous benefits from sharing partner stretching and massage throughout your pregnancy. Use your bouncer as a base to stretch from, as you guide your partner's hands to those areas of tension that need firm pressure. The feeling of another person tuning in and caring for your body, especially in the months following the birth, when you are giving out so much of yourself, is extremely nurturing. Massaging and stretching with your partner is a wonderful way to show care and feeling for each other. And most importantly, if you'd like a shoulder rubbed or a knot pressed out, don't forget to express your needs!

159

REMEMBER: POSTURE!
● Keep your knees soft and shoulders relaxed.
● Aim to keep your back straight and neck in line with your spine.
● Always return to a starting position without arching or straining your back.

2

POST-NATAL GRADUATION

CONGRATULATIONS!

With your baby finally in your arms, those first few days will be filled with emotional charges of excitement, love, appreciation and delight. But don't be surprised if it doesn't all feel like joy and glory. Although the experiences involved as you get to know your baby are full of rewards, it's not unusual to feel totally overwhelmed by the birthing experience, and the fuss around you, or to experience feelings of 'let down'. On top of sometimes unexpected emotions, fatigue, broken sleep and additional responsibilities of motherhood can create further strain.

STRIKING THE BLUES

Most new mothers feel a little weepy, traditionally around the time milk supplies settle in. As hormonal balance see-saws during this period, your moods may swing from exhilaration to exhaustion in a flash. You may feel confident one minute and uncertain of your capabilities the next.

While everyone offers advice on the best way to cope, remind yourself that your instinct as a mother will provide the best guide for what you and your baby truly need. The more rest you can fit in after the birth, the better you will cope and the sooner you will recover your equilibrium.

Hearty Healing

SITZ YOURSELF

Sitz baths are a must as you take steps to healing your perineum, following the birth.
❶ Either use a bidet or take a sterilized basin and fill it with warm water.
❷ Mix in 3 drops of lavender and 5 drops of cypress essential oil.
❸ Completely bathe your entire pelvic area including your perineum and anus.

❹ The lavender stimulates the production of white blood cells to keep infection at bay and stimulate healing, while the cypress is astringent causing the wound to heal over.
❺ Follow this procedure every time you urinate or pass a bowel motion.

ANGELIC ARNICA

A homeopathic remedy, arnica combats bruising and soreness, speeding the healing process. Following an episiotomy, which involves the cutting of your perineum during delivery, it may also be wise to bathe your wounds with a few drops of calendula and hypericum tincture in some warm water as a base. They work well with arnica as a remedy.

ESSENTIAL BATHING

When you are tired and blurry-eyed, treat yourself to a good long soak in a bath with essential oils of your choice (p. 133). Clary sage and rosemary will give you a burst of energy and refresh you. Jasmine is soothing and will calm anxieties. Geranium is a powerful rebalancer, while lavender soothes and heals.

BACH FLOWERS

Bach flower remedies are also helpful to get you through various emotional transitions. Choose the remedy to suit your particular needs. Rock rose is an excellent remedy for panic. Elm is wonderful if you are feeling overwhelmed. Olive will rejuvenate you if you are feeling drained of energy and exhausted.

NECESSARY NOURISHMENT

A healthy well-balanced diet is essential to you and your baby throughout this entire period. Wholefoods will keep you nourished and strong. The secret of a quick and energetic recovery following birth, is to let yourself be thoroughly pampered by family and friends, nourishing your needs from all levels.

LASTING SOLUTIONS

● If you have had ongoing problems with stress incontinence, you will notice incredible improvement with six weeks of regular bouncing. Like any other muscles, if you don't use them you lose them. Your pelvic muscles will deteriorate

without regular bouncing sessions.
● Your initial bouncing programmes are designed to strengthen and restore muscular tone so that by the time you begin to bounce again, the impact will be minimal.

REST UP

The Chinese and Zulus are among the cultures who insist the mother should rest and be nurtured for at least forty days following birth. Don't make the mistake of rushing around too soon, when you should be lying low. Your uterus, the muscular sac that holds your baby, naturally shrinks back to normal size within six weeks following birth, indicating that by then, you should be ready to resume a more complete spectrum of physical activity.

RESOLUTION PLAN

On the Road Again

~

FOR THE FIRST WEEK FOLLOWING THE BIRTH YOU MUST REST, ALTHOUGH AFTER A FEW DAYS YOU CAN START TO DO A FEW PELVIC TILTS AND PULLS, PRACTISING THEM SUBTLY AS YOU LIE AROUND.

❶ THE BONY FRAME AT THE BASE OF YOUR BODY IS KNOWN AS YOUR PELVIC GIRDLE. IT CONSISTS OF FOUR SETS OF BONES, JOINED TOGETHER BY MUSCLES AND LIGAMENTS, WHICH BECOME SOFTER DURING PREGNANCY, DUE TO HORMONAL SECRETIONS, WHICH ENABLE YOUR PELVIS TO EXPAND IN SIZE SO YOUR BABY CAN BE BORN.

❷ WHEN YOUR BABY IS BORN, YOUR PELVIC MUSCLES ARE STRETCHED TO THEIR LIMIT. THEY HAVE A DEEP AND SUPERFICIAL LAYER, WITH THREE OPENINGS: THE URETHRA FROM YOUR BLADDER, YOUR RECTUM AND ANUS FROM YOUR BOWEL, AND YOUR VAGINA FROM YOUR UTERUS. IMAGINE THE MUSCLES THAT SURROUND THESE OPENINGS REPRESENTING A FIGURE 8. EVEN THOUGH THE MUSCLES ARE INTERCONNECTED, WORKING AS ONE UNIT, DEPENDING ON WHETHER THEY ARE SLOW OR FAST TWITCH, SOME WORK IN LONG BURSTS WHILE OTHERS WORK IN BRIEF SPURTS.

WORRIES ABOUT LEAKAGES

Over 85% of women suffer the occasional leakage for the rest of their lives after giving birth. Bouncing offers a powerful way to reset the gaps, turning those fast twitch muscles into slow, to work in your favour. Tapping the additional G-Force at the bottom of every bounce offers the best and fastest way to switch your fibres.

❶ When you begin bouncing again, the additional pull on the cells and organs of your pelvis, encourages them to tighten up and perform to command.

❷ You can purchase stress incontinence pads at first, if you have an ongoing problem. These are often all you need to give you the confidence to set out on your bouncing programmes, which will then rectify the problem.

❸ Most dribble leakages occur because you haven't allowed the necessary time to bounce back. If you have had an active birth, your pelvic muscles should return to normal quickly. Usually problems set in if you have had interference during the birth.

Early Days . . .
Taking Control

In the days following birth, practise a few of the following techniques to strengthen and tone your general condition. Your body is often your best guide as to what you are ready to do. During these early days you can slowly begin to practise the same routines that you called upon throughout pregnancy. You need to gently work on your back and abdomen and routines that are going to mobilize and release tension in and around your shoulders.

BRIDGING THE GAP ▼

● Lie back on the bouncer, completely relaxed, legs bent, feet parallel on the floor. Breathe deeply.

● Pull up on your tummy muscles at the end of each exhalation, holding for a count of 3.

● Release your abdomen as you breathe in, filling it with air.

● Alternate this routine with your pelvic floor routine. Pull in and up, tightening the grip on your anus, urethra and vagina all at the same time, but not tensing your abdomen. Hold for a count of 3. Repeat the entire sequence × 8, gradually adding to the number of repeats as you become stronger.

● Lying back on the mat, exhale as you lift your right foot off the floor, raising your knee towards your chest. Keep the small of your back pressed into the mat.

● Breathe in fully as you hold the knee lift, exhale again as you lower your foot to the floor.

TUMMY TRIMMER

● Strengthen your tummy muscles starting with techniques from Bridging the Gap. Gradually build in routines from abdominal conditioning in the Starbound Workout. Balance these with techniques to strengthen your back muscles, like Flutter Legs.

PREPARING YOUR PLAN OF ACTION

● Include your baby in your bounce sessions. The sooner they get used to the fact that these are part of the daily routine the easier it will be for you to create space to bounce independently.

● Place them in a position where they can watch while you bounce. Beanbags are an excellent baby chair initially.

● Include them in sessions while you are conditioning. A baby on your tummy makes a great resistant weight!

● Once they begin to crawl around, they love to chase after toys and balls you can throw about for them while you are bouncing.

● Plan your post-natal sessions to strengthen your back, and tone your tummy.

● If you slowly work to recover your strength and mobility you should be ready to step up onto your bouncer again, around six weeks following the birth.

● In the first few weeks following birth, you can use your bouncer to stimulate lymphatic drainage and to massage your breasts. Any movements up until the six week mark, should take place with your feet flat to the mat in the Rhythm Bounce.

TOPICAL TIPS

❶ Keep all routines simple to begin with.

❷ Begin every session with Perfect Pelvic Pinching.

❸ Always empty your bladder before bouncing.

❹ Initially use one-star techniques with single-foot strike landings.

❺ All of your organs and systems are readjusting to the additional G-Force, so build up gradually.

❻ Use techniques from other Starbound programmes.

PLUM TUMS

Don't despair if your tummy doesn't return immediately to the streamline shape you once knew. It takes six weeks for your uterus to contract back to normal size, and then you have to allow for toning and tightening.

You have four layers of muscles forming your Granny's Corset:

● 2 superficial muscles – running up and down.

● 2 pairs of obliques, internal and external.

● 1 pair of transverse abdominal muscles.

Because muscles are weakest in front, as they stretch throughout pregnancy, your linea alba – a thin band of fibrous tissue, which is normally about half-an-inch-wide – softens. Later in pregnancy, your recti abdomini often separate, removing the support they normally offer your back.

BABY BACK ZIPPER

This is an excellent sequence to follow when you are feeling the tension in your upper back and shoulders, due to the extra strain of carrying your baby about with you.

● Sit on the bouncer rim, legs apart, feet flat to the floor.

● Slowly lean forward, allowing your head and arms to hang loosely.

● Keep your breathing full and even, into your abdomen, contracting your tummy at the end of each exhalation.

BACKSTOP!

It is always a good idea, around eight weeks following birth, to have an osteopath check the balance of your back and pelvic areas. Especially if you have given birth reclining, your pelvic bones have been forced apart by the passage of your baby's head. This may inhibit your joints from working to full capacity while increasing the possibility of osteopathic lesioning in your lower back.

DON'T BREAK YOUR BACK

❶ Constantly remind yourself to check your posture throughout the day and when you exercise.
❷ Remember to breathe as fully as possible utilizing techniques from Totally Breathtaking (p. 135).
❸ Carry your baby in a sling, centrally on your front or back, to avoid loading the weight to one side.
❹ Your sacroiliac joint is often the site of niggling tension in your back. Use Camel Humps, Swiss Roll and Around the Bend (pp. 158–9).
❺ As you strengthen those abdominal muscles you provide the firmest possible support for your back. Practise Abdominal Doming and Granny's Corset.

PERFECT PELVIC PINCHING

When you are on the move again, you can practise your Perfect Pelvic Pinching anywhere. You will find it helpful to practise Perfect Pelvic Pinching if you are about to sneeze or cough, as an extra safeguard against leakage. When you are ready to bounce again, always practise this technique at the beginning of every bouncing session, remembering to empty your bladder beforehand.

❶ Imagine a string running up through your vagina, anus and urethra, towards your navel.
❷ Pull in and up with your pelvic muscles, tightening your grip on this imaginary string.
❸ Hold the tension for a count of 3, then slowly release your tension on these muscles.

❹ Remember, it is contraction followed by relaxation that strengthens these muscles.
❺ Repeat in sets × 8 throughout the day, gradually building up the number of pinches you perform at any one time.

Back on Your Bouncer

Following your six week check, you will be ready for more bouncy action. There are a few considerations to bear in mind, to make your transition back to bouncing a successful one. Most new mothers feel immense frustration trying to fit 'exercise time' into their new schedule. A bouncer in the house means you can make the most of even a few minutes at a time. This is often all you need to lift your mood and balance your emotional responses.

FLUTTER LEGS ▾

Lie on your tummy on the bouncer, with hips flat and aligned, resting on your elbows to support your upper body, hands holding the rim. Exhale as you lift your right leg, keeping your hip flat. Inhale, returning to starting position. Repeat alternating legs. As you lift, keep your head released, with your chin tucked into your chest, remembering not to lift too high.

RAZOR BLADES ▸

Tummy flattener and waist wittler.
Lie back on the bouncer, bend your knees with your feet on the rim. Exhale as you slide your right hand toward your right foot, bending in from your waist. Hold for a count of 3 and repeat. Hold your tummy in as you slide forward, releasing as you relax the contraction.

● Although these techniques are perfect for post-natal recovery, they can be used at any time within your Starbound Workout.

Better Breasts

Your body is designed not only for giving birth, but to provide nourishment through breast-feeding. Research leads to the obvious conviction that 'breast is best', not just for baby, but for you as well.

Breast-feeding will aid your role of mothering in many ways. Apart from the naturally close physical bond it creates between mother and baby, breast-feeding secures the release of many hormones to help you get on with the job. Not only do breast-fed babies have a healthy sense of security about them, but they are offered extra protection from illness and infection.

Your breasts are mainly fatty tissue, with a little glandular tissue tucked away. As your pregnancy progresses, your breasts enlarge along with milk-producing glands. Wear a good supporting bra throughout pregnancy, and for as long as necessary after the birth.

SLOW MILK FLOW

If your milk flow is low, try not to worry. Anxiety is only going to make matters worse. Follow some deep breathing and relaxation techniques, check your diet, and gently bounce throughout the day. If necessary consult your practitioner for advice.

❶ Fennel tea stimulates milk production. Lemongrass tea and essential oils are also ideal stimulants.
❷ Bathe in 5 drops of essential oil of lemongrass.
❸ Press your reflexes to stimulate lactation.
❹ Check that you are feeding your baby fully. If you are removing the baby from the breast too soon, you will diminish your supplies.

LYMPHATIC LACTATIONS

Your breasts are loaded with lymphatics. The vessels must be constantly drained to avoid a backflow from building up in your valves, so keep them well exercised at all times.

To nourish your baby well, you have to keep lymph on the move. Fat cells, in themselves, are the perfect warehouses for toxins, which are released into your circulation as fat supplies are called upon as sources for lactation. If you bounce your way through breast-feeding, you literally clear the debris that will otherwise influence the quality of your milk supplies.

As bouncing keeps lymph and fluids on the move in your breasts, the balance of your hormonal input and production will be stimulated. Your moods are more likely to be relaxed and positive and your immune function will definitely be primed for better performance.

WEIGHTY WEANINGS

If you wait for the right time and allow breast-feeding to come to a natural end, it shouldn't be a traumatic experience for either you or your baby. When you do stop feeding, hormonal patterns will swing for a while, as your system readjusts.

It is helpful if you continue to stimulate and massage your breasts to keep your circulation on the move. A baby naturally ravages the breasts in the latter stages of breast-feeding, which in itself, offers natural protection to the mother, helping to empty the smaller vessels, preventing lymph and fluids from stagnating.

It is a good idea, when weaning, to stay on a very low intake of saturated fats.

● When you are weaning, use your bouncer. In the Rhythm Bounce, massage your breasts, on the sides by your ribs, into the centre and upward at the same time.
● Support your right breast, cupped between your thumb and index finger. With your left hand, begin massaging in small circular motions, working from your shoulder, into your armpit, and then out, around your breast, up towards your collarbone. Repeat to the other side.
● Practise elbow presses and pectoral presses (p. 99). Squeeze your elbows together in front of your chest, then release your arms to your sides at shoulder level. Repeat × 8.
● Include a variety of techniques for mobilizing your shoulders and neck.

● Try to practise mobility and stretch techniques every few hours.
● Any techniques using controlled arm movements will help to stimulate movement of fluid in your upper body. Peccy Presses, Curlylocks, Swivel Hinge, Horses in the Stable and Breaststroke (pp. 99–101) are all excellent techniques to help keep your breasts healthy.

TOPICAL TIPS

DRENCHING DEPRESSION

If you happen to be among the 10% of new mothers who suffer from severe post-natal depression, your Starbound programmes should help you regain control. Feelings of exhaustion are often triggered by an imbalanced intake of nutrients in your diet, as well as malnourishment on social, mental and emotional levels. An accompanying lack of oxygen can make things a lot cloudier on a grey day.

Natural inertia weighs us down and it is even more difficult to overcome when you are stressed or depressed. Rather than fighting an uphill battle, let your bouncer take you for a ride! Head for the bouncer before you start indulging in tranquillizers. Feelings of depression and aggression are often related to your hormonal swings and reaction to stress. A bounce will release your aggression, lethargy and unhappiness, clearing your circulation of hormonal residue, that may be bathing your body cells. You will immediately receive a lift in spirits as you bounce.

❶ Treat yourself to some essential oil of jasmine. It is a wonderful spirit lifter as well as a natural tranquillizer.

❷ Relax in a bath, containing 3 drops of jasmine and 3 drops of geranium, for a perfect pick-me-up.

❸ Press your reflexes for the glands (p. 32).

3

A BONNY BABY!

A NATURAL BOUNCER

Babies are probably the most naturally energetic of us all. When not asleep, they are in a state of constant frenetic motion, using all of their muscles for a purpose. With a baby in the house, you'll soon discover your bouncer is the most versatile piece of nursery equipment at your disposal. Many a grizzly baby has been calmed from colic and teething pangs, thanks to a gentle bounce. As your baby moves in unison with the rhythm of your own body, coupled with the natural rhythm set up from the bouncer, the calming influence that it exerts has been hailed as close to miraculous by many grateful parents.

In the womb, you were aware of pulsating rhythms, as you moved to and fro, gently bouncing around in a safe and protected environment of fluid. A new baby who is rocked and cradled is always more content than one who lies bound in stifling stillness.

ROCKABYE BABY

When you use the bouncer to help calm your baby down, you relax yourself and unwind at the same time. Have you noticed that your baby often seems to get wound up just at that point in the day when you are losing your tether? This is the perfect time for you to spend a couple of minutes on your bouncer practising cross-crawl techniques from Brainy Blitz (p. 144), before you let your brain go into 'overload'.

When you need to use your bouncer to 'rock-a-bye baby', the following hints may be helpful.

Stand in the Rhythm Bounce gently setting up a motion. Rock and hum softly to your baby, gently swaying in time with the motion. Gently massage your baby's back at the same time.

BACKRUBBER ▾
Sit on the bouncer, with your baby lying along your legs on his tummy. Gently bend his legs so they are in the frog position, feet facing in and knees opening out. This helps to ease any abdominal discomfort he may be feeling. Set up a gentle rhythm, by moving the bouncer base. Gently rub and massage his back.

TWISTIES
Stand on the bouncer, moving gently in the Rhythm Bounce. With your baby held firmly against your chest and on your shoulder, gently massage his back while you twist from left to right.

DISTRACTING PLOYS

When absolutely all else is failing and you are at your wits end, grab your baby and gently bounce! It is often just the shock to the system they need to stop them in their tracks. Often the change in rhythm, and general distraction, is enough to focus their attention away from the discomfort.

Your bouncer is also the perfect nappy changing surface. With a towel or plastic mat thrown over the surface, changing time becomes a treat, not a trauma. When the grizzles begin, you can bounce them away.

BABY GYMNASIUM

Before your baby becomes a champion on the bouncer, he will spend many happy hours using the frame as a base to pull up from. Before you know it, he'll be walking around it, climbing onto it, and learning a host of skills. As long as he is well supervised and the springs are well covered, it won't be long before baby is teaching you a thing or two. Babies love to bounce on their bottoms, and when they are strong enough to stand, they love to hold your hands and dance a little jig on the bouncer mat.

4

BOUNCY OFFSPRING

LEAPS AND BOUNDS

When bouncing is encouraged as a natural activity at home, children move forward in leaps and bounds. They establish natural patterns for channelling energy supplies, while acquiring skills through play which reinforce brain balance, coordination and learning reflexes. Better nerve and muscle coordination will prove an additional bonus as moods and immune systems sustain their natural high!

LIFE INSURANCE

The best insurance policy you can take out on behalf of your children is to provide them with a quality foundation for a healthy future. Changing behaviour is no easy task, so setting patterns which lead to positive lifelong habits, relating to exercise, is your responsibility as a parent.

PARAMOUNT PRIORITIES

Are your children suffering through a lack of regular physical activity? Physical education is placed at the bottom of the list for many schools when they assess priorities in reference to the curriculum. At home, millions of children spend far too many hours glued to the television.

Children of all ages need year-round opportunities for regular physical exercise. This should include aerobic training, at least three times a week, for over twenty minutes a session. The majority of children in their pre-teens spend only a few minutes each day in activities that are vigorous enough for them to reach their aerobic target values.

HYPERACTIVITY? HYPOACTIVITY!

While the catch-phrase of the eighties bandied about over cups of tea was 'hyperactive', the concern for the nineties should more realistically be 'hypoactive'. On average over 60% of children spend most of their time in a state of 'hypoactivity' with heart rates of less than 110 beats per minute. Nearly 40% of their time passes by in so-called moderate activity, with heart rates less than 160 beats per minute, still failing to produce the required conditioning effect for sound health.

BUNDLES OF BLAME

Bundles of extra energy needn't be a negative sign. 'Hyperactivity' is a term coined to cover a multitude of sins, from head-banging in toddlers, to tantrums in ten-year-olds. Not enough thought rests with the fact that hyperactivity is an essential element of a natural lifestyle. Our children are dealing with chemical exposures in large cities, foods laced with toxins and numerous artificial ingredients, and other triggers leading to nutritional deficiencies. But unnatural recreational practice, with a simple lack of hyped-up activity at the top of the list, is the very weight that tips the scales and disturbs the balance.

POSITIVE PARAMETERS

Children love to work to positive parameters. So that you keep their enthusiasm fired, you have to be sure to provide a 'do' for every 'don't' you issue. If you have to deliver the warning, 'Don't jump on that bed' be prepared instead, to offer the positive alternative of 'Jump on your bouncer!'

Hours of fun and positive expression will be enjoyed by your children over the years as they bounce.

Rather than busting the bedsprings, and having their instinctive urges to bounce squashed at an early age, offer your children the encouragement and channel to release their energy and vent their expression as the needs arise.

Childhood is crucial for laying down healthy cells, bones, tissues and patterns of circulation, all of which develop rapidly. Nothing short of healthy doses of oxygen, balanced supplies of nutrients and regular

● Inactivity in childhood and early life, fuels the risk of ill health. Recent surveys reveal that if a park is more than ten minutes walking distance from her home base, a mother won't reach it with her small children.

● Children naturally and spontaneously jump every day if there is a bouncer available. Amazing benefits can be tapped in line with their levels of fitness, motor and learning skills, and their health in general.

bouts of activity, provide the stimulus for the development of healthy frames.

Children love to bounce in class to tap a common group rhythm. Many children who can't beat time in an ordinary floor class, suddenly emerge confidently and in tune on their bouncers. Simple skills like 'step, clap, turn around, step, clap', fall into place on the bouncer, in an instant, whereas they might take months in a similar learning situation on the floor.

CATCHING CRAZES

The teenagers, who carry the craze wave along, are right up there on their bouncers. I spend many a happy hour with my younger friends, choreographing routines, getting them familiar with the 'bouncing high', as we call it. Parents experience a great sigh of elation as teenagers in the household take to the bouncing blitz. From jazzy jives and jolly jingles to the latest wave in rap rhythm, there's a beat to get every teenager on the bounce.

PUBERTY BLUES

The activity of very early childhood is blotted out too quickly as we are expected to buckle under at school and prove our scholarly capabilities. The need to move is suppressed, and often completely wiped out.

Teenage years are notorious for spotty skin and emotional confusion. Both relate to hormonal imbalances due to insufficient circulation and glandular metabolism. As hormones become trapped in circulation, stagnating tissue fluids and lymphatics become breeding grounds for debris and bacteria that seek escape through the skin. The resolution plans offer the perfect foundations for the eradication of these problems. Within six weeks following the necessary dietary changes, accompanied by regular bouncing programmes, spotty skins can become a thing of the past. While bouncing teenagers tell of relief at the improved appearance of their skin, relieved parents marvel at the change of tune in their moods!

STUDY BREAKS

Spells of study can be perfectly interspersed with a bouncing tune-up.

● Practise cross-crawl techniques to get both sides of the brain working in unison (p. 144).

● Include some breathing techniques (p. 115) into your sessions combined with techniques for mobilizing shoulders and the upper back. When you are studying for exams these seem to be the areas that take the most strain.

● Take a bouncing break every forty-five minutes.

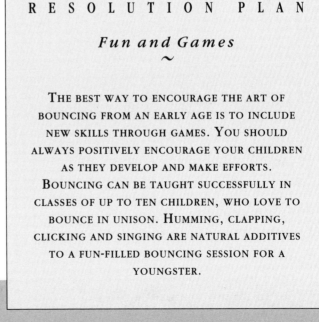

> ### RESOLUTION PLAN
>
> *Fun and Games*
> ~
>
> THE BEST WAY TO ENCOURAGE THE ART OF BOUNCING FROM AN EARLY AGE IS TO INCLUDE NEW SKILLS THROUGH GAMES. YOU SHOULD ALWAYS POSITIVELY ENCOURAGE YOUR CHILDREN AS THEY DEVELOP AND MAKE EFFORTS. BOUNCING CAN BE TAUGHT SUCCESSFULLY IN CLASSES OF UP TO TEN CHILDREN, WHO LOVE TO BOUNCE IN UNISON. HUMMING, CLAPPING, CLICKING AND SINGING ARE NATURAL ADDITIVES TO A FUN-FILLED BOUNCING SESSION FOR A YOUNGSTER.

EXPLORING SPACE

❶ In a class or as individuals, children love to explore their own potential to move in space.

❷ Always encourage correct posture and body alignment as they move, so they can refine their skills.

❸ As with any other activity, they have to learn and practise new skills until they become perfected. You can devise many games and activities to help strengthen their confidence and enthusiasm.

ACTION RHYMES

Be creative and devise your own games to emphasize skills. Choreograph them into simple routines and action songs. Work with children to devise their own rhymes and movements.

The following are examples of action rhymes my six-year-old daughter frequently enjoys.

BOUNCING BALL

I CAN JUMP HIGH LIKE A BOUNCING BALL.
(Bouncing high)
I REACH FOR THE SKY AS I GROW VERY TALL.
(Opening arms in a circle, fingers outstretched)
WHEN I COME BACK TOMMY TIPPY TOES,
(Into the Ballet Step)
I BECOME MICKEY MOUSE
(Looping hands to ears to make big ears)
WITH A BALL ON MY NOSE.
(Free dance with knee lifts clocking the mat)

CLAP AND CLICK

CLAP YOUR HANDS 1, 2, 3
(In Rhythm Bounce)
CLAP AND CLICK AS YOU SPIN WITH ME.
(Tap each foot in 1/4 turns progressing to clicking fingers at the same time)
CLAP YOUR HANDS 1, 2, 3
(Stepping onto the ground)
CLICK AS YOU CLIMB THE MONKEY'S TREE
(Climb onto the bouncer making monkey sounds)

JACK IN THE BOX

JUMP LIKE JACK WITH LEGS SO WIDE.
(Jumping Jacks)
QUICKLY JUMP FROM YOUR BOX.
(Big high jumps)
NOW RUN AND HIDE.
(Run and hide)

CLAPPING RHYTHMS

Either in a group or with a single child:

● Establish a bouncing routine so that feet are marking time.

● When they have settled into the footwork, clap a simple pattern that they can imitate.

● Next, they have a turn to clap a pattern for you.

● The game goes on with patterns being clapped and repeated back.

● You can make the game trickier by having everyone follow the footwork of the leader as well.

I SPY...

As you bounce, take it in turns to play I Spy, choosing objects from two different levels in the room.

● Vary the game, spying objects by their letter, colour or substance (animal, mineral or vegetable).

● If there is only one bouncer available, the person who guesses correctly moves to the bouncer. Adapt your rules to suit the situation. It is quite easy to have a group of ten children and only one bouncer and still to facilitate positive learning.

FAIR BALL!

There is a lot of fun to be had with a ball. Try using different sized beach balls as you bounce. They offer perfect bouncing speed and are safe to use indoors. Make up new rules for each game you play.

● Throw the ball to each other, seeing how far you can count before the ball is dropped by someone.

● As with the above, but use the alphabet instead of numbers.

● You can always recite the times tables, to the rhythm of the bouncer, which the children seem to really love.

● Play donkey, with children in a circle; each time the ball is dropped, the child gains a letter; after six drops the word 'donkey' is spelt and the child is out.

● Make up simple coordination games. Perhaps, throw the ball, clap your hands and turn around, ready for the return catch.

MINI AEROBICS

● Use your bouncer as part of a mini-aerobic circuit for the children, either inside or in the garden. Set up a course that the children can follow.

● They seem to enjoy marking themselves against time.

● If they can read you can write their instructions down, listing the activities.

● Be creative when choosing the other activities to form the circuit. You might like to include: ping pong balls to be thrown into a small bin; skipping activities; 'french elastic', placing a joined strip of elastic between two chairs, or children; throwing hoops onto a stand; rolling a ball into a bucket on its side.

TREASURE HUNT

Another favourite game to keep the children occupied for hours is to devise a bouncing treasure hunt.

● On each clue there are bouncing routines to perform before hunting the next clue.

● Make the instructions clear on the clues and plant them around the house or the garden.

● All kinds of tempting prizes can lie at the end of the hunt, but keep them healthy or you are defeating the purpose.

BRAIN BOXES

Include cross-crawl techniques and routines in your child's programmes as well as skills for visual stimulation.

● They can play Magic Paintbrush sketching with the paintbrush attached to the tip of their nose as they bounce. Rather than you dictating what to draw, make it a guessing game. They draw and you guess!

● Blinking games can be fun, and coordinated with alphabet learning. For example, recite ABC, blink, DEF, blink, and so on.

● Encourage games that help children loosen their tight spots and tensions. Help by playing, cuddling and tickling the tensions away.

BOUNCING BOUNDARIES

● So the bouncer can be used safely certain rules have to be stated loud and clear, to create defined boundaries, and prevent accidents, or misunderstandings. These are:

● Always bounce to the centre of the mat, never on the spring cover.

● Only one child on the bouncer at a time.

● Jumping from the bouncer to other furniture, or vice versa, is an invitation to injury.

● Never bounce in socks, tights or slippery shoes.

● Never bounce if you have food or chewing gum in your mouth.

● Your bouncer is not a trampoline and no acrobatic tricks should be performed.

● Any of the safety pointers that apply for adults apply for children as well (p. 26).

SENIOR CITIZENS

TIPPLE ON OXYGEN

Don't doze your latterdays away! Whatever your age, it's never too late to start improving the quality of your health. If your incentive to 'get up and go' has become dampened, it's likely the quantity of oxygen you need to keep you inspired has also diminished accordingly.

Research reveals that the ability of your organs to function gets progressively worse, after the age of thirty, at a rate of about 5% every ten years. This falls right in line with an associated decrease in activity and the corresponding depletion of rich supplies of life-giving oxygen.

PRIDE AND PURPOSE

Elderly folk often need encouragement to find the purpose to remain active, which in turn will help prevent many illnesses and ailments from creeping in. To reap the benefit of a ripe old age, you need to remain mentally sharp and physically alert. Although 'elderly' is a term that officially refers to those in society over the age of sixty-five, many qualify much earlier, due to disease and discomfort. It is usually the case that those who enjoy bright and breezy health until late in life, have remained busy in purpose, with a well-balanced spectrum of exercise, food and social interaction.

WHAT GIVES?

Over 45% of the elderly suffer problems with muscles and bones. An alarming 65% are plagued with problems concerning hearing and vision. It's also disturbing that over 20% lose control of their urinary functions in the latter days of their life. The list of baffling statistics includes a frightening 27% of senior citizens ending their days with cognitive difficulties, such as Alzheimers disease. Brain functions slow down mainly due to an inhibited lack of oxygen to the central nervous system. Old people's residences and hospital wards often reflect the complete depression of spirit and mind that many of our elderly endure. As the mind and nerves cloud up the body has no choice but to slowly degenerate. Many people rust up before they wear out, due to a simple lack of spirit, love, activity and true purpose in their lives.

BOUNCING BACK

Many elderly people have turned the quality of their lives around with a simple daily bounce. Heart and soul return to many residences for the elderly when bouncing units are placed in recreation rooms.

Sheer enthusiasm is reflected in hundreds of letters I have received. The health and fitness of many has blossomed as they have bounced back to a fullness of energy and vitality. These comments from Esther Reiger, of Auckland, New Zealand, in her mid-eighties, reflect her appreciation of the new surge of energy she has mustered all thanks to her bouncer:

'When recovering from major surgery, following my eighty-third birthday, my son gave me a bouncer. I started with the Rhythm Walk just a few minutes at a time, several times a day. I use a balance bar because my balance isn't one hundred per cent. I am now walking an hour with a group, before lunch, and the same amount of time afterwards. At last I am fit and well, finally enjoying life. Age is no barrier to bouncing. Doing rhythmical exercises to music keeps me supple.'

Perhaps the most touching comment I have received was from an elderly grandmother. She was delighted that the lump on her leg which had bothered her for years was finally vanishing, her double chin was disappearing and she was thankfully able to sleep through the night, due to a little bounce before she retired. However, the thing that impressed her beyond all else, was that her grandchildren loved bouncing as much as she did! Bouncing is a form of exercise that can finally bridge the generation gap.

BRILLIANT BALANCE

● Perfecting your balance requires the development of skills. If you need support use a balance bar.

● Either face the bar, holding it as you perform your techniques, or turn side on to the bar holding it with one hand which leaves the other free for movement.

● Any movements performed to one side should be repeated to the other side so turn and hold the bar with your other hand.

● Remember your posture. Keep your back straight, abdomen gently contracted and buttocks tucked slightly throughout. Shoulders should be relaxed, elbows soft and hands released while you hold the bar for balance.

TOPICAL TIPS

● If you haven't been active for many years, take it very gently. It is better to use your bouncer for a few minutes at a time, gently easing your body back into more vigorous activity. Many elderly people prefer to simply walk on the bouncer mat, using it as a treadmill, than to actually bounce. As you hold the balance bar, begin by walking for a few minutes. If you want to add some double-foot strike landings, stay low to the mat in one-star Rhythm Bounce techniques.

● Many elderly people prefer to bounce in groups. Gather a few friends and meet in each other's homes, or use a local hall. You can chat away, using your balance bars for support, if necessary.

● Remember to plan your session according to the required programme structure. Always include a complete warm-up and stretch routine into your sessions.

● Include stimulation of your reflexes, especially if you suffer any niggling ailments.

● Include other exercises from Starbound programmes. You will find great peace and strength when practising relaxation and release techniques. Keep a rug close by for when you are relaxing at the end of a session, so that you stay warm and comfortable.

● Use your Starbound programmes to spark the spring in your step. If you are worried about your balance, or feel extremely stiff, start out bouncing with a balance bar for support.

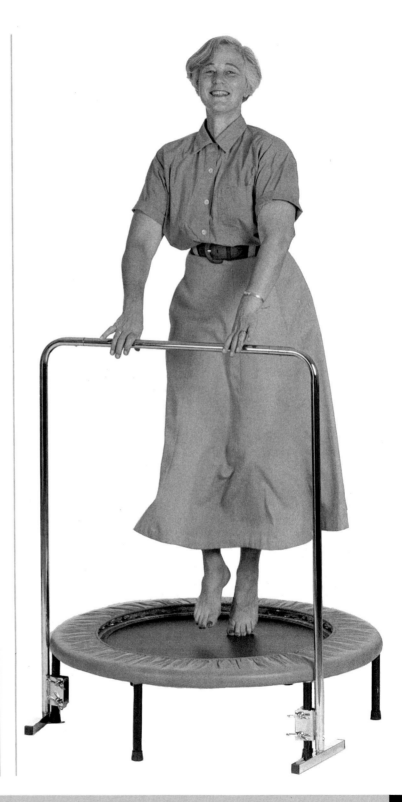

● When using a bar keep your routines low. Roll through your feet with a toe-ball-heel strike keeping your knees soft when you land.

● Learn to assess the intensity of the session by becoming familiar with the Borg Scale of Perceived Exertion (p. 49).

● If you suffer high blood pressure never perform conditioning techniques with your head lower than your heart. Always change the position of your body from horizontal to vertical very gradually.

As you bounce numerous benefits to your well-being accrue, offering your body an extraordinary power for regeneration and rejuvenation. Many people have switched to bouncing to keep disease at bay and have experienced relief as colds, allergies, menstrual discomforts and other niggling complaints gradually disappear. Many who have suffered chronic disorders report remarkable improvements thanks to consistent bouncing every day. The following A to Z outlines tips to help you with specific illnesses and problems you may be experiencing. However, the range of ailments helped through your bouncing programmes is by no means limited to those I have selected here. There are many steps you will take if you want the words in this book to empower your life and work in your favour. The first step is a simple one – the step you need to take each day up onto your bouncer.

ACHING JOINTS

Many people suffer aching joints on waking. Circulation has been sluggish overnight, wastes have accumulated and oxygen supply to your tissues has been reduced. Accumulations of waste deposits around your joints must be removed.

Topical Tips
● Bounce gently in the Rhythm Bounce and also in the Pulse Base (p. 128) ● Use essential oils of eucalyptus, ginger, juniper and lavender ● Stay with predominantly alkaline foods (p. 115)
● Start the day with a Lemon Zinger (p. 118)
● Reduce tea and coffee to one cup a day.

ADDICTION

Whatever the addiction the use of gentle techniques to stimulate the removal of toxins is a definite bonus. Although the following outline is specifically geared to breaking the cigarette chain, it can be adapted for numerous other addictive withdrawal programmes.

It is easy to begin smoking, twice as easy to become addicted, and yet not nearly as easy to kick the habit. With your bouncing programmes as support, to help you through the transition period, you can ring the changes.

The first thing to do is to decide on your plan of action. Are you going to give up in an instant or are you going to gradually cut back, until cigarettes are no longer worthy of consideration? You have to find the approach that suits your present habits, personality and lifestyle. Remember to ease your body through transition, rather than strain it. Give yourself definite supports that you know will help you through the tempting moments. You will be dealing with surfacing toxins. The following pointers should help.

Visualization Support
When you replace your smoking habits with more positive patterns, use this visualization format whenever you feel the need to focus on your intentions.
● Bounce for a few minutes to centre and free your breathing patterns ● Enter a state of relaxation in Innerspaces (p. 132) ● Travel back in your mind to the time when you first began to smoke. Visualize the scene, recall associated memories. Why were you smoking? How did you feel? ● Focus on reasons that prompted you to develop your habit ● At the end of each visualization, contemplate what you want to achieve. Visualize your body and mind free from all attachment to cigarettes ● When you withdraw from the meditation, bounce for a few minutes to bring your awareness back to deep and full breathing.

Topical Tips
● Bounce and gently stimulate the reflex zones for your lungs (p. 32) ● As you bounce: elimination of wastes and toxins from your system is sped up; fluid uptake of your lymphatics increases, helping to prevent the fluid retention that often appears when withdrawing from cigarettes; you absorb more oxygen and accelerate the release of the wastes; depending on the height, speed and amount of effort you put into each bounce, your lungs will function at a corresponding plateau; both the volume you inhale and exhale will increase, ensuring swifter removal of wastes and toxins from your system; chemical triggers of your addiction can be brought under control as you refresh your circulation; hormonal production and blood sugar levels are stabilized, helping to strengthen your physical and mental outlook.

Balancing Fluids
When you stop smoking you may experience extreme bloating in your abdomen. Your body is retaining fluid to surround and dilute poisons that are being released into your system. Because you can only eliminate a certain amount at any one time the fluid remains to cushion your systems from the toxic load. The longer you have smoked the longer the load is likely to take to disperse.

● The more you bounce the faster the elimination of these toxins occurs ● Any additional weight you have gained is not only due to a higher food intake, but also to the increased build up of fluid throughout your body ● The toxic load is removed as you guard your food and fluid intake cautiously, combined with regular bouncing ● Bounce your way through craving moments. They are brought under control as you raise your circulation and dose up on oxygen, both of which will help to remove chemical triggers from your brain ● Plan a careful combination of food and fluid to balance toxins and melt the cravings away ● Always start the day with a Lemon Zinger (p. 118). If you are feeling an acidic reaction in your stomach, this will help ease you through and rebalance your system ● Distilled water, fruit and vegetable juices are the best spring cleaners ● Alpine and herb teas may be helpful if you suffer any constipation throughout the withdrawal period. ● Drink fluid between bouncing sessions.

Food
● Once a week you will benefit by following one of the simple cleansing regimes from Detox. Dimensions (p. 111). Design your food and fluid intake from your Five-Star Files (p. 116) ● As you withdraw from cigarettes your system will become more acidic. Plan to eat a predominantly alkaline menu (p. 115). Celery, lettuce, cucumbers and peppers plus any of your basic 'rabbit' foods are excellent snacks. Not only are they highly alkaline but they also contain a high water content to flush your tissues. Munch on them whenever you are tempted to smoke ● Stock up on all supplies of Vitamin C. Good food sources: currants, citrus fruits, fresh vegetables, kiwi fruit, sprouts, milk ● Fruit is a powerful cleansing agent. Always keep an apple in your pocket ● Cut back on: coffee, tea, sweets, white flour products, red meats. They are all acid forming and will hinder elimination of toxins from your system ● Use your bouncer several times a day in short bursts ● Bounce in your target zones at least three times a week, to improve the functioning of your heart and lungs ● Stroke zones for your elimination organs at least twice daily (p. 109) ● Incorporate techniques into your sessions that activate your breathing patterns (p. 115) ● Choose supports to nurture yourself with throughout transition. Use Time-Out periods to reaffirm your intentions ● While you are in the early stages of withdrawal, stroke the lymphatic reflex zone for your spleen (p. 33).

AIDS
(Acquired Immune Deficiency Syndrome)

A person carrying the H.I.V. virus cannot cope with a host of infections, which weaken immune response and cause immune system damage. A weakened immune system is likely to fall prey to a host of other diseases. Stress, poor food intake and lack of exercise are major factors to counteract, to ensure the immune system stays on top.

Topical Tips

● Bounce daily with several small sessions to keep your circulation on the move ● Refer to Immune Response (p. 184) ● Stroke lymphatic reflex zones daily (p. 30) ● Use Flower Power (p. 133) and essential oils to balance your response to emotional trauma and upset ● Follow your Five-Star Plan for Triumphant Transformation (p. 113) ● Plan Time-Out sessions for meditation, relaxation and prayer (p. 128).

ALCOHOL

Alcohol is a carbohydrate and will have the same effect on your body as sugar, causing a speedy rise and fall in your sugar metabolism. Unknowingly, many alcoholics use alcohol to treat a low level of blood sugar. The associated high occurs when blood sugar is raised.

Topical Tips

● As your body processes alcohol it releases toxins, which need to be eliminated. Bounce, but not while you are directly under the influence of alcohol ● As alcohol is processed in your liver, enzymes need a consistent supply of vitamin B1 to perform their duties. Good food sources: wholemeal bread, nuts, beans, pasta, wholegrains, liver, pork ● Continuous consumption of alcohol will overburden your liver and kidneys, and deplete your zinc and magnesium supplies; this in turn strains your heart and weakens nerves. Good food sources – zinc: lean meats, fish, oysters, beans, wholegrains, eggs; magnesium: nuts, soya beans, milk, fish, green vegetables, wholegrain cereals ● For a hangover use essential oil of rose. Drink several glasses of water throughout the day. Bounce several times stroking the zones for your elimination organs (p. 109) ● If you are withdrawing from alcohol seek the support of a group such as A.A. Consult a health practitioner, who can guide your food and fluid consumption ● Draw up a food plan to counteract the chemical changes you are facing in transit: high protein foods are excellent if you are craving a drink; tomato, vegetable and fruit juices also raise your blood sugar level, but are released slowly into your cells; avoid all refined carbohydrates and sugars.

ALLERGIES

Allergies are hypersensitive reactions of particularly the digestive and immune systems to a variety of substances. Such disorders are extremely common. Hayfever, sinusitis, hypoglycemia, fluid retention, migraines, skin rashes and asthma are among the symptoms that often surface due to allergic response.

Topical Tips

● Several times daily, bounce for a few minutes in the Rhythm Bounce stroking the reflexes for your glands (p. 30) ● Stroke lymphatic reflex zones regularly to enhance immune function.

ALZHEIMER'S DISEASE

Regular bouncing will positively influence anyone who is suffering with this condition (or pre-senile dementia). As mental functions deteriorate, behaviour changes according to fluctuations in mental state. Causes may range from slow viral infections to high levels of toxins, especially from aluminium. This is known to be highly toxic to your nervous system and is likely to produce changes in your brain structure.

Topical Tips

● Adapt techniques from Brainy Blitz into bounce sessions (p. 144) ● Check levels of B12 in your diet. Good food sources: liver, meat, sprouts, fish, milk ● Avoid cooking in aluminium ● The very elderly or unstable will need to use a balance bar for support.

ANAEMIA

Iron is stored in and released from your spleen, which lies under your heart to the left of your abdomen. Your spleen is an important immune organ and is strongly linked to the workings of your lymphatics. As you bounce, the stimulation of your spleen is boosted, your lymphatics are powerfully activated, and the additional supplies of oxygen-rich blood will work to ensure better nutrient absorption. Vitamin B1 and iron are often in short supply in cases of anaemia. Iron is best absorbed in the presence of Vitamin C and is essential for the transfer and transport of oxygen. With the average diet containing only 75% of the required iron, iron deficiency is thought to be the world's most common form of nutritional starvation. Often associated with learning difficulties and behavioural problems in children, low levels of iron also become a cause of concern when a woman is pregnant.

Topical Tips

● Don't drink coffee with your meals. One cup of coffee reduces the absorption of iron by up to 40%.

If you suffer from iron deficiency, stay away from coffee for an hour before a meal and wait at least two hours following a meal ● Check sources of iron in your diet. Good food sources: meat, liver, seafood, egg yolk, legumes, nuts, cereals ● Combine your iron intake with Vitamin C. Good food sources: citrus fruits, currants, milk, fresh vegetables, sprouts ● Stroke reflexes for your spleen, twice daily. Use the neurovascular reflex zone programme daily (p. 141).

ANAL FISSURES

More common than you would think, recurring anal fissures plague the comfort of many, often coinciding with bouts of constipation.

Topical Tips

● Use a sitz bath with 5 drops of cypress and 3 drops of lavender, every time you pass a bowel motion or urinate ● Bounce very gently to stimulate the peristaltic action of your intestines, pressing your neurovascular reflexes for constipation ● Perfect Pelvic Pinches will help to strengthen the muscles of your pelvic floor (p. 164).

ANOREXIA NERVOSA

Every effort must be made to convince anyone you suspect is suffering from anorexia nervosa, or any other eating disorder, to seek medical attention and therapy. In serious cases anorexia is usually complicated by great emotional confusion, and can lead to severe starvation and even death. Bulimia is another food related disorder, in which the sufferer overeats and then vomits, or purges the system with laxatives to get rid of food.

Internal organ injury is a regular feature of both anorexia and bulimia, resulting in an upset electrolyte balance. People with these problems often feel a lack of control over the patterns in their lives, or are afraid to accept control. Self-denial or the repression of emotions are known to coincide with an urge to remain child-like.

Distorted eating habits – these include periodic starvation and compulsive eating – need to be replaced with more positive patterns. Within therapeutic rehabilitation, bouncing programmes can be very positive, helping reset the internal rhythm of organs, and their functions. Digestive organs are gently coerced back into operation, while internal massage plays its role.

Topical Tips

● Stroke reflexes for your glands (p. 30)
● Use techniques from Spacing Stress Out (p. 128) ● Aim to bounce gently as you rebuild your strength. Use reflex and sound work to re-establish your inner enthusiasm.

177

APPENDICITIS

Few people suffer from appendicitis or diverticulitis, where inflamed pockets in the gut cause irritation, if food is unrefined. Appendicitis involves the small tube-like appendix becoming blocked with faeces, inviting inflammation and infection. If you suffer severe grumbling rumbles, you know the time has come to take matters in hand before acute conditions set in.

Topical Tips

● Bounce gently in the Rhythm Bounce, stroking zones for elimination organs (p. 109) and colon (p. 33) ● Eliminate most refined foods from your diet ● Create new food habits based on the Five-Star Plan (p. 113) ● Plan your menu to include sufficient high fibre ● Practise Abdominal Doming and Granny's Corset twice daily (p. 137).

ARTHRITIS

It is said there are as many different types of arthritis as there are victims. The term arthritis means the inflammation of a joint. The two main categories are referred to as Osteoarthritis and Rheumatoid Arthritis. Within these two categories there are differing forms of disability and severity. Treatment often involves drugs to suppress pain, but these can produce unwanted side-effects. Underlying causes must be removed for improvement and healing to take place. The worst thing you can do if you want to eliminate side-effects from arthritis is to sit around, nursing your wounds. You need to gently 'get on the go'. Letters I have received from around the world provide written testimony that people are experiencing relief from their arthritic symptoms with a simple bounce, once or twice daily. Don't sit around if there's a bouncer in the house!

Rheumatoid Arthritis affects at least three times more women than men. Fatigue, aching joints and loss of appetite are often the first signs. Inflammation progressively damages the structure of joints, causing deformity in the fingers, knees and back.

Osteoarthritis is the most common form of arthritis, and tends to gradually creep up on the sufferer. Stiffness may flare up, followed by a period of remission.

Junctions between two bones are known as joints. Shoulders, elbows, wrists, hips, knees, ankles and spinal joints can all be affected by arthritis. You tend to suffer most where circulation is at a stand-still. When toxins, wastes and inorganic substances become stagnant, joints are more likely to become inflamed and swollen. The more difficult the joint is to use, the less flexible it becomes, along with the muscles that enable the movement.

As you bounce more calcium is absorbed and deposited in your bones, making them stronger. The additional strengthening and toning of your muscles, ligaments and tendons, enhances the stability of your joints.

The cartilage in your joints doesn't have a direct blood supply. Compression of the joint itself creates the impact through which nutrients and oxygen are delivered, and wastes carried away. Degeneration occurs without sufficient nourishment and cleansing. When you bounce you gently stimulate the fluids surrounding your joints, encouraging lubrication of inflamed tissues and the cleansing of wastes and toxins.

The swelling, pain and heat of arthritis, due to inflammation, are often reduced in a mild bouncing programme, as more fluid becomes lymph-obligatory. Many cases of arthritis may be offset by a viral condition, when antigens invade and cause the initial inflammation. It is thought they may lie in wait for years before attacking, when they sense that conditions are ripe for survival. Instead of becoming the soldiers you need, many defender cells are thought to become confused by the attack of the antigen. They become the agents of destruction themselves, turning on your joint, damaging the cartilage and the joint lining.

The bony ends of your joints are sealed in by a thin membrane, known as synovial lining. Debris collects and breeds in these areas, often damaging underlying tissues. Once triggered by a virus, or an antigen, inflammation can be self-reinforcing. As inflammation increases, pannus, the jagged growth that builds up in your joint linings, stockpiles and can start eating into your cartilage.

The following conditions may all trigger the development of arthritis: ● Inflamed membrane of your joint ● Inflamed ligament attachment to your bones ● Crystal chemicals in fluid surrounding your joint ● Bacteria in the intercellular fluid, surrounding your joint ● Breakdown of the cartilage of your joint ● Inflammation of your muscle tissue ● Local injury ● General poor nutrition, with an excess of acidity in your system.

A balanced approach integrating gentle bouncing programmes with stress release techniques and plans for Triumphant Transformation, will serve to help the problems. Activation of the fluid surrounding your joints will encourage the removal of wastes and trapped plasma proteins will be carted away in your lymph. Gentle, vibrational bouncing stimulates fluid surrounding your joints, offering lubrication to inflamed tissue, and circulation exchange. As you bounce the efficiency of your immune system is increased and elimination of urea is activated by better circulation. Bones, ligaments, tendons, muscles and joints are strengthened, and your joints are nourished due to improved circulation.

Surgery involving arthritic conditions often relates to problems associated with inflammation. Relief of pressure on nerves, removal of swollen joint linings, and tendon repair, are among the causes for operations. Symptoms are often improved or removed with gentle bouncing programmes. If swollen synovial tissue presses on nerves and causes discomfort, gentle bouncing helps reduce inflammation. If tissue surrounding your joint is inflamed, a gentle bounce will activate the cleansing of the tissue.

Topical Tips

● Plan to bounce gently at least twice daily. The swelling associated with your condition should gradually reduce. Rhythmical compression of the synovial fluid surrounding joints will produce a host of positive side-effects that set healing in motion ● If arthritis is virally activated, immune function needs to recover a strategic position. Bounce gently to activate your lymphatics ● If you are suffering wear and tear on your joint, the gristle is too weak, and will benefit as it is cleansed and strengthened. Gently vibrate in the Rhythm Walk or Bounce, stroking your reflex zones ● If your muscles and joints are inflamed, plasma proteins are probably trapped, inviting more fluid. Bounce very gently ● Insufficient synovial fluid in your joints means poor circulation. Warm-up thoroughly before you bounce ● If you suffer crystallization of urea or gout, circulation is stagnant. Cut out rich, refined and processed foods, sugar and salt. Eat more fresh fruit and raw vegetables, and drink more fresh water. Bounce and stroke reflex zones for elimination ● Use a balance bar to stabilize your posture and give you confidence ● If your joints are inflamed, vigorous bouncing will make them worse, not better. Use the Rhythm Bounce and Rhythm Walk as the basis for your programme ● Never bounce on a joint while it is hot and inflamed or overly swollen. Wait for it to die down, and then use your bouncer ● As you become fitter, develop your programme to contain a warm-up which gradually expands into Bounce Target Zones ● Never allow yourself to become fatigued when you bounce ● Avoid high tension bouncing, or routines that require force across a joint ● Heat can help reduce muscle spasm, while improving the flow of blood and lymph to your muscles and joints. Take a shower before bouncing, or apply a warm compress to any pain for additional release ● If your arthritic condition is in your knees, you can perform simple mobility movements sitting on your bouncer. Any full bouncing would be limited to the Rhythm Bounce and Rhythm Walk. Monitor your reactions to different techniques and plan your sessions accordingly ● Remember that bouncing reduces the impact on your weightbearing joints by up to 85%, while still offering your joints the benefits in terms of compression and circulation.

Ankylosing Spondylitis

This is a form of arthritis which causes inflammation to the outside of the joint, where tendons and ligaments are attached to the bone. Most other forms of arthritis affect the inside of your joint. This complaint particularly affects the vertebrae in the spine, hindering the range of movement in the affected spinal area. Pain and stiffness is often more severe in the morning, then eases throughout the day. This is helped with a gentle vibrational bounce. Although anti-inflammatory drugs ease symptoms, you may gain the same relief by gently bouncing. The following tips should serve as reminders.

● Check your posture throughout your bouncing sessions ● Sleep on a firm mattress with no pillows ● Lie on your tummy on the surface of your bouncer. Lazy Lizzies, Snakes and Ladders, Ping Pong and Starlight Express can all offer release from tensions.

Topical Tips

● Follow a food plan that is predominantly alkaline (p. 115) ● Keep intake of saturated and animal fats to a minimum (p. 113) ● Take one to two teaspoons of coldpressed linseed oil daily ● Avoid all foods that restrict your absorption of minerals. These include: tea, coffee, bread, bran ● Check your supplies of selenium, copper, zinc, iron and manganese. Vitamins A, B, C and Betacarotene must be in good supply. Zinc supplies need to be in balance, to activate immune response to virus and bacteria ● A small copper bracelet worn on your wrist allows small quantities of copper to be absorbed through your skin. Because copper has anti-inflammatory effects, many people find this a helpful aid ● Arthritic conditions are fired if there is too much acidity in your system. With an excess in acid, your kidneys are forced to work on overload. The more severe your condition the more they will be strained. Activate the lymphatic reflex zone for your kidneys (p. 33).

ASTHMA

Most cases of asthma are triggered by a multitude of factors. Irritation, emotional stress, physiological trauma and reactions to diet can all be individually responsible for an asthmatic condition, or can combine to make matters worse. Of chief importance, when aiming to bring asthma attacks

under control, is the activation of the lymphatics. Under an asthma attack, the air passages in your lungs are narrowed by mucous secretions and spasm. Regular bouncing should help to keep the mucous membranes clear of accumulating fluid, helping to avoid this.

Topical Tips

● Work toward three sessions each week in your Bounce Target Zones to increase the depth and rate of your breathing ● Stroke the reflexes for your lungs (p. 32) ● Include techniques from Spacing Stress Out (p. 128) in your daily bounce sessions ● Choose a variety of techniques from Totally Breathtaking to enhance your breathing patterns (p. 135) ● If you feel an attack coming on, use Granny's Corset or Abdominal Doming ● If you suffer exercise induced asthma, bouncing offers a perfect base from which you can gently graduate your programmes. Within days of starting their bouncing programmes, many people are able to put their ventilators to one side ● Check your nutritional balance. 50–100mg a day of vitamin B6 is of proven value for asthmatics.

AUTISM

Controlled bouncing programmes provide excellent exercise for autistic children. You need to distinguish between play and exercise: use the latter as a form of therapy where specific skills are taught and refined. Because autistic children react to ritualistic repetitive behaviour, any over-stimulation only reinforces a psychotic state in which they are likely to cut off from the real world, as we may experience it. Many authorities on autism have suggested that the state is genetically orientated. More recent theories are surfacing to suggest that many autistic children have suffered 'breakdowns' at an early age, sometimes relating to situations they experienced as very small babies. When this occurs at such a young age, patterns related to the formation of speech and other physical skills don't get the chance to develop.

Topical Tips

● The best way to utilize bouncing is by reinforcing patterns of cross-crawl, to encourage balance of each side of the brain to the body ● Create programmes from Brainy Blitz (p. 144) to ensure these patterns set in ● By using nursery rhymes, poetry and songs in a fun-filled way, the therapist or parent should easily discern when to ring the changes before over-excitement sets in ● Practise sound and breathing techniques (pp. 130, 115).

BELCHING

Habitual or periodic belching can be due to too little gastric acid and to pepsin, which results in bacterial growth. This causes food to ferment, producing gas. Usually a sign of digestive malfunction, you have to plan your food intake thoughtfully.

Topical Tips

● Prepare to eat only in situations where you are truly relaxed. Food must be thoroughly chewed into a paste before you swallow. Refer to Table Manners (p. 116). Avoid drinking any liquids for at least fifteen minutes before you eat and for thirty minutes after your meal. Never eat and drink at the same time, as this dilutes stomach acids ● In the Rhythm Bounce stroke the reflexes for your colon (p. 33) ● Regular bouncing sessions regulate your digestive functions, facilitating passing of wind ● A series of colon washes will help to reset your equilibrium as you create a transition plan to overcome the belches ● Combine food carefully. For top quality digestion, avoid combining proteins and starches in the one meal (p. 115).

BLEMISHES

Acne and blemishes are often a sign that glandular and elimination systems are 'out of synch'. Your body is throwing off wastes faster than your systems are able to eliminate them. Bounce every day, aiming for several small sessions. Stimulate the zones for your elimination organs (p. 109) twice daily. Your glandular reflexes are also important (p. 32).

Topical Tips

● Follow the Detox. Dimensions (p. 111) to cleanse. Then move into the Five-Star Plan (p. 113) to replace ● Prepare all food as freshly as possible, preserving natural fluid content whenever possible ● Eliminate all saturated fats from your diet ● Drink several glasses of water daily, between meals ● Tea tree oil provides fast and effective treatment for clearing boils, pimples and acne ● Place 3 drops of essential oil of lavender in 100ml of base oil of almond or apricot, or alternatively in pure distilled water. Dab it onto your skin with a cotton wool ball to help rejuvenate skin cells ● Vitamin C is essential for maintaining and improving skin conditions. As an antioxidant, it cleanses your tissues of electrically unevenly charged particles, known as 'free radicles', which damage your skin cell walls, weakening them and allowing bacteria, viruses and toxins to enter ● Other antioxidants, vitamins E and

A, and minerals zinc, selenium and manganese, are also essential for healthy skin ● Don't use soap on your face or neck ● Cleanse, tone and nourish your skin daily with natural products ● Wear a hat instead of using a harsh sunscreen. Anything you put on your skin is going to be absorbed into your blood and lymph. Be sure ingredients that you put on your skin are absolutely pure.

BLOOD PRESSURE

Blood pressure basically drives your circulation, so it is essential to keep it in healthy balance. Both the force of your heart as it contracts, and the pressure of the contractile muscles in your vessel walls, stimulate the pressure of your blood. Many problems with high blood pressure, referred to as hypertension, will be eliminated as you move through transition for Triumphant Transformation. Cut back on processed foods, which lead to an overabundance of sodium and a decrease in potassium. When your cell generators are activated, blood pressure is helped to stabilize. When you bounce, blood is directed away from inactive organs and muscles, to where it is required. Many conditions cause your arteries to constrict. Poor food, lack of exercise, stress, salt, sugar, and shock are among the factors that will cause constriction to occur. Use your programmes to eliminate the causes.

Topical Tips

● If you have high blood pressure, check with your practitioner, regarding your exercise parameters ● Over a period of time, your blood pressure should definitely improve, if you follow bounce programmes consistently ● In turn, this will reduce the risk of heart disease, strokes and kidney diseases ● If your blood pressure is high, overstate the value of your heart rate readings when you begin your programmes. Use the Borg Scale to determine your bouncing intensities. Work very gently to begin with ● Check your risk triggers for hypertension. These include: obesity, stress, saturated fats, refined sugar, smoking, the pill ● Increasing your heart rate to around 120 beats per minute (Borg Scale 12), as you bounce, should produce a substantial reduction in your blood pressure for up to ten hours. If you suffer hypertension, aim to bounce at least once daily at around this rate, to recover your normal level ● Use Time-Out daily. Take a positive stance towards problem solving. Use the Five Steps (p. 129) to deal with any problems as they arise ● Within your programmes move gradually from vertical to horizontal postures. Keep your head parallel to or above your heart at all times ● Stroke the reflexes

for your heart and circulation (p. 141)● Essential oil of clary sage will regulate high blood pressure. Lavender will lower blood pressure and act as a nerve and heart tonic ● Any tension that alters your glandular output and response will aggravate the stability of your blood pressure ● Adapt techniques from Totally Breathtaking (p. 135) and Spacing Stress Out (p. 128) into your programmes.

BREASTS

Breasts contain numerous lymphatic drainage routes. This is partly due to the fact that your nipples provide a most welcome entry for many invading micro-organisms, particularly during lactation. Thanks to the numerous lymphatic vessels permeating your breasts, your lymph nodes can provide the necessary surveillance for defence. You need to get your lymphatics working really well to ensure protection against cancer and other breast diseases. You don't just catch cancer. Conditions have to be ripe for the replicating cells to spread. If your lymphatics are in prime shape, the chances of cancer catching you out are slim.

Breasts are both glandular and vascular. When you produce milk, your breasts require vast supplies of nutrients and oxygen to function properly. Obviously, your lymph needs to be drained quickly, so filtration from your blood can be continuous and can aid in the production of milk. Lymph carts much of the debris away from your tissue spaces and certainly removes it from all of the larger molecules.

We have different types of cancer of the breast, and different types of lumps, including fatty tissue, blocked lymph nodes and fibrocystic lumps, which are often tender around menstruation and menopause. Major damage is caused through metastases. After the primary cancer develops in your breast, small cancer cells go wild and invade your lymphatic vessels; from there they are carried to nodes in your armpit, where secondary growths often develop. Metastases cause death if malignant tumours as single cells stem off from the original tumour, spreading to other parts of your body through your fluids. Lymph nodes often show evidence of war against malignant cells, and trouble often strikes as the tumour takes over the lymph node itself. If you follow your bounce programmes regularly and consistently, you will ensure the regular and consistent drainage of your breasts.

Topical Tips

● Include stretches and conditioning for your breasts in your programmes. Excellent techniques to ensure the activation of your breasts include: Shoulder Rolls (p. 34); Crocodile Walk (p. 34);

the Conductor (p. 42); Heading Out (p. 97); Starlight Express (p. 94); Seagulls (p. 96); combinations from Armed Forces, such as Peccy Presses (p. 99), Pulling Anchor (p. 99) and Horses in the Stable (p. 101) ● As you bounce, you stimulate flow in the lymphatics in your breasts. For additional stimulation stimulate your lymphatic zones (p. 30) ● Cut right back on saturated and animal fats (p. 113) ● Have any fears or lumps checked by a practitioner, especially one who is familiar with your lymphatics ● Essential oils of jasmine, ylang ylang, sweet fennel and geranium are excellent rebalancers for your breast functions.

BRONCHITIS

Respiratory systems are irritated by pollution, cigarettes, infections and allergies. Many physiotherapists encourage the use of a bouncer to activate the secretion of phlegm from your lungs and associated systems. Nick Ewert, clinical physiotherapist, explains that gentle bouncing brings movement and vibration into your chest area, encouraging deeper breath to help loosen the secretions so they can be coughed up and cleared. In the course of a normal day, breathing tends to be shallow and slow. Bouncing offers the necessary stimulation to deepen your breathing.

Topical Tips

● Avoid inhaled allergens: cigarettes, house dust, animal fur, grasses and pollens, moulds, mildews and chemicals ● Avoid ingested allergens: food additives, colourings, preservatives, aspirin, wheat and yeast based products, refined carbohydrates and sugar ● Bouncing encourages the stamina of your respiratory system. Mucus is drained as chest muscles are strengthened. Parasympathetic nervous responses are calmed and harmonized ● If you are suffering a severe viral bout of bronchitis, lie low, rest up, and wait until you have your strength back. Then draw up a resolution plan to prevent further attacks ● Bounce gently to gather strength during rehabilitation ● Stroke the reflexes for your lungs (p. 32) and elimination organs (p. 109) ● Select techniques from Sounding Off (p. 130) and Totally Breathtaking (p. 135). You'll find Abdominal Doming (p. 187) particularly helpful ● Essential oils of marjoram, lemon, eucalyptus and benzoin are especially beneficial for any bronchial or chesty complaints ● Dose up on vitamin C, and check your intake of zinc and B-Complex ● Yellow or greenish phlegm usually indicates that infection has set in. Seek advice for recovery from a practitioner.

CANCER

The combination of poor nutrition, stress, a weak immune system and lack of exercise offer perfect conditions for the onset of cancer. In the case of breast cancer, the role of fat in your diet is overwhelming, but on the other hand, factors such as genetic conditions can predispose a person to cancer. For every case, it seems, there is an absolutely individual reaction and history.

Topical Tips

● Your immune function is vital. Stroke reflex zones daily ● Bouncing increases the rate of the oxygenation of your tissues, thus flooding your body cells with oxygen and nutrients. Even if you are undergoing treatment for cancer, you will benefit from fresh supplies of oxygen as you bounce. Your emotional and mental states will be uplifted in tune with your spirit ● As you intensify the supply of oxygen to your lungs, you will help to prevent lung cancer from developing. Too much LDL cholesterol stifles the activity of your white blood cells, which scavenge your cancer cells. Because this affects their immune response, cancer cells can take over ● Anaerobic bacteria, which live in the last few feet of your colon, can convert their excretions to female hormones called oestrogens, and also to a cancer-producing substance referred to as 'deoxycholic acid'. If these products are laid down, they can be responsible for cancer in your colon. Anaerobic bacteria cannot survive in the presence of the enriched oxygen you invite in as you bounce. In fact it poisons the bacteria, allowing your more friendly aerobic bacteria to survive instead. An abundant supply of oxygen to your cells is an essential element in the prevention of cancer ● Remove saturated fats from your diet ● Eat more high fibre. Follow the Five-Star Plan (p. 113). By drawing up resolution plans to ensure quality habits for your health, combined with a general selection of techniques from the various programmes, you will be offering yourself the best possible preventative medicine for cancer.

CANDIDA

Candida offers a classic example of micro-organisms going out of balance, creating problems for your health when they get the upper hand over those micro-organisms that would normally keep their enemies in check. In a normal bowel, three to four pounds of micro-organisms co-exist, probably weighing more than your brain. Micro-organisms are strictly common souls. They eat from the same table as us. They are synibodes. We help each other. We put down food for them, as they produce useful chemicals for us, breaking down the food we eat and making it more digestible. They even produce chemicals to control the patterns of micro-organisms, by and large, keeping infections out. How many other things they produce, we don't know, but there have been chemicals isolated from them that have anti-tumour, and therefore anti-cancer, activities.

As the candida yeast proliferates, if it gets the chance to puncture your gut wall it can adopt fungal form, growing like a lyceum. If your gut wall becomes invaded, there is always the danger that large food molecules will pass through, where they are recognized as antigens by your immune system. This invasion can set up allergic responses. Some people react by becoming hyper-sensitive. If you do over-react, symptoms such as asthma, eczema, veticaria, irritable bowel syndrome and possibly psoriasis may surface.

Not only do a wide range of disorders have their roots in an overgrowth of candida as it runs rampant, but candida announces its presence when something has happened to tip the balance of micro-organisms in its favour. If you don't react at all, you can't control the situation by keeping them in check or killing them off. As they take over a large part of your bowel, they produce toxins which enter your system, starting to interfere with your immune system. If it does get to this stage, it can either move throughout your entire body, or the chemicals that it produces will, creating toxicity within.

If it gets the chance it will thrive in your bowel, vagina, mouth, and even your false teeth. There is a male syndrome, and male and female partners reinfect each other. Athletes foot, ringworm, dandruff on your scalp, and even abdominal upsets, may be due to other yeasts, but often indicate that candida is present. Men may show these symptoms, while carrying doses of candida that have the potential to reinfect.

Topical Tips

● Your immune response is important. If you are suffering a candida attack, aim to bounce several times daily, for a few minutes at a time. This will stimulate your white blood cell count to engulf micro-organisms and to strengthen your immune system. ● Your lymphatics cart away the debris more quickly, preventing further toxic load. As the cells start to die off, it is possible to develop 'Herxheimers reaction': organisms burst, spilling their toxins into your system in one short sharp dose ● Minor digestive disturbances, such as flatulence and loose stools, often occur as a result of 'die off' of unhealthy micro-organisms. As you bounce these symptoms are diminished, due to increased lymphatic response and enhanced digestive processes. Remember, stagnant lymph implies stagnant toxins. Your wastes must be removed ● To clear the problem from the roots, you would be wise to take a four-fold approach – 1. Food Plans: Following a strict diet won't clear the problem up by itself, but it will give those micro-organisms a terrible migraine, making it difficult for them to bounce back. Candida thrives on all fermentable foods which make you feel bloated. Avoid all yeasted foods, concentrated orange juice, bread, alcohol, sultanas, grapes etc. Limit dairy produce – cheese, milk and associated products. Garlic and unrefined olive oil will stimulate healing. Check iron and zinc supplies in your diet. An extra 2 grams of vitamin C 3 times daily will stimulate healing. Combine your foods thoughtfully to minimize bloating and other symptoms of uneasy digestion. Fresh leafy vegetables often contain natural anti-fungal properties. Gradually cut out tea and coffee during your healing period ● 2. Consult your practitioner: You will need some form of drug treatment, preferably two weeks after your change in food intake. See your practitioner concerning this phase of the treatment ● 3. Bounce: Follow your usual bouncing timetables, but add several sessions daily, of short bounce routines, to stimulate immune response and to fight the 'die off' ● 4. Acidophillus: When your intestinal tract becomes more efficient, your immune system will thrive. Acidophillus is one of the key organisms in your bowel flora, similar in type to bulgaricus, from which yoghurt is made. Many women treat their thrush by douching their vaginal area with yoghurt, not realizing that although bulgaricus is suited to living in the airing cupboard, acidophillus is suited to the normal temperature of the bowel. As you put the normal organisms back into your bowel, they should take hold, multiply, and become a larger population. Acidophillus has many positive influences. It inhibits the growth of harmful, toxic micro-organisms, whilst helping to detoxify harmful material from your diet. At the same time, it increases your body's natural immunity for fighting bacterial, fungal and viral infections and inhibits the growth of 'candida albicans'. Acidophillus inhabit digestive tract, mouth, throat, oesophagus, stomach, intestines and vaginal mucosa. It's best to take acidophillus orally during treatment phases, in powder form that is acid-resistant, so that organisms are not destroyed as they pass by the acids in your stomach.

181

CHOLESTEROL

A combination of a natural food plan with regular bouncing programmes, to manage stress and body chemistry, will keep your HDL cholesterol at a healthy level. Although between 200 and 800mg of cholesterol may be eaten daily, your body naturally manufactures cholesterol at a rate of about 2000mgs daily. It is essential to many aspects of metabolism, hormone production, bile formation and the synthesis of vitamin D.

Topical Tips

● Bouncing stimulates the production of HDLs which carry the cholesterol away, thinning your blood (p. 114) ● If you smoke, your body will have more difficulty dealing with fats in your bloodstream ● Check your intake of dietary cholesterol. Cut back on saturated and animal fats ● If you have a high ratio of LDLs, bounce every day, with short bursts in between, to utilize the free fatty acids floating about in your bloodstream.

COLDS

Depending on the nature of your cold, decide whether you should continue to bounce through it or not. If an infection is heavy and viral, you should rest up and give your body every chance to fight the invaders, encouraging a quick recovery.

Topical Tips

● Certain colds are often simply your body going through a cleansing crisis. As you bounce gently you find mucus, wastes and other debris being eliminated more quickly. Follow your instincts and use your bouncer as often as you feel the urge in a very gentle Rhythm Bounce ● Follow the Detox. Dimensions to activate a thorough cleansing (p. 111) ● Top up on your vitamin C supplies ● Stroke the reflexes for your elimination organs (p. 109) ● Drink a Lemon Zinger several times daily (p. 118).

CONSTIPATION

If the natural rhythm of your bowel movements is slowed down, hard stools often become a problem – difficult to pass and infrequent. Constipation can be an ongoing or one-off affair. Immediately you bounce, peristaltic waves in your intestines are activated, food passes through more quickly and wastes are released. Your intestines are automatically internally massaged and the pressure exerted by your abdominal muscles on your bowel is intensified.

Topical Tips

● Practise Abdominal Doming and Granny's Corset (p. 137) ● Include conditioning routines daily for your abdomen ● Limit your intake of tea. It can

cause constipation ● Pure cold-pressed olive oil acts as a lubricant to your system ● Drink several glasses of cleansing fluids daily ● Prepare your food with the minimum processing ● Stroke the reflexes for your elimination organs (p. 109) ● Stay with natural high fibre content in your food (p. 114).

CORONARY HEART DISEASES

A variety of diseases may afflict you, affecting your heart, blood and vessels. Recuperating from attacks requires strict guidance in a therapeutic programme. You must seek advice and direction from a professional practitioner or therapist. Bouncing programmes can be used to improve conditions once attacks have occurred and to help prevent the onset of further attacks. If you suffer with angina, you must monitor your heart rate and the intensity at which you bounce carefully.

The oxygen demand of your myocardium, which is part of your heart, depends on individual blood pressure and heart rates. As you progress with training, your heart rate is often lowered, with a noticeable reduction in myocardium demand. Symptoms of angina occur at higher intensities of exercise, so keep your bouncing intensities lower and gradually increase your efforts. If possible, have a clinical reading to assess your safety limits and levels.

Following the initial stages of recovery from heart attacks, which will be under strict supervision, work through your bouncing routines with a clinical therapist who will let you know at what stages during recovery you should start to bounce, and will help monitor intensities. Many people use a bouncer in the third stages of their cardiac rehabilitation programme. The same training principles apply for those recovering from cardiovascular diseases to those who are free of symptoms. Your heart muscle has to be strengthened gradually over a period of time. Clinical rehabilitation staff can initially monitor your progress on treadmills and will adapt your programmes to your bouncer on request. Exercise stress tests should be carried out, accompanied by electrocardiograms before you begin to bounce.

Recovery from heart disease requires a positive approach restructuring your lifestyle and habits. By the time you get to your bouncer your confidence and knowledge of the performance levels you can carry out, should be well established.

Topical Tips

● Stroke the reflexes for your heart (p. 33) and lungs (p. 32) ● Plan clear transition guidelines to change those habits causing the trouble. Bouncing

Back to Square One (p. 120) should reset your obesity levels. Spacing Stress Out (p. 128) will help to bring your reactions to stress under control ● If you bounce regularly and enjoy healthy living habits, you should never have to worry about the build up of wastes on the walls of your arteries, which eventually may lead to strokes, heart attacks, arteriosclerosis, and circulatory diseases ● Bounce to keep LDL cholesterol under control, and check your dietary intake ● Keep alcohol to a bare minimum or give it up altogether ● Keep your blood sugar levels stable by staying with a natural diet of unrefined complex carbohydrates (p. 117) ● Stroke the reflexes for your thyroid (p. 32). An underactive thyroid may reduce your fat metabolism, increasing the level of fats in your blood ● Get regular doses of sunlight.

CYSTIC FIBROSIS

One in three thousand babies are affected by this condition, which interferes with the lungs, pancreas, and digestive function. Children often suffer chest infections, and are small for their age. Mucus has to be removed from their systems regularly, for which they are turned upside-down and drained.

Topical Tips

● Bouncing beforehand will help to loosen up the secretions in the lungs before draining, and will naturally aid in the balance of fluid systems ● Essential oils of rosemary, sandalwood, frankincense and black pepper are helpful for this condition ● Practise Alternate Nostril Breathing (p. 136).

DEPRESSION

Psychiatric illness and depression are stoked by many underlying factors. If you suffer any ongoing bouts of depression, consult your practitioner. You should have a complete physical and neurological checkup to include laboratory analysis, to cover nutritional assessment, urine tests for kidney disorders, infections or diabetes. Metabolic imbalances of your kidneys and liver should be checked and you should be screened for infections or anaemia. Any underlying emotional tensions and conflicts have to be worked through, so do seek help. You will find your bouncing programmes loaded with techniques for self-help and positive growth patterns. Depression is naturally lifted as you bounce. All you have to do is get yourself to the bouncer!

Topical Tips
● Essential oils of clary sage, camomile, hyacinth, cypress, geranium and jasmine will lift your spirits immediately ● Select techniques from Totally Breathtaking (p. 135), especially Alternate Nostril Breathing and Hummm (p. 136) ● Relaxation in Innerspaces (p. 132) will keep you in balance
● Seek remedies from your Flower Power (p. 133).

DIABETES

An abnormal amount of glucose in the bloodstream is the most common feature of diabetes. This occurs as the pancreas fails to produce sufficient insulin to supply the needs of your body. The level of insulin usually rises after food and declines a little following exertion. Controlled and regular bouncing should help your case.

Topical Tips
● Stroke the reflexes for your pancreas (p. 33)
● Stay away from refined food products ● Practise Alternate Nostril Breathing and other breathing techniques (pp. 135–7).

DYSLEXIA

The reading and writing of letters the wrong way around creates learning difficulties, with the left and right hemispheres of the brain in confusion. Therapists are including the use of the bouncer within the framework of their programmes, combined with cross-crawl and techniques for improving visual capacity. When use of the bouncer is regular and consistent, symptoms of hyperactivity often associated with this condition are usually quickly relieved.

Topical Tips
● Peep Po, Crystal Gazing, Stare Bears and Magic Painting are excellent for programme fillers (p. 148) ● Hopscross, Kite Flying, The Nutcracker and Jerky Jugglers (p. 144) all help to unravel brain/body patterns.

EAR PROBLEMS

Many ear problems have their roots in poor elimination of wastes and an accumulation of congested fluids. Both of these conditions are improved as you bounce.

Topical Tips
● Haaa, the Bounce Vibration, Hair Raisers, Scary Spiders, Miss Muffet and Sticky Webs are all helpful (pp. 130–1) ● The Headspinner, Jawstrings, Lock-jaw and Face Shaker provide excellent release from ear tension (pp. 140–1).

ECZEMA

Your skin depends on a healthy supply of nutrients, coupled with oxygen from the vessels in underlying tissues. Eczema is often characterized by inflamed itchy eruptions, breaking into a weepy rash when severe. Food allergies are often the prime suspect. With regular bouncing, most people with eczema show marked signs of improvement.

Topical Tips
● Stimulate your reflexes for all elimination organs (p. 109) ● Stroke the reflexes daily for your lymphatic zones (p. 30) ● Detox. Dimensions (p. 111) followed by the Five-Star Plan (p. 113) will ensure optimum nutrition.

EMPHYSEMA

Because this condition destroys the small air spaces in the lungs, the ability to absorb oxygen and release carbon dioxide is restricted. As you bounce, any activities such as whistling, singing or humming – see sound techniques (p. 130) – will help to develop the capacity of your lungs.

Topical Tips
● Carefully graded bouncing, building up gradually in intensity and time provides the perfect exercise regime for emphysema sufferers ● Stroke the reflex zones for your lungs (p. 32) ● Press your neurovascular reflex points for your chest and lungs following your bounce session (p. 141) ● All techniques from Totally Breathtaking (p. 135) will help to set you off into healthier breathing patterns. Improvement can be remarkable as you bounce
● If you need to stop smoking refer to Addiction (p. 176) to break the habit.

FATIGUE

If you are prone to fatigue, it could just be that you are not getting sufficient doses of oxygen. A few minutes on your bouncer may reset the balance. Be positive and invite energy in, rather than slumping in a chair, depressing your oxygen supplies.

Topical Tips
● Avoid all saturated fats (p. 113) ● Allergies often instigate fatigue; evaluate possible areas for concern ● Stimulate your glandular reflex zones daily (p. 30) ● Essential oils of clary sage, rose, gardinia and melissa are excellent energy boosters.

FLUID RETENTION

Swelling of your ankles and feet are often the first sign that you are retaining fluid. Drink several glasses of water daily, and ensure your fluid intake stays high. A gentle approach to your bounce programmes will help quickly. Correct the underlying causes of your problems.

Topical Tips
● Cut out salts, sugars, and refined carbohydrates. Refer to the Five-Star Plan (p. 113) ● Press your reflexes for elimination (p. 109) ● Assess and clear up any allergic reactions you may be suffering from ● Avoid diuretics at all costs. They may seem to help initially, but your body makes biochemical adjustments to deal with the tablets. When you stop them, your fluid retention will be worse, not better
● Essential oils of peppermint, lemon and geranium are great fluid rebalancers.

GALL BLADDER

The underlying organs of your colon and liver need to be activated if you are suffering gall bladder problems. As you bounce, congestion will be broken down. Diet plays an important part in the prevention of gallstones.

Topical Tips
● Stay away from saturated fats, unrefined products and processed foods ● Stimulate the reflexes for your gall bladder, liver and colon (p. 33) ● If you are presently experiencing attacks, bounce gently several times daily.

GOUT

Gout surfaces due to a disturbance in the production, destruction and elimination of uric acid. This occurs when your body fails to break down protein sufficiently. Often there is immense pain in the big toe, as it becomes swollen and inflamed. Water is retained in your body. Insoluble uric acid salts accumulate in the tissues surrounding your joints as wastes build up in your body. There is often no residual pain between attacks although larger deposits of uric acid accumulate sneakily, with inflammation creeping in.

Topical Tips
● Detox. Dimensions is an essential transition zone if you are suffering from gout (p. 111) ● Drink plenty of natural fluids, particularly the Lemon Zinger (p. 118) ● Steer clear of foods containing purine: Kidneys, liver, sardines, sweetbread, anchovies, meat extracts. Eggs, milk products, lentils and beans should be restricted ● Press the reflexes for your digestion, absorption and elimination (p. 109) ● Essential oils of camphor, cypress, geranium and juniper will ease symptoms and help prevent attacks.

HAEMORRHOIDS

When you bounce you strengthen the underlying muscles of your anus. Veins that become congested and protrude from your rectum can cause extreme pain. Sometimes they bleed, and can even require surgery.

Topical Tips

● If your haemorrhoids are painful, avoid double-foot strike landings on the bouncer. Stay low in the Rhythm Walk, which can form the base for your routines ● As you are on the downward bounce, pull in the muscles of your pelvic floor, and for men the anus ● The use of 5 drops of lavender mixed with 5 drops of cypress in a sitz bath is an excellent aid in healing. Repeat every time you pass a bowel motion or urinate ● Stroke your reflex zones for elimination (p. 109) in the Rhythm Walk ● Perfect Pelvic Pinching (p. 164) and other routines for your pelvic floor will really serve you well! ● Work on avoiding all factors that encourage constipation. Try Triumphant Transformation for food planning to encompass high fibre. Cut intake of saturated fats and processed and refined carbohydrates, to ensure your system maintains a healthy balance ● Colon hydrotherapy offers an excellent aid for healing and treatment.

HEADACHES

The causes of headaches are as numerous as the changes in the weather. If they are consistent, you must consult your practitioner and seek diagnosis. Tension headaches are most common and often surface because head and neck muscles are over-contracted. They are also commonly associated with withdrawal from stimulants such as coffee and cigarettes. Most people experience relief from recurring headaches when they follow bounce programmes regularly.

Topical Tips

● Stimulate your neurovascular reflex points daily (p. 141) ● Facial tension releases are important as soon as you feel a headache coming on. Try Lock-jaw or Face Shaker (p. 139) ● Remove any tension from your neck with gentle massage ● Eyestrain often leads to tension headaches. Concentrate on techniques from your Delightful Eyes resolution plan (p. 148).

HORMONE REPLACEMENT THERAPY

Giving oestrogen or progesterone in the form of injections, pills, implants or skin patches, is becoming a popular treatment for menopausal problems. They are said to prevent hot flushes and help prevent osteoporosis. The long-term risks and side-effects are still unclear, although research indicates treatment may increase the risk of endometrial cancer. Fibroids may deteriorate under this treatment along with other symptoms that often appear with the use of the pill. If you are utilizing the therapy, your bouncing programmes will help to disperse excess fluids and eliminate the feelings of bloated tenderness in your abdomen.

Topical Tips

● Stimulate the reflex points for your liver (p. 33) ● Daily practice of Abdominal Doming and Granny's Corset will stimulate your abdominal region (p. 137).

HYPOGLYCEMIA

The dipping of your blood sugar level swings hand in hand with other symptoms at the time of the dip. Tension, nervousness, fatigue, depression, dizziness, headaches, muscular tensions and even black-outs can occur if the situation is severe. Sufferers often feel tenderness in the upper abdomen, on the left hand side, where the pancreas is situated. If your blood sugar level falls too low, your adrenals come out to play, excreting adrenalin to boost your system: your body then has to deal with this, which places extra strain on your liver. Symptoms are most common in the middle of the morning and in the afternoon, usually between two and five hours after you have eaten.

Topical Tips

● Eat a diet high in unrefined foods and fibres, and aim for Triumphant Transformation with your Five-Star Plan (p. 113) ● Eat your meals at regular times each day, to enable your internal bodyclock to rebalance ● Cut right down on tea and coffee. They cause a rapid rise of insulin from your pancreas, followed by a rapid drop when their effects wear off ● Refer to Addiction (p. 176) to quit smoking cigarettes. They also cause too much insulin and glycogen to be released into your bloodstream ● As you bounce you encourage the use of sugar by your body cells, without requiring insulin, which means you avoid having to counterbalance your body's adrenal response ● Press the reflexes for your glands (p. 30), to enhance their tone ● Press the reflexes for your pancreas (p. 33) ● Use Spacing Stress Out routines to help bring your mood swings under control (p. 128) ● Marijuana, alcohol, cocaine and cigarettes set up a false elation when the initial burst of sugar they stimulate hits your bloodstream. The reactive fall in blood sugar only aggravates your condition.

IMMUNE RESPONSE

Fluid Intake

● Drink fenugreek tea, brewing your own by adding hot water to one teaspoon of granules. This acts as a ginseng tonic to your lymphatics, containing an oil-based cleansing action. Your lymphatics gather fatty deposits, especially those from your liver and intestines, and need a regular spring clean. Several combined herbs make an excellent cleansing brew. A couple of cups a day for three months and you will really notice the difference ● Have the following combination mixed at any quality health store or herb supplier: juniper, hawthorn, birch, lemongrass, rosemary, horsetail, cherrystalks. Steep two tablespoons in a pot of boiling water and simmer for a few minutes ● Matte and nettle tea are both great purifiers for your lymphatics ● Drink a Lemon Zinger (p. 118) daily.

About The House

● Keep fabrics as natural as possible. Many skin irritations are due to man-made fibres which not only aggravate the surface condition but demand immune response. Carpets, curtains, bedlinen and the clothes you wear may all influence your state of health ● Allergens such as house dust, pollen, cat hair, house gas and non-natural cosmetics all demand immune response. Every demand will eventually sap your strength.

Healthy Healing

● To stimulate immune function follow the Lymphatic Reflex Zone programme (p. 30) ● Diuretics and water retention tablets may temporarily deplete your excess fluid, but won't help to get it on the move. The best way to relieve water retention is to bounce very gently in the Rhythm Bounce (p. 29) several times daily ● Your lymphatics can be damaged by operations or other injuries leaving permanent scars. Oedema may surface years later. If you are in the danger zone take extra precautions. Avoid excessive heat. Temperatures over 38°C will strain your lymphatics. Heat causes blood proteins to escape from your capillaries, causing oedema. Avoid saunas, overly hot baths, showers or compresses, and tanning in the hot sun. If you suffer any wounds place antiseptic salve immediately around the skin. Essential oil of lavender helps to build up the white cell count to speed healing. Tea tree oil is the modern 'wound wonder'.

As You Bounce

● You keep your lymph circulating through your nodes offering them the chance to filter aliens

● You create excellent conditions for the reproduction and stimulation of lymphocytes ● As you work up a sweat this helps to rid your body of unwanted antigens. With a rise in temperature white cells produce endogenous pyrogen, releasing it into your bloodstream to attack bacteria ● Waste products and toxins are removed from your intercellular fluid (along with antigens and disease producing bacteria) into your lymphatics where they are hopefully rendered harmless in your nodes ● Brief bursts of bouncing increase your white blood cell count helping affirm your resilience to infection and disease ● Damaged cells produce metabolic wastes which may be poisonous if they accumulate. By moving the proteins on as you bounce, you return them to the lymphatics before they cluster ● Fatty deposits build up in the nodes and lymph vessels as well, creating blockages in your lymphatics. Trouble looms if a backlog of lymph flow causes proteins to cluster. If damage occurs to your valves as lymph piles up, implications can be serious for your immune system.

INSOMNIA

As you bounce away your tensions and anxieties, you'll begin to sleep more easily. Bounce gently, fifteen minutes before retiring.

Topical Tips

● Practise Innerspaces (p. 132) before retiring in the evenings ● Use the Five Steps (p. 129) for problem solving if your sleeplessness is hiding an inner anxiety ● Essential oils of lavender, jasmine, geranium and orange are excellent for calming and relaxing you before sleep.

IRRITABLE BOWEL SYNDROME

Pain in your colon, and disorderly bowel habits – diarrhoea, constipation, tummy rumbles, flatulence and belching – are major symptoms of this syndrome. The bowel is easily irritated by coffee and tea, stress, psychological triggers, and poor food. Your bouncing programmes help to redress the balance. See In Transit (p. 108).

Topical Tips

● Merge techniques from Spacing Stress Out (p. 128) to form patterns for settling and calming your bowel ● Press reflexes for elimination daily (p. 109) ● Draw up a full transition plan to eliminate the underlying causes.

JET LAG

Bounce several times a day leading up to a flight, and then again at the other end if you can find a bouncer! Your circadian rhythms are reset more quickly, due to the toning of your glandular systems. Time zone fatigue, as jet lag is often called, interrupts your body metabolism. Tests performed on international travellers show they suffer a 20% drop in alertness, between 15% and 25% reduction in concentration and 10% reduction in muscular strength, by the end of their travel. A bounce at the end of a flight brings your body more quickly through full cycle, restoring natural energy.

Topical Tips

● Stimulate your glandular reflexes (p. 30) ● Work with your sound techniques (p. 130) ● Eat as many raw and natural foods as possible on flight ● Eat meals at the same time as usual ● Allow 20 minutes between food and fluid intake ● Drink more fluid to counteract fluid retention, but avoid alcohol.

KIDNEY STONES

Minerals and chemicals forming insoluble crystals from substances normally present in urine, accumulate to form kidney stones. They vary in size from tiny deposits to stones a few inches in diameter.

Topical Tips

● Drink several glasses of distilled water daily ● Plan meals high in natural fibre (p. 114) ● Limit your consumption of alcohol, sugar, salt and refined carbohydrates ● Stroke the reflex zones for your kidneys (p. 33) ● Follow Detox. Dimensions (p. 111) and then move into the Five-Star Plan (p. 113).

LUPUS

Systemic Lupus Erythematosus is a disease that affects your joints, muscle tissues and other body organs. Regular bouncing helps ease inflammation and swelling which often develops around the joints. Fatigue is a common symptom of the complaint, so you must never strain yourself. Develop your bouncing programmes to restore your energy and stamina. Immunosuppressants are commonly used to treat more severe pain.

Unfortunately they also dampen immune response, lowering your body's resistance to infections. If you use your programmes to keep inflammation at bay, this is an additional advantage.

Topical Tips

● Essential oils of cinnamon leaf, camphor, black pepper, benzoin and eucalyptus all help to balance the symptoms ● Stroke the reflexes for your elimination organs (p. 109), lymphatic zones (p. 30) and neurovascular points (p. 141) ● Plan a highly alkaline food intake (p. 115).

M.E.

(Myalgic Encephalo Myelitus)

Over the last few years M.E. has really hit the headlines, often referred to as 'post-viral fatigue'. Symptoms do vary, but excessive fatigue seems a common thread in most cases.

Following a virus, incomplete recovery leaves some people feeling unable to cope with even bare essentials. Vertigo, blurred vision, ringing in ears, muscular aches and pains and emotional weakness in general, push a battle-worn body to the point of exhaustion.

Coming to terms with the syndrome as it affects you, means accepting your limitations for a while, encouraging your body to recuperate with total bedrest. Many sufferers equate exercise with getting fit and well, and rush out to exercise, thinking it will pull them through. To recover from any viral infection, you have to allow your body total time-out to heal. With M.E., severe fatigue is often experienced after a bout of exercise, due to the lactic acid released from your muscles. This accumulates in the early stages of exercise and builds up around your muscle cells.

Topical Tips

● Bouncing offers a perfect form of exercise throughout your rehabilitation. A boost of oxygen to a weary system is welcomed at a threshold intensity and duration suited to the individual. You have to work for short, gentle spells, followed by a complete period of relaxation and release at the end, no matter how short the session ● Stroke your lymphatic zones (p. 30) and press your neurovascular reflex points (p. 141) ● Draw up a transition plan that will encourage your total rehabilitation. You will need to work toward Triumphant Transformation to change your food patterns ● Camomile, lavender, juniper, geranium, sage, melissa and peppermint will help you through the recovery phase.

MENOPAUSE

Fatigue, depression and hot flushes are among the indications that menopause is striking.

Topical Tips

● Stroke the reflex zones for your glands (p. 30) and kidneys (p. 33) ● It is vital to plan your programmes to include daily Time-Out sessions (p. 128). Include positive affirmations and visualizations into your sessions. At this time you have to make special efforts to stabilize a positive attitude ● Practise Abdominal Doming (p. 137).

MENSTRUAL PROBLEMS

Pre menstrual tension takes on several forms. Common symptoms include mood swings, irritability, nervous tension and worry. It isn't unusual to feel depressed and generally out of sorts. Many women crave sweets and eat impulsively. The worst side-effect for many is the terrible sensation of feeling bloated due to fluid retention.

Topical Tips

● Regular bouncing will help to balance your hormonal secretions and glandular functioning, while eliminating the cramping that often accompanies your period ● Check your levels of magnesium are high enough. Low levels are thought to interfere with hormonal metabolism as well as influencing your blood sugar. Select techniques from Spacing Stress Out (p. 128).

MIGRAINE

Migraines are usually more deep-rooted in association with the circulation of fluids to your brain. They often begin as a one-sided headache, accompanied by vomiting and nausea, an intense aversion to light and blocked energy. Fluid retention, mood swings, fatigue and cravings often precipitate an attack. Research shows that blood platelets cluster together more than usual during an attack. If you have the normal warning signals, use your bouncer to activate your lymph, stimulating the dispersion of trapped plasma proteins through the necessary channels.

Topical Tips

● Follow the Pulse-Base (p. 128) ● Concentrate on Spacing Stress Out techniques, particularly Jaws and Innerspaces (p. 132).

MULTIPLE SCLEROSIS

If you are struck with multiple sclerosis you need to pay attention to the stimulation of your nervous system. M.S. fluctuates in severity, and many people go into remission for periods of time. If you can bounce with a balance bar, the extra boost of oxygen to your system and the rhythmical motion as you

bounce will help to stimulate all systems, keeping you fresh mentally and physically.

Topical Tips

● If you can stroke your reflexes as you bounce, this will help ● Press neurovascular reflex points while you are sitting (p. 141) ● Activate your breath with techniques from Totally Breathtaking (p. 135) ● Essential oils of clary sage, sage, pine, melissa and hyssop keep you refreshed and alert.

MUSCULAR DISEASES

Whatever your muscular ailment, supplies of oxygen rich blood to your tissues will help you get the best out of your remaining muscles, increasing your mobility and stimulating your circulation.

Topical Tips

● Use a balance bar if it helps your confidence ● Stroke your lymphatic reflex zones daily (p. 30) ● Neurovascular holding points (p. 141) will also improve nerve and blood supply to your muscles ● Enjoy a selection of breathing techniques from Totally Breathtaking (p. 135) ● Use essential oils of cypress, pine and marjoram.

OSTEOPOROSIS

Due to a loss in mineral content, bones become thinner. While they require nourishment and sustenance from oxygen and nutrients, your bones depend upon the stress impact on each cell to generate strength. Your bones act as a reservoir for calcium, of which about 1% is floating about in your tissue fluid. Calcium is required by your tissues for their metabolic processes. Bones support a fine network of capillaries flowing through them. As you bounce you activate the flow of these nutrients to all bony tissues. Vital blood vessels within your bones are cleansed and wastes are removed. Gentle bouncing programmes suited to your individual capacity will provide a healthy challenge to your bone cells, with a minimum strain to your skeletal structure. When you tone your bones you are toning your muscles at the same time. You are not only preventing further bone loss, but you are also encouraging the formation of new and sturdier bone mass. Even short bounce sessions influence the calcium balance in your body. Bouncing is an exceptional method of exercise for both preventing and treating osteoporosis. There is every evidence that bone mineralization is organized in the most favourable way, to give strength to the bone in the direction to which the force is normally applied. Tapping the forces of gravity as you bounce

increases and intensifies the amount of work performed by your bones and therefore strengthens them. Men are at risk as well as women. About one in eight men suffer osteoporosis and nearly one in three elderly women.

Topical Tips

● Stroke your neurovascular reflex points (p. 141) ● Use a balance bar if you are at all unsteady on your feet ● Plan your programmes so that you have a complement of bouncing, conditioning and stretching. ● Aim toward Triumphant Transformation. Eat as many vegetables as possible close to their natural state to ensure the mineral content is intact ● Cigarettes and coffee leach your body of calcium. Aim to give them up.

PHYSIOTHERAPY REHABILITATION

Physiotherapists use bouncers in a variety of situations to stimulate the speed and quality of healing. It provides a safe and protective base for enabling patients to ease their body back into shape, following injury and surgery. Bouncing can be used in a training programme for rehabilitation, or for aerobic conditioning. As a form of warm-up bouncing is excellent, and also great for someone in the advanced stage of rehabilitation, wanting to get back into some serious training.

Topical Tips

● In the early days following surgery you must rest completely. You can start to recover by slowly walking on the surface of your bouncer. Keep all movements to a single-foot strike at first – then progress into a more complete bouncing programme ● Knee and ankle injuries are well protected through rehabilitation as you move gently on your bouncer ● With an acute sprain, after two or three days' rest, begin to walk gently on the mat to exercise the injured area. This also activates your lymph, to remove trapped plasma proteins and wastes from the scene of the injury. A bouncing programme should always be built up gradually, with emphasis on single-foot strike landings before you begin double-foot strike landings.

POLYNEURITIS

A number of factors can lead to the failure or abnormal conduction of nerve tissue, causing numbness, pins and needles, weakness, and loss of sensation in your body. B12 deficiencies are believed to be a major cause, as is toxic overload, infection and diabetes.

Topical Tips
● Plan to move through the Detox. Dimensions (p. 111) to your Five-Star Plan (p. 113) ● Stimulate your neurovascular zones (p. 141) and your lymphatic reflexes (p. 30) ● Use techniques from Totally Breathtaking (p. 135) and Spacing Stress Out (p. 128).

PSORIASIS

On average your skin cells have a twenty to forty day lifecycle. As they age they travel to the surface of your skin, through various layers, so the dead cells can be shed. With psoriasis, your skin ages between every two to seven days, with dead cells surfacing so quickly that they become entangled with the living cells. This is what gives your skin a scabby and patchy appearance. As plaques appear on these patches of skin, they are itchy and uncomfortable. Hereditary, emotional, allergic, and stress factors all appear to trigger reactions.

Topical Tips
● Your bouncing programmes will help to both prevent and cure ● Work through Detox. Dimensions (p. 111) into the Five-Star Plan (p. 113) ● Cut back on all saturated and animal fats (p. 113) ● Aim for quality and quantity of fresh vegetables, fruit and natural fibre ● Don't use soaps or unnatural creams or perfumes on your skin ● Time-Out daily is essential (p. 128). Take yourself quietly through release and relaxation techniques, utilizing meditation and the Five Steps for solving problems (p. 129).

PSYCHIATRIC DISORDERS

Mental illness is a disease, just like any other illness. There is often a strong underlying physical cause. Glandular imbalances or a malfunctioning kidney or liver often lie at the bottom of mental disturbance. There is every possibility that viral infections may also play their part in many mental diseases. The psychological lift that you receive as you bounce is of great benefit. A greater feeling of self-control, enhanced self-image and esteem, are factors that create positive repercussions. The physical counterparts are also an obvious bonus.

Topical Tips
● Work with techniques from Totally Breathtaking (p. 135). Brainy Blitz is full of great ways to activate the two sides of the brain. Try Jerky Jugglers and the Nutcracker (p. 145) ● Sage, patchouli, bay, geranium and basil are among the oils that will harmonize and benefit the mind and emotions. Techniques that bring calm and relaxation from Spacing Stress Out should be learned and utilized in therapeutic situations (p. 128).

SCIATICA

A distinct pain running down your leg, from your buttock to behind your knee, is often the first indication that you are suffering from sciatica. It is usually caused by a pressed nerve, creating acute pain or, in less severe cases, discomfort.

Topical Tips
● Walking on the mat of your bouncer may help relieve the pain ● Bouncing in the Rhythm Walk or Bounce, very gently stretch then release your hips and buttocks ● Essential oil of camphor, ginger, lavender and marjoram combine to make an excellent massage oil.

SINUS PROBLEMS

Complaints related to the fluid balance of your eyes, ears, nose and throat should ease as you bounce. Any initial discomfort through these channels may occur as your body throws off wastes and toxins. Gentle bouncing stimulates the drainage of the channels in your inner ear, helping to prevent infections and rebalance the inner vestibular apparatus, which helps to maintain your balance.

Topical Tips
● If your sinus conditions are extreme, bounce for short periods only – about two minutes at a time ● Stroke the reflex zones for your eyes (p. 32) ● Activate your elimination reflex zones (p. 109) ● Sound techniques (p. 130) work wonders for your sinuses ● Essential oils of sandalwood, orange, cedarwood, cypress and hyssop are among those that will rebalance your sinuses, helping to eliminate catarrh. Massage your feet daily after bouncing.

STROKE

Many stroke patients in rehabilitation programmes are enjoying positive results following regular participation in bouncing programmes. People have reported the stimulation of feeling in their legs again, even with other people bouncing for them.

Topical Tips
● If you have been severely disabled, you will need to seek assistance from a friend to help with the bouncing (p. 105) ● Utilize techniques from Brainy Blitz (p. 144) ● Numerous techniques from Face Savers (p. 139) are excellent for activating facial muscles. Steamrollers and Puffing Billies are excellent examples of techniques that are beneficial ● Stimulate your neurovascular reflex points (p. 141) ● Activate your breathing with techniques from Totally Breathtaking (p. 135).

THYROID DEFICIENCY

An underactive thyroid gland can produce many changes including dry skin, palpitations, weight gain and mental confusion. Overstimulation of the gland will bring about heart failure, weight loss or palpitations.

Topical Tips
● Aim to include breathing techniques into your session ● Stimulate the reflexes for your pituitary and thyroid glands (p. 32) ● Select techniques from Spacing Stress Out (p. 128).

VARICOSE VEINS

On its return journey your blood flow is controlled by a series of valves, which may become weak, causing blood to pool in your legs, with varicose veins surfacing. Over a period of time, as you bounce, you should notice improvement in your veins. One of the reasons for this is that new routes are forming for the blood to flow back to your heart. Your veins perform a milking action, with the help of your calf muscles and then your abdominal muscles and finally your diaphragm, to press your blood upward and return it to your heart.

When you bounce you not only activate the return of lymph and blood to your heart but you also stimulate the working of both calf muscles. They are powerfully and rhythmically contracting in repetition nearly one hundred times a minute. This cannot but help to tone the quality and strength of the supportive tissue and muscles in your legs.

Bouncing offers the perfect opportunity to ease your blood back to your heart, without placing excessive pressure on your veins. As someone reminded me in a letter recently: if bouncing is having such a visibly powerful effect on these veins, it must be having a similar effect on literally thousands of kilometres of veins and capillaries, winding their way through your body, even though you can't see the visible effects.

Topical Tips
● Soak your legs in a solution of warm water and calendula essential oil ● Fabulous Feet (p. 153) offers techniques you can use for your legs and feet ● Practise the Legshaker (p. 153) every day, and treat your legs to a gentle massage once a week. Never apply firm pressure on swollen or damaged veins. Gentle upward stroking will keep the flow in your legs on the go!

INDEX

ACKNOWLEDGEMENTS

My special thanks and deepest respect go to my editor Alice Millington-Drake, who has worked so thoroughly and supportively to develop and structure Starbound, with amazing precision and clear insight. Without her efforts and sacrifice this publication could not have been organized so creatively in so short a space of time. Michael Dover has supervised the production brilliantly. For his efforts I promise him a bouncer! Alongside the entire team at Orion, I particularly wish to thank Richard Hussey, Emma Way and Susan Lamb.

I would like to thank everyone who has set aside time for interviews and to help with my research. In particular, my thanks to: Janet Balaskas, International Active Birth Centre, London; Sarah Bunting; Brian Butler, Academy of Kinesiology (UK); Dr Damien Downing, Journal of Nutritional Medicine (UK); Hephzi Felton, Childsense; John Francis; Kathy Fulcher, London Sports Medicine Clinic; Jenny Hammond, Caeteris Education Centre, Auckland (New Zealand); Ken Holme, Churchill Centre, London; Dr Harry Howell, National Guild of Clinical Nutritionists and British Association of Lymph and Colon Therapists; Paco Irving; Dr Brian Kaplin; Dr Robert Michael Kaplin; Jon H. Leigh, General Council and Register of Naturopaths (UK); Rev. Dr William Martin; Sue Miles, Raphael Clinic, London; Mary Malloy, Biodynamic Institute (UK); Veronica Peck; Dr Craig Sharp, British Olympic Training Centre; Rosemary Steele, Kirleon Institute (UK); Dr Andrew Wade, London Hospital Medical College; Sue Waterhouse; Hildegard Whittlenger, Vodderschule, Alpenbad (Austria); Julie Wilson.

My special thanks for their continuous support to Jed Alward, Ailsa Barry, Gil Dove, Victoria Goldsmith, Kathy Gustafson, Peggy Manton, Gunhilde Molving, Ross Reiger, Philippa Turville, my parents, and, of course, Romani, who devised names for many Starbound techniques.

The author and publishers would also like to thank the following companies for the use of their garments: Monsonego, 24 Walpole Street, London SW3; Speedway, 50 Long Acre, London WC2; Stirling Cooper Ltd., 27 Duke Street, London W1.

191

STARBOUND ENTERPRISE

I have established Starbound Enterprise to meet the needs of the many enquiries that I have received in the course of my research. My aim is to offer a range of services and products designed to encourage your ongoing participation and enthusiasm for bouncing.

There are STARBOUND^{SM} coach training courses, club memberships, seminars and workshops. You may also wish to order from a range of STARBOUND™ bounce units, balance bars, video and audiotapes, wallcharts, and other products for home delivery.

For order forms, prices and further information please send a stamped, self-addressed envelope to Starbound Enterprise at one of the addresses below. (Enquiries from countries not listed should be directed to the U.K.). I regret that personal correspondence cannot be entered into.

U.K. and Europe
P.O. Box 3505
London NW5 2HZ

New Zealand and Australasia
P.O. Box 305
Orewa
North Auckland
New Zealand

STARBOUND™ and STARBOUND^{SM} are registered trade and service marks for Starbound Enterprise.

A variety of bounce units are also widely available in leading sports shops, department stores and other outlets.

With very best wishes and good luck with your bouncer
Michele Wilburn